You Know
I'm Right

More Prosperity, Less Government

Michelle Caruso-Cabrera

with a foreword by Larry Kudlow

Threshold Editions

New York   London   Toronto   Sydney

Threshold Editions
A Division of Simon & Schuster, Inc.
1230 Avenue of the Americas
New York, NY 10020

First Threshold Editions hardcover edition October 2010

THRESHOLD EDITIONS and colophon are trademarks of
Simon & Schuster, Inc.

For information about special discounts for bulk purchases,
please contact Simon & Schuster Special Sales at
1-866-506-1949 or business@simonandschuster.com.

The Simon & Schuster Speakers Bureau can bring authors to
your live event. For more information or to book an event
contact the Simon & Schuster Speakers Bureau at
1-866-248-3049 or visit our website at www.simonspeakers.com.

Designed by Joy O'Meara

Manufactured in the United States of America

10 9 8 7 6 5 4 3 2 1

Caruso-Cabrera, Michelle.
    You know I'm right : more prosperity, less government / Michelle
Caruso-Cabrera.
        p. cm.
    1. United States—Economic policy—2009- 2. United States—
Social policy—1993- 3. Health care reform—United States.
4. United States—Military policy. 5. Responsibility—Political
aspects—United States. I. Title.
    HC106.84.C37   2010
    330.973—dc22   2010022653

ISBN 978-1-4391-9323-5

To the three greatest influences on my life:

My parents,
Wellesley College,
and Milton Friedman

— Contents —

— Foreword —

The best social-welfare policies are the ones that create good
new jobs. Smart politicians know this. And it was the late
President Ronald Reagan who taught me this thirty years ago,
back when I served as Associate Director for Economics in his
Office of Management and Budget.

He also taught me that the best way to create good new
jobs is to unleash the entrepreneurs who operate in the private
economy. Reward their success through low tax rates. Stay
out of their hair by keeping government regulations to a minimum. Give them room to prosper by putting government on a
short leash—by limiting its size, scope, and spending. Broaden
their markets by keeping trade free and open. And protect
their spending power with a reliable currency and by holding
inflation in check.

No wonder the Gipper was the most successful president in the post–World War II era. His policies worked. The
citizenry was happy. The nation prospered mightily. Jobs were
plentiful. Reagan was so successful, and America so bountiful
because of his policies, that the Soviet Union was blown out
of the water, relegated to the dustbin of history.

In short, Reagan knew that free-market capitalism is the
best path to peace and prosperity. That's my creed, too. And

it's a view shared and embraced by my friend and CNBC colleague Michelle Caruso-Cabrera in her new book, *You Know I'm Right*.

Michelle has written a hard-hitting book that illuminates the supremacy of pro-growth economic principles. And she has done so at a time when the nation is reeling from the lingering effects of a deep recession and the presidential policy mistakes of recent years.

Michelle is less interested in partisan politics and much more concerned with restating and reapplying Milton Friedman's theories of capitalism and freedom, which Reagan made the centerpiece of his program. As I read it, that's her mission, and she sets to it at just the right time—for we must not forget how we got into this mess, and how we can climb back out.

This is America, Michelle reminds us. We are an exceptional nation. Our system of democracy and freedom can overcome the mistakes of the past, just as it has so many times in our gloried history. But a soup-to-nuts road map is essential.

Go back to Reaganism, she exhorts. Then build on it even more. Use Reagan's supply-side, market-oriented plan as a guide to solving today's high unemployment, massive job losses, and stagnant growth. Pessimism and unhappiness are in the air today, just as they were three decades ago. But optimism can be restored by returning to a classical liberal economy built on market supremacy and strictly limited government.

Michelle doesn't hide the fact that Ronald Reagan is her all-time favorite chief executive. Her second favorite? Bill Clinton. It was Clinton, she points out, who joined (however reluctantly, but cleverly in a political sense) with Newt Gingrich and his Contract with America movement to reform welfare, expand free trade, and balance the budget through economic growth and tough spending cuts. Okay, I can go with that. After all, the Clinton-Gingrich Era was really Ronald Reagan's third term, wasn't it?

As the Obama administration moves deep into its second year—with its unprecedented government controls over the economy; its massive spending, deficits, and debt-borrowing; its higher taxes on businesses and our most productive earners and investors; and its reregulation of near every nook and cranny of the private sector—the so-called economic recovery languishes, while doubts about our standards of living and wealth turn grave.

Michelle says no, no, no, and no to all this. Statism, redistribution, and European-socialism lite are not the answers. Instead, Michelle argues that we must slash the budget across the board by eliminating or curbing the cabinet departments, agencies, and programs that are unnecessary in the new age of information technology.

She says end the public-sector unions, whose outlandish pay and benefit schemes—at nearly twice the compensation levels of their private-sector counterparts—are picking taxpayer pockets and moving us toward bankruptcy. She says reform the health-care and Social Security entitlements through consumer choice and personal ownership. She says use vouchers and school choice to solve our problematic education system.

To some ears, Michelle's policy proposals will sound radical. But I regard them as sensible and long-overdue reforms. Every step of the way, her key points summon the proven doctrines of consumer choice, personal responsibility, and market competition.

Michelle Caruso-Cabrera's splendid book, *You Know I'm Right*, is all about economic freedom in pursuit of life, liberty, and happiness. She knows that the principles of freedom set down by the Founders must, as Reagan frequently reminded us, be at the very heart of American recovery.

Lawrence Kudlow
New York City
July 9, 2010

— Introduction —

I never used to be a political person. In fact, I used to hate talking about politics. I sometimes wish I weren't covering it now, but I have little choice because politics and business have become increasingly intertwined. In the past I interviewed CEOs to discuss how they made their companies grow. These days on CNBC I ask CEOs how they'll deal with new invasive policies being dictated by Washington. And although I used to rarely interview politicians, now they're on the air every day. Government just keeps getting bigger and it increasingly regulates the ordinary affairs of American business.

What I've learned from the BP oil disaster, the housing debacle, and the financial collapse is that government is over-regulating our lives, and yet it's never going to protect us. I believe we can do more with less. I believe I'm right when I say less government means greater prosperity for everyone in this great nation. And I don't just mean the wealthy—I also am referring to the middle class and those struggling just to put food on their families' tables.

During the last election, as our nation and others around the world were on the brink of economic disaster, I looked at both the Democrats and the Republicans and thought, *We're in big trouble here.* Neither political party was looking out for our economic interests. Neither was doing it right. There was a fundamental crisis of leadership.

So I decided to write this book—and not to attack just the left of the political spectrum, because I'm equally frustrated with the right. I always thought I was a Republican, until the party got too caught up in social issues that government shouldn't be dealing with and lost sight of more important fiscal ones. So neither political party seems to be on the right track to fix our economy. I'm writing this book to urge American leaders to reduce the size and role of government in both our private lives and our free-market economy. It's time for politicians of both parties to get the country back on track and it's time for the rest of us to take a little personal responsibility for the mess we find ourselves in.

That's right, I'm not just blaming Washington, either. I think the media is to blame as well. I know you probably think I'm about to trash the so-called liberal, left-wing media, but I'm not. I'm taking everyone to task—including the so-called right-wing media.

Lou Dobbs, for example, used to call himself a Republican. Then he claimed he was an independent. Whatever his label, he wasn't in favor of the free movement of labor, capital, and goods. He took his extreme stance on immigration simply to tap into the socially conservative population. It was not a fiscally conservative position. He was a populist opportunist when he should have been a voice for the conservative movement.

Right-wing talk radio and TV aided and abetted the GOP by focusing on social issues rather than fiscal ones and in doing so wasted an opportunity to fight for the goals of the Goldwater and Reagan-era Republican Party. How much time did shock jocks spend covering nativity scenes when they could have been asking President George W. Bush why he kept spending and expanding government? Why were these right-wing pundits with such powerful platforms wasting an opportunity to fix the fiscal mess our nation faces? Where were the right-wing pundits, who are suddenly all about small government now that President Obama has taken office, when President George W. Bush went on a spending spree? The conservative media needs to start embracing policies, not politicians.

So that's what this book is about. It's about fixing the way we do business. It's about how we as a society should look at government. And by the time you've finished, you'll know I'm right.

— 1 —

Mind My Business, Not My Bedroom

I want a government that stays out of my pocketbook and stays out of my private life. I find it frustrating that the Democrats think I want to keep paying for their big government and endless spending projects. But I am equally annoyed that the Republicans turned their backs on a voter like me and now think it's okay to run my personal affairs at the expense of fiscal issues. So as a voter, I'm partyless. I'm left out in the cold. And frankly, I'm feeling a little unwanted—unwanted from a philosophical, political standpoint, that is. I'm not alone. There's a major problem with the political system in the United States today: neither party truly represents a growing number of middle-class Americans.

Where does a fiscal conservative and a social liberal go? For me, neither the Republicans nor the Democrats represent my values and beliefs. Neither envisions reduced spending and less government involvement in the private lives of the American people.

I am part of a new and growing crowd of "sort-of" Republicans. I am far too fiscally responsible to want to reach out and hug the Democrats. Their social spending will keep the next several generations laden with debt. At the same time, I am too fiercely independent to embrace the Republican Party, because I want people to be free to make their own choices about their personal lives. I don't want Washington insiders to tell me what to think and how to behave in the privacy of my home.

There are a lot of us that don't like the tax-and-spend approach to budgeting but also believe in, for example, a woman's right to choose. Michael Petrilli at the Hoover Institution said it best when he used the term "Whole Foods Republican"—someone who embraces a progressive lifestyle, but not progressive politics. It's not a great place to be. No matter where I turn to for leadership, I have to compromise. Over the past decade, both parties seem to have been hijacked by social issues such as abortion, the environment, and gay marriage. These issues don't define us as a nation, so why do they define our two political parties?

Here's the thing: I believe in low taxes, and a small, non-intrusive government. I don't really care if gays want to get married or not. I don't smoke pot, but frankly, I don't care if you do. Of course I want us to live in a healthy environment. But that doesn't mean we stop drilling for oil. I believe in God, but I don't think everyone else must accept my God. In fact, I don't think religion should have anything to do with governing at all. I also know we can be good neighbors even when the family next door looks different.

By that, you might think I'm a Democrat, but the Democratic Party is out of control when it comes to spending and intrusive government programs. They have a never-ending appetite for taxpayer dollars to advance their causes. I don't believe in socialized health care. In fact, I don't believe that government can fix much of anything. But members of the Democratic Party consistently claim the moral high ground by calling themselves compassionate in order to justify excessive spending on social initiatives. There is nothing compassionate about running the country into the poorhouse. By abandoning any form of fiscal responsibility, the country will soon be unable to afford to support anyone. Democrats need to understand that the most compassionate country is one that allows people to make their own choices and live with the benefits and consequences of those choices.

The Republican Party of the last ten years has courted the religious right at the expense of fiscal conservatives who believe that less government is better government. It has embraced programs designed to do social engineering much in the same way the Democratic Party has always done. Why is it that the Republicans seem more concerned about creationism in the schools and debating stem-cell research than they do about balancing the budget? Simple solution: let's not tell educators how to educate or fund any research. That is not the role of government.

Things didn't used to be this way. Republicans were the party of Barry Goldwater and Nobel Prize–winning economist Milton Friedman, who believed in free markets and a limited role of government. It was the party of Ronald Reagan, whose emphasis on less government and less spending became the heart and soul of Reaganomics. These men would be aghast to see what has happened to their party.

Now both parties have abandoned those of us who believe in a secular state with a government that limits its spending and regulatory intervention in the economy. The government has no place in the bedrooms of the nation, and it should not distort the economy with rules, susidies, and tax policy. It needs to represent those of us who believe in personal responsibility.

If a strong independent emerged in the next presidential election, I might embrace him or her. But under the current primary and electoral college system, a viable independent is unlikely to happen.

Ronald Reagan represented my views. He was my favorite president. My second favorite? Bill Clinton. Even though according to their party affiliations, they would seem to be polar opposites, in reality they were very similar. Just as strange, George W. Bush and Barack Obama share an emphasis on using big government to fix everything, which makes them oddly similar.

If the government got out of the business of making social and moral choices for us, not only would it be more efficient, but legislators would also have more time to focus on fixing the economic well-being of the nation. Milton Friedman was right when he said government has just four roles: it should protect our freedom, provide law and order, enforce private contracts, and foster competitive markets. Government shouldn't tell you who you should share your bed with, which god (if any) you should worship, or whether or not you should use marijuana. In a free society, people need to make those choices themselves.

The other big problem with big government: overregulation. Paradoxically, underregulation didn't cause this current financial fiasco we're in. Overregulation got us here. The recent economic disaster that we've just experienced is a direct result of abandoning the core principles of Reaganomics: less government, less spending. Instead, the last Republican administration spent vast sums of money and inflated both the size of government and its red tape. During his time in office, President George W. Bush did things that were fundamentally leftist in nature, such as imposing steel tariffs, expanding entitlements for the elderly, and encouraging home ownership for everyone. Even those who didn't have enough income to afford a home were able to buy one. And look where that got us.

The United States is a world leader. Democracy, the rule of law, and the rights and freedoms entrenched in our Constitution make us the envy of friends and foes around the world. But if we want this great nation to continue along on this path and if we want to ensure that we are a prosperous nation, we need to get back to these core values and principles: less government and more personal responsibility.

Look at this current recession and the rash of foreclosures: it's heartbreaking to see so many people lose their homes. Washington wants to blame business, but let's face it, in many ways government is responsible. The tax structure encouraged and facilitated home ownership even when people couldn't afford it. Fannie and Freddie fueled the mortgage market. The Federal Reserve created cheap money with low rates. Taxpayer dollars were used to create a system that made it possible to buy a home with no down payment.

The business community, particularly the banks, made its share of mistakes, too: the ratings agencies that rubber-stamped mortgage securities did us no favors, and the lazy fund managers who didn't do their homework and just kept buying junk made the problem worse. But government officials promoted home ownership as if even the unemployed should be entitled to buy a house. Americans bought into this fantasy, thinking that a worker making $45,000 a year could afford a $300,000 home. The mortgage brokers and the banks had a big hand in that, but logic should have prevailed on an individual level. Homeowners need to take responsibility, too. Don't buy what you can't afford.

Economic policy truly matters—not just to big business but also to the everyday lives and livelihoods of moms and dads trying to support their families. It is the basis for every aspect of our lives in this country. The government needs to stop trying to command and control the economy, and the government can only be smart about that if it focuses on getting smaller and purges social issues from its agenda. That way the government could emphasize personal responsibility and create a foundation that allows anyone in the country to achieve success.

So people like me—people I call "the great unwanted middle"—are in a real predicament. We have nowhere to turn in 2012 unless one of these parties decides to return to these fundamentals: smaller, not bigger, government and less involvement in our personal lives. I know I'm right when I say, "Whoever wants to be our next president should campaign on one line: I'll stay out of your private life and out of your pocketbook."

— 2 —

Ronald Reagan Had It Right

I will always love Ronald Reagan. After he was elected president my parents stopped fighting.

The 1970s were awful. I vividly remember the tension in my house growing up because my parents fought over money a lot—something as simple as buying gas sparked a debate. My dad explained to me the windfall-profits tax that Jimmy Carter had imposed on the oil companies and how, if Reagan won the election, it would go away, and how it would be easier to buy gasoline. I was into that stuff at a very young age.

Well, Reagan won. In the simple way a child views the world, my family's life got a lot better. Happier. Once my parents felt they had control of their money—and their lives and livelihood—they were so much more relaxed. I wasn't conscious of it at the time, but I learned implicitly how much economic policy matters to our everyday lives. Ronald Reagan taught me that.

If only we had someone like him now who believed in the American people as much as he did.

It was called a revolution for a reason. In his eight years in office, President Ronald Reagan worked to return America to a system of less government, one based on the belief that American citizens are smart enough to control their own futures and destinies. His rise to leadership and his style of governance personified what it meant to be American. What could be more American than believing in the power of the individual and believing that an economy based on individualism leads to strength?

Reagan believed political freedom could only be achieved when government stayed small in the lives of its citizens. He believed that democracy could not be separated from true economic freedom. Reagan knew that people and businesses know what's good for them. He understood that legislators and regulators are not the people who generate jobs in America. Entrepreneurs and business leaders are. He also believed that if they make mistakes, they have to live with them, and that the government shouldn't bail them out. The best welfare program: a job.

If we had more presidents like Reagan, we would never have gotten into the trouble that we did with real estate, because he never would have advocated home ownership at any cost, as Clinton and Bush did. He hated subsidies because they were provided with taxpayer money but rarely benefited the taxpayer.

Reagan knew that the money you make is your money— and what you do with it is your personal choice and responsibility. Excessive government and regulation is essentially a roadblock on the highway to progress and prosperity. As a nation, we've wandered too far away from Reagan's revolution and we need to get back on track. We need to reembrace Reagan's fundamental economic approach to our policies and governance so that we can get back on the road to prosperity he paved for us thirty years ago.

When Reagan took office, the country was in a "worst since" era, just like the one we're climbing out of now. The country was feeling the repercussions of an oil embargo, which led to price controls by Nixon in 1973 and consequently massive lines at the pumps. The stock market was nearly stagnant for the decade before Reagan took office. The Dow gained a mere 4.8 percent, which, adjusted for inflation, was basically less than zero. Inflation was the highest it had been since World War II. Interest rates hadn't been higher since the Civil War, and incomes for the average American were tanking, while high taxes were simply choking household budgets. Unemployment in the 1970s was around 7–8 percent.

By the end of his eight years in office, Reagan had turned the economy of the United States around. He had created 16 million new jobs and put cash in the pockets of Americans both rich and poor. Unemployment fell from 7.5 percent to 5.4 percent.[1] Reagan liberated the U.S. economy, unleashed tremendous wealth and growth for both wealthy and lower-income families, and created a new optimism for the entire population.

Reagan reminded the nation of this key economic truth: a nation is more prosperous and a government more powerful when there is less government, less taxation, and little involvement in the personal lives of everyday Americans. Reagan was elected on a platform from which he didn't deviate throughout his presidency. He came into office with a strategy: lower taxes, reduce regulation, establish monetary stability, and control federal spending (which he tried to do through a failed constitutional amendment to balance the budget). His presidency was defined by a laserlike focus on what was a radical notion at the time: that Americans should keep the majority of the money they earn.

And so he lowered taxes dramatically, and guess what happened—contrary to critics at the time, tax revenues went up, not down. Why? Because the economy improved. Tax revenues go up when taxes go down, plain and simple. This is an especially important point for the naysayers of today, since they think higher taxes are somehow better for the economy.

The Tax Reform Act of 1986 simplified the income tax code, lowered the top tax rate, and reduced the number of brackets, effectively making a flatter tax system and broadening the tax base. When Reagan came into office, the top marginal tax rate was 70 percent. To his credit, Reagan persuaded Congress to lower the top marginal tax rate to 50 percent in 1982 and 28 percent in 1988. The result? Tax revenues climbed from less than $351 billion in 1980 to more than $615 billion in 1989.[2]

More wealth was generated for everyone. Instead of going into government coffers, earned dollars became part of the real economy—people had more money to buy homes or cars, to educate their children, to travel, to save for retirement. Jobs were created as people spent more. Reagan demonstrated that cutting taxes ensures the growth of an economy and in the process provides more tax revenues from more people.

The evidence is in the numbers. With Reagan in office, tax receipts climbed dramatically because the economy boomed: the nation's GDP went from $3 trillion to $5 trillion.[3] Fewer taxes under Reagan resulted in more growth—more tax revenues actually came from a larger tax base, not higher taxes. There were more people making more money and generating more wealth. All this occurred because the individual had been freed from handing over more than half of his money to the government.

It's important to understand that tax cuts are not part of a right-wing conspiracy designed to make the rich simply get richer. In fact, cutting taxes to stimulate growth isn't a uniquely Republican idea. One of the most revered Democratic presidents in our nation's history, John F. Kennedy, supported and enacted significant tax cuts. Here's how he explained it in a November 20, 1962, news conference. "It is a paradoxical truth that tax rates are too high and tax revenues are too low and the soundest way to raise the revenues in the long run is to cut the rates now. . . . Cutting taxes now is not to incur a budget deficit, but to achieve the more prosperous, expanding economy which can bring a budget surplus." [4]

Two months later he repeated the point in his annual budget message to Congress. "Lower rates of taxation will stimulate economic activity and so raise the levels of personal and corporate income as to yield within a few years an increased—not a reduced—flow of revenues to the federal government." [5]

When Kennedy came into office, top marginal tax rates were roughly 90 percent, with effective tax rates of 70 percent. Back then, to be in the top tax bracket as an individual you made $200,000. Today, to make it into the top bracket, you'd have to earn $373,000, and if we still had the same level of taxation as in 1960 you'd be handing over $261,000. [6] But that's how it had been for nearly twenty years, since 1945. JFK pushed through a cut, which lowered the top rate to 70 percent. And just as we saw under Reagan, tax revenues went up, not down. In 1961 the government took in $94 billion. Seven years later, after the cut, that number grew to $153 billion.[7]

Tax historian Dan Mitchell has done some great research. His analysis shows consistently that when we cut taxes, we generate higher tax revenues. Kennedy and Reagan weren't a fluke. He points out that in the 1920s, after the government cut top tax rates from 73 percent to less than 25 percent, we had an economic boom. Revenues in 1921 were $719 million. By 1928 they were at $1.164 billion, an increase of 61 percent.[8]

During that time, Treasury Secretary Andrew Mellon pointed out that when tax rates are high, people with money withdraw it from productive businesses and investments and instead put it in things like "tax-exempt securities or other methods of avoiding the realization of taxable income." So everybody loses because "the source of taxation dries up."[9] Mellon knew the government was better off, and brought in more revenue, when it taxed capital less rather than more.

People think tax cuts mean the rich actually pay less money. History has shown that in fact, after tax cuts the rich pick up a greater percentage of the nation's tax burden. Mitchell points out that in the 1920s, the 1960s, and 1980s the wealthiest Americans ended up paying more of the nation's tax bill, not less. In 1921 the richest people paid around 45 percent of all taxes.[10] By 1928 they were paying 78 percent of all taxes. (The richest people back then were those who made more than $50,000.) Here's a way to look at it: less taxes per person actually increases the number of people that are wealthy. Therefore, over time, more people have more money and therefore pay more taxes. The tax base expands.

Under Kennedy, the richest people went from paying 11.6

percent of the nation's overall tax bill to 15.1 percent. And ditto for Reagan. In 1980, the top 10 percent of tax filers paid 48 percent of all taxes—and in 1988 they paid 57.2 percent of all taxes.[11] Even though individually their taxes rates were cut, the richest Americans overall, as a group, picked up the greater portion of the tab for the entire nation's tax bill.

Look at what happened to the wealthiest 1 percent of earners—the superwealthy—under Reagan: In 1980 the top 1 percent paid only 17.6 percent of all the nation's taxes. By 1988 that same group was paying 27.5 percent. By the end of the Reagan administration that 1 percent of the population was paying more than a quarter of the nation's tax bill.[12]

Not only that, but the taxes paid by poor families under Reagan were also reduced. The tax rate was cut back for people filing taxes in the lowest income bracket.

For the first time in history, the effective tax rate for individuals in the bottom 20 percent of those filing taxes went negative. In other words, not only did they not pay payroll taxes—they paid none—but they also got additional money back because of the earned income tax credit, an initiative that was started in 1975 but greatly expanded under Reagan. It was designed to help offset the burden of Social Security taxes for poor families. Nearly every president since has expanded the earned income tax credit, particularly George W. Bush. It was an idea championed by Milton Friedman, who wanted it to replace all welfare programs. The idea was to make it more profitable to work rather than collect welfare.[13]

Consider some experiments around the world with simple, low tax regimes: After communism fell in Eastern Europe, a few countries emulated the West and set up progressive tax structures. Others decided to go a different route and introduced a low, flat-tax structure where everyone pays the same low rate on income. The result? The countries that adopted a flat tax—for example, Slovakia, Lithuania, and Estonia—experienced much higher economic growth than their neighbors who had adopted progressive tax structures, which tend to punish the wealthy investor class. After introducing the flat tax, Lithuania saw its unemployment rate fall and its overall standard of living rise, as well as a major decline in tax evasion. More evidence that lower taxes, and the flatter regime advocated by Reagan, have a positive effect on the economy.

Reagan's pal, then British prime minister Margaret Thatcher, shared the same perspective on taxation. When Thatcher came into office, the tax on unearned income in her country could reach 98 percent, leaving few interested in investing in Britain.[14] Why would you risk investing money? Even if the investment were successful, you'd only get to keep 2 percent of your profits.

Reagan's other mission was to cut spending in every government department except national defense. This led to knock-down, drag-out fights with Congress. Reagan would frequently tear into his foes. In March 1985, after vetoing that year's farm bill (subsidies to farmers), Reagan explained, "The bottom line is that someone in Washington must be responsible. Someone must be willing to stand for those who pay American's bills. And someone must stand up to those who say, 'Here's the key, there's the Treasury, just take as many of those hard-earned tax dollars as you want.' "[15]

One of my favorite speeches by Reagan on the subject of spending took place on April 24, 1985. It was an address to the nation on the federal budget and deficit reduction. He said, "The answer to a government that's too fat is to stop feeding its growth.... The simple truth is: No matter how hard you work, no matter how strong this economy grows, no matter how much more tax revenue comes to Washington, it won't amount to a hill of beans if government won't curb its endless appetite to spend. . . . You know, sometimes big spenders in Congress talk as if all the money they spend just kind of magically appears on their doorstep, a gift from the Internal Revenue Service. . . . Well, there is no magic money machine. Every dollar the government spends comes out of your pockets. Every dollar the government gives to someone has to first be taken away from someone else. So it is our moral duty to make sure that we can justify every one of your tax dollars." [16] I don't think we've heard speeches like this since Reagan left office.

In fact, spending under Reagan fell in most departments in his first three budgets. In his first budget, he proposed 5 percent baseline cuts in every department except defense. He did the same for his second budget. He didn't get all the cuts he wanted from Congress in either attempt, but at least he proposed cuts in baseline spending. George W. Bush, on the other hand, proposed big increases going into the budget process. The basic fact is that the real nondefense discretionary spending under Reagan decreased his first three years in office by 14 percent. Reagan slashed spending across the board— agriculture, commerce, education, labor, and energy—and he used his veto power over budgetary matters three times during the first three years in office. Compare that to supposedly Republican president George W. Bush, who did what most Democrats are accused of: he entered office with a surplus and left with a deficit.

I suspect for some of you reading this there is an eight-hundred-pound gorilla in the room. When critics talk about Reagan, one of the first points they bring up is the huge deficit—the largest in peacetime (that is until now). They usually attribute it to excessive defense spending. They'll say that while Reagan sliced taxes and spending in other budget areas, he upped spending on defense with programs like his famed Star Wars project. All that is true, but it's not the entire story.

What critics never mention is the role of inflation. The automatic increases in Medicare and Social Security shot up dramatically before and during the Reagan era; when it came to entitlements, there were far more government outlays than any economist from either side of the aisle anticipated.

So defense spending contributed to the Reagan deficit, but not as much as you think. In 1982 defense spending was $185.9 billion, and in 1983 it went up to $209 billion, a gain of nearly $25 billion. Compare that to mandatory spending on entitlement programs that year, which posted a gain of $30.5 billion from the previous year. In fact, from 1981 to 1989, nearly every year, increases in entitlement spending surpassed increases on defense spending. And in 1980, the year before Reagan came into office (a year of massive inflation), mandatory spending on entitlements shot up a whopping $40.7 billion, while defense spending went up only $12 billion. So Reagan inherited a bigger deficit than anyone had predicted.[17]

Also contributing to the Reagan-era deficits was a huge decline in tax revenue because the Federal Reserve purposely brought on a recession to try to tame inflation.

Inflation had been horrendous for a decade. As far back as 1969, prices were rising at an annual rate of 6 percent. In 1974, inflation was a staggering 11 percent (in part because of the oil embargo), but even in 1980, with no oil embargo as an excuse, inflation was 13.5 percent.[18] Compare that to today— your four-dollar latte just became forty-three cents more expensive. Granted, these numbers look good in some countries, but not in the United States. Price gains at that level cripple the economy and prevent the middle class from providing for their families. Wages simply can't keep up with rising prices. Price gains eat away at savings and investments as well. For example, if you've saved money for retirement and there is a spike in inflation, the money you've saved no longer buys you what you thought it would.

President Jimmy Carter appointed Paul Volcker to head up the Federal Reserve in 1979 in order to deal with the inflation problem, and Reagan kept Volcker in place. Volcker raised interest rates dramatically to break inflation. It seems like an obvious thing to do, but at the time it was groundbreaking.

I interviewed Volcker for CNBC when Ronald Reagan died. He showed me what the Fed had been doing with interest rates on a daily basis. The Fed was moving interest rates by a full point on some days. Think about that—we run full weeks of coverage on CNBC about whether or not the Fed is going to move a quarter of a percentage point from the meeting three months before. Back then Volcker and the Fed were moving the rates by a full percentage point from one day to the next.[19]

The jump in interest rates had severe and direct effects on the U.S. federal budget and deficits. High interest rates caused the worst recession since the Great Depression (sound familiar?) and that led to a dramatic drop in tax revenues, particularly at the corporate level.[20] But it took a few years of high interest rates before inflation began to fall. As a result, the cost-of-living adjustments for those receiving Social Security and Medicare went up much more sharply than anyone had predicted. The numbers, in fact, were staggering: 10 percent in 1979, 14 percent in 1980, and 11 percent in 1981.[21] The final assault was that high levels of interest rates led to much higher interest payments on the debt for the federal government as well.

There is a fair and worthy discussion to be had about our overall defense spending. Those of us who praise Reagan shouldn't have blinders on when it comes to this topic. However, it is fair to say we gained a lot from the levels of defense spending under Reagan. When I interviewed Milton Friedman for CNBC, he told me that Reagan contributed to the fall of communism by engaging the Soviet Union in an arms spending race.[22] One could argue we broke the back of the Soviet Union, which, due to its weak communist economy, couldn't keep pace with our defense spending.

Reducing government control of the economy—or regulation—was a tough pill for the nation to swallow, but Ronald Reagan believed Americans should make choices for themselves and give power to the markets to drive the best outcome: get the government out of the business of telling Americans how to run their businesses. Reagan ran on the ticket that free markets would help lower the cost of living for Americans far more than the government could. What he did with oil prices is emblematic of his vision. In 1981 he said, "Our national energy plan should not be a rigid set of production and conservation goals dictated by government. Our primary objective is simply for our citizens to have enough energy, and it is up to them to decide how much energy that is, and in what form and manner it will reach them. When the free market is permitted to work the way it should, millions of individual choices and judgments will produce the proper balance of supply and demand our economy needs."[23]

One week after he took office, Reagan removed government price controls on oil that had been in place since 1973.

People were terrified that if price controls were removed, the cost of oil would soar even further, reducing money available in the household budget for food and clothing. He removed the cap that companies could charge. The price of oil fell from $36 a barrel at the start of his presidency to $12 a barrel in 1986. Gas prices were nearly cut in half in the same time period—which, with inflation adjustment, made the price of gas cheaper than at any time since the 1950s. The removal of price caps led to higher production and greater supply. Keep in mind that this happened during an economic boom, which traditionally should drive prices higher due to increased demand. Reagan trumpeted these changes not as a triumph of government and politics, but as a victory for free markets, and as he said, for freedom itself.[24]

Reagan was correct to remove the price caps. In 1986 he told Congress, "Our renewed energy health is a testament to the ingenuity of the American people and the strength of American businesses, large and small. We have rightly placed our trust in our people and the belief that we were not running out of energy, only imagination. We have reduced regulation, wherever and whenever possible. We have placed our confidence in the marketplace, rather than government, to make key economic decisions about energy."[25]

Oil wasn't his only deregulatory accomplishment. He dismantled the Civil Aeronautics Board (CAB), which had regulated airline routes and fees. Airline deregulation had begun under Carter, but Reagan finished it. Now we have market-based pricing on airlines, which is why it's so much more affordable to fly today. The airlines have certainly suffered, but the American consumer has won (yes, I know sometimes when you fly it doesn't feel like it, but that's because the government never deregulated the airports, as it should have).

Reagan removed the Interstate Commerce Commission, which had regulated freight shippers, and he broke up AT&T, which at the time was the nation's largest public utility. Reagan's goal: create more competition. He pushed for market-based pricing in both natural gas and electricity markets.[26]

Reagan didn't just deregulate private industry—he took aim at the government as well. While he reduced regulation on business, he limited the ability of government to expand its regulation on society and the business community. He signed an executive order that made it harder for federal agencies to create more red tape. Before a new rule could be instituted, it had to be justified with a cost-benefit analysis, making it more challenging for bureaucrats to bureaucratize. This measure, still applicable today, has been very effective. A few of examples given in a *Washington Post* story demonstrate this point: Reagan's initiative prevented an expansion in bilingual education (not for the government to decide), additional labeling on chemicals, and a new airbag rule. Pages of regulation dropped under this initiative as well—from 13,700 pages under Jimmy Carter to 9,400 under Reagan.[27]

You might think from reading this that I think Reagan was a perfect president, but Reagan didn't get everything right. He did a complete reversal on Social Security. Back in 1964, when campaigning for Barry Goldwater, Reagan argued that individuals should have the right to opt out of the program if they were saving on their own. Early in his own political career, he campaigned on and advocated for personal accounts so that individuals could save on their own. It was a political loser for him, and many believe it is a key reason he lost the 1976 Republican nomination. So in 1983 he did something that was probably opposite to his views and beliefs: he signed a new law that raised the payroll tax and the retirement age to qualify for Social Security. Note that this didn't solve the problem; it only delayed it.

Reagan critics will say he was anti-abortion. Yes, he was. But he didn't do much about it. Even the liberal-leaning *Washington Monthly* observes that under Reagan "the conservative desire to outlaw abortion was never seriously pursued."[28] In fact, he only gave lip service to the discussion.

In a speech to the nation on January 11, 1989, Reagan summed up his presidency better than I can. He called for less—not more—government as a path to liberty and freedom. Reagan said (and don't laugh, but this speech makes me tear up), "Back in the 1960s, when I began, it seemed to me that we'd begun reversing the order of things—that through more and more rules and regulations and confiscatory taxes, the government was taking more of our money, more of our options, and more of our freedom. I went into politics in part to put up my hand and say, 'Stop.' I was a citizen politician, and it seemed the right thing for a citizen to do. I think we have stopped a lot of what needed stopping. And I hope we have once again reminded people that man is not free unless government is limited. There's a clear cause and effect here that is as neat and predictable as a law of physics: As government expands, liberty contracts."[29]

He was right.

— 3 —

My Second Favorite President

Bill Clinton left the gay population in the closet with Don't Ask, Don't Tell. But in my opinion, he was in the closet himself: from a fiscal standpoint, he was a closet Republican, more right-leaning than George W. Bush. That's why, next to Ronald Reagan, Bill Clinton is my favorite president of all time.

The Bill Clinton we knew in Washington had all the makings of a card-carrying member of the GOP, but was a two-term Democrat. He is on my favorites list because Clinton's greatest achievements were effectively from the Republican handbook. He supported free trade and presided over a balanced budget and welfare reform. Unlike his successor, George W. Bush, Clinton was committed to the economic values, goals, and principles . . . of the right. Clinton might choke if he read this, but he shouldn't. Why should he be concerned about labels when we really should be focused on the issues? More of today's leaders should govern with the same disregard of party lines and partisanship.

There were several big achievements under Clinton's eight years in office that effectively prove my point and the point of many fiscal conservative social liberals like me. Not only did Clinton preside over a balanced budget, but he also was one of the few presidents who left office with a budget surplus. He and Reagan both presided over a decline in nondefense discretionary spending. Both the North American Free Trade Agreement (NAFTA) and the World Trade Organization agreement came into being with Clinton at the helm. Dramatic welfare reforms took place under Clinton, too—he reduced entitlements for those capable of working but uninclined to do so. While I disagree with doing law-and-order initiatives at the federal level, Clinton also dramatically increased the number of police officers on the street.

All in all, Clinton was an old-fashioned Republican and, not surprisingly, he achieved all of these conservative initiatives with a Republican Congress.

Free Trade

Clinton was an avid free-trader. He liberalized international trade in such a way that it is relatively entrenched and secure from protectionists who want to try to dismantle it in the future. In fact, you could say that Clinton did more to liberalize trade markets and entrench capitalism around the globe than any other American president. We can't give him credit for the fall of communism—Reagan took care of that for us—but we can argue that unlike any other president, Clinton has opened the door to the spread of global capitalism (and with it democracy) on an unprecedented scale. Who could have imagined that countries like China, Saudi Arabia, and Russia would clamor to gain access to trade initiatives adopted under the Clinton administration?

President Clinton's free-trade mantra looked like Ronald Reagan's. Reagan was the one whose administration first signed a free-trade agreement with Canada in 1988, which laid the groundwork for the NAFTA. And it was in 1986, under Reagan, that the trade talks for the WTO began in Uruguay. Clinton ensured the successful completion of these two Reagan initiatives with the passage of NAFTA and the WTO agreement.

NAFTA became law in December 1993. But it wasn't a sure thing. Clinton had to convince congressional legislators it was the right thing to do. There was a great deal of uncertainty. Democrats were very concerned about the environment and labor, while Republicans hammered at whether this free-trade deal was really fair. Clinton, however, got the job done. And he did so without pandering to the special interests that wanted to entrench their protectionist ideals.

Because of NAFTA, it's estimated that trade with Canada and Mexico is up a whopping 300 percent, to approximately $1 trillion. Canada and Mexico buy more than one-third of our exports. American jobs depend on liberal access to their countries. More than 110,000 small and medium-size American companies benefit from NAFTA by exporting to those countries. More than a third of all U.S. agricultural exports go to Mexico or Canada. Thanks in large part to NAFTA, Canada is the biggest buyer of U.S. wheat, poultry, oats, eggs, and potatoes. It's the second-largest export destination for beef, pork, apples, and soybean meal.[1]

Mexico had even higher tariffs than we did on many products. Mexico used to impose tariffs of 10 percent on U.S. goods, while the United States only placed a tariff of 2 percent on Mexican goods coming in. Those tariffs went away, and now as a result of NAFTA, Mexico is the top U.S. export destination for beef, rice, soybean meal, apples, cheese, and dried beans. It's the second-largest export market for corn and soybeans.[2]

The WTO agreement also played a significant role in trade liberalization on a global scale. Unlike any agreement in the past, the Clinton administration instituted a free-trade pact that covered not only goods, but also intellectual-property rights and services that benefited the United States more than any other nation. The agreement was comprehensive and built upon the original General Agreement on Tariffs and Trade of 1947. It was a Reagan initiative that was signed, sealed, and delivered by the Clinton administration.

What do these free-trade deals mean for the average American? The most recent data available suggests that the average American family of four benefited by $350 to $930 annually because NAFTA raises the nation's GDP and, in the process, increases the family income while lowering the costs on consumer goods.[3] NAFTA and the WTO agreement keep Americans working. Clinton's free-trade initiatives mean jobs throughout the United States. Take the state of New York. According to the most recent data available from the U.S. Department of Commerce, New York exported over $80 billion in merchandise in 2008, up over 43 percent from only four years earlier. And according to the figures most recently available from 2006, almost 20 percent of employment in New York State is dependent on exports.[4]

Remember, it isn't just about the trade data and statistics. It's about how the Clinton administration entrenched these international agreements in the global arena to safeguard them against future interventions by protectionists. The NAFTA created a binding dispute settlement to protect investors from arbitrary interventions by the Canadian or Mexican governments. This provision means that American investors can sue these foreign governments for unfair regulatory measures. For example, in 1994, when the Canadian minister for the environment tried to remove MMT from use in gasoline in Canada because it was allegedly affecting auto emissions, the United States fought back in court, as per NAFTA provisions, forcing the Canadian government to back down and recognize the interests of the American investors at stake.

Similarly, at the WTO in Geneva, a binding dispute settlement system has been successfully put in place to allow the United States to challenge governments that restrict American exports across their borders. Countries listen to the trade court's decisions or face the threat of revoked trade concessions and limited access into the States. Officials in Washington, for example, have successfully litigated on behalf of American drug manufacturers and magazine publishers, forcing the Canadian government to alter its existing trade practices in order to boost growth of American exports.

Welfare Reform

Without a doubt, welfare reform is one of the crowning achievements of Bill Clinton's closet Republican presidency. It changed the very nature of federal assistance, and it changed it for the better. The lives of those truly in need were improved and the taxpayer shouldered a much smaller burden. By using a classic incentive system, it dramatically altered what had become a nearly permanent underclass in America and significantly reduced the size of the program and the tax burden it imposed on hardworking middle-class Americans.

It's not just right-wingers who harp about personal responsibility. Granted, it was Newt Gingrich and his Contract with America that pushed Clinton into welfare reform. Still, in 1996, Clinton signed the new welfare measures into law. Appropriately named the Personal Responsibility and Work Opportunity Reconciliation Act, this measure effectively modernized assistance, the goals and principles of which had originated during the Great Depression years. Until the Clinton reforms, welfare benefits were uniform across the country. Regardless of what state you lived in, you had access to the same entitlements, with few to any obligations. Equally significant, there were no time limits attached. Sadly, this meant that one could become a welfare recipient for life.

But with the passage of the new law, the rules of the game changed. Control of welfare money was handed over to the states, which were only given two mandates:

First, the recipient had to begin working within two years of receiving the assistance. This ensured that welfare was there for those in need, but at the same time, it also meant that recipients had a reason to continue to look for work.

Second, there was a five-year time limit on assistance. Welfare was no longer for life. The eligibility allowance had a cap. The government would be there as a support but only until one could get back on his or her feet.

Another result of the changes: states were now allowed to deny increased coverage to mothers who had additional children while already on public assistance. This reduced the incentive for women to have children just so they could get a bigger check.

Republicans at the time felt it didn't go far enough, but looking back, the results were fantastic. In two years the numbers of those receiving assistance dropped dramatically. By June 1998, families receiving welfare fell to 2.98 million—a considerable difference from the 4.73 million that were on assistance in 1995.[5] By three years into reform, a huge number of adults had left the public assistance payroll and reentered the workforce. Although the numbers varied, anywhere from 62 percent to 87 percent of a state's unemployed rejoined the workforce. The across-the-board change was both impressive and shocking.

Because the state governments were free to use the money from the federal government in ways they determined served their local needs best (providing they met the two key mandates of work and time limits), they developed a lot of opportunities and incentives to get people back to work. A state-by-state look offers a window into the importance of personal responsibility and preventing abuse of taxpayer dollars.

As time went by under the new welfare regime, researchers at the Heritage Foundation were able to glean insights into what made some state programs more successful than others in terms of getting people off the public payroll and back into employment. States that implemented two key features of back-to-work initiatives ensured that more individuals were successful at finding work. First, those state governments that applied stringent sanctions on people who did not comply with the programs' requirements, such as job training or community work, were more successful than those that did not. States such as Idaho, Wisconsin, and Wyoming docked an individual's entire welfare check at the first instance of noncompliance. If a welfare recipient didn't show up for work or at the welfare office just once, his or her benefits were docked. Those states saw their welfare caseloads drop by 77 percent, 74 percent, and 66 percent respectively. In other states, such as Rhode Island and Minnesota, that had very weak sanctions and only partially docked a person's paycheck, caseloads dropped by only 5 and 11 percent. In fact, in Hawaii, another weak-sanction state, officials saw the number of cases *increase* by 10 percent.[6]

A second key feature found in successful state programs involved the timing of the work requirement. Again, states such as Idaho and Wisconsin insisted people immediately enter the workforce by doing community work like street sweeping or by attending the welfare office for job training on a daily basis. This was significant because it reduced fraud from the beginning of the reforms. It showed that there were some households getting multiple checks under different names. "Phantom" recipients can't show up at the work site or welfare office on a daily basis. Sometimes people who didn't even live in a jurisdiction would be able to collect checks because it was so easy prior to the reforms.

This system also uncovered an even more common form of welfare fraud: people who worked and still received a check from the government. Orange County, California, found that more than one-third of its welfare recipients also had a job. Immediate work requirements make it nearly impossible for people to participate in daily assigned activities at the welfare office and still report to work. So they had to choose.

An immediate work requirement also reduced the attractiveness of being on welfare and doing nothing. Now that you had to actually do something every day to get that check, the value or benefits of welfare fell sharply, making getting a job a more attractive option. Researchers at the American Enterprise Institute believe this prepared recipients of aid for the real world of work, where they would be accountable for their actions. The AEI said recipients were taught self-control, responsibility, and persistence, all hallmarks of eventual self-sufficiency.[7]

A lot of critics of welfare reform say that the only reason welfare rolls dropped so dramatically at the time was that the economy was booming. But in fact, some of the states with the highest unemployment saw the greatest reduction of those on welfare. Far more important was the way each state implemented the changes.

Many Democrats called Clinton's welfare reform "cruel." Give me a break—it was hardly that. Overnight, welfare became about job training and job placement. And when those who had gotten jobs were asked whether the following statement was true—"my life was better when I was on welfare"[8]—the overwhelming majority said no.

Clinton's policy had another effect, one that arguably improves the lives of the poor considerably. Researchers found that children are far more likely to end up on welfare if their parents are on welfare, and that this is true regardless of race, gender, and family income. In other words, children whose parents' income came from welfare were almost twice as likely as children of employed parents of the same income level to become high school dropouts, and spent 200 percent more time on welfare as adults themselves.

One University of Michigan study found that even when a family receiving welfare had a *higher* income than an equivalent nonwelfare family, there were negative effects on the children. An increase of $1,000 per year in welfare received by a boy's family decreased his future earnings by as much as 10 percent. The study compared families whose average nonwelfare incomes were identical, so each additional dollar in welfare represented additional financial resources.[9] So a child in a welfare home will grow up and earn less than a child raised in an even poorer family where the parents are working.

Still, many viewed these welfare reforms as harsh and unfair. Examples were touted to show how people faced undue hardship under the new regime. And fair enough: some of these cases were true. But Clinton's welfare reforms were all about personal responsibility and were ultimately compassionate for most people. Self-reliance, hard work, and less government intervention in the economy changed the lives of many—for the better.

A Budget Surplus

When Clinton left office, there was a budget surplus. As the *Wall Street Journal*'s Stephen Moore also said, I will give him credit for this because he was there, although he did not actively set out to balance the budget. When you look at the budgets he sent to Congress, he proposed much bigger increases than the Republican Congress was willing to give him. He wanted much more in social spending than he finally got. The great budget battle between Clinton and Newt Gingrich in the summer of 1995 had significant consequences. Clinton had to submit five—yes, five—budgets before he went along with the Republican Congress. But in 1996, as happened under Reagan, nondefense discretionary spending went down.

That is the beauty of divided government.

It is worth reviewing the results because they are so, so

pretty: In 1992, Clinton faced a budget deficit of $290 billion, and there was no good news in sight. It was estimated that Clinton was looking at a $455 billion budget deficit by 2000.[10] Future prospects were, shall we say, bleak. Clinton inherited a George H. W. Bush budget with too much spending.

By Clinton's second term in office, the trend set by his predecessor had been reversed. Not only was there a budget surplus annually, but it was used to reduce the debt for all Americans. The budget surplus in 1998 was viewed as a considerable feat at $69.2 billion and legislators across party lines agreed that the 1999 surplus of $122 billion was even more significant. But in 2000, Clinton's last year in office, the surplus was an inspiring $230 billion.[11] Even after adjusting for inflation, these budget surpluses were the largest in history and considerable by any measure.

Yes, Clinton benefited from a booming economy, a decrease in defense spending, and a Congress that wouldn't rubber-stamp his spending wishes. But he could have been worse. When you look at President George W. Bush in the ensuing years, Clinton was downright sensible.

Clinton's Failures

In other ways, President Clinton, despite his successes, disappointed me. He signed the Defense of Marriage Act—not quietly, but in the Rose Garden, with fanfare. A strange move for a president who campaigned as an advocate for gay rights. More government intervention into our private lives? And it was a measure that was at odds with the more open tone of the Democratic Party.

Those who don't agree with me that Clinton was a closet

Republican will certainly cite his efforts at health-care reform. They are right. There is nothing Republican about what he tried to do with health-care reform. It was classic big government, big spending at its finest. I will give him credit for giving up far sooner than you-know-who when he realized it was something the American people did not want.

What he saw as a success and I think was a failure was his huge push in 1992 to extend home ownership to more individuals. He and the congressional leadership pushed Fannie Mae and Freddie Mac to buy risky loans: mortgages with very low down payments for home buyers who would thus be devoting a huge chunk of their monthly income to their monthly payments. It's the seed of the debacle we face now.

Family Values

Yes, I know, Bill Clinton clearly failed one of the tenets of modern-day Republicanism—the one that emphasizes family values and constantly recalls the sordid details of the Monica Lewinsky affair and the "blue dress." You remember them. Unfortunately, we all do.

But while I fundamentally disagree with his conduct, I don't want to confuse his personal life with his public accomplishments. Don't get me wrong: I agree with everyone who thinks Bill Clinton's family life was in a complete state of disarray, that he humiliated his wife and daughter, and that he showed questionable judgment. I don't disagree.

But why should I care about his family life if his public life and the conservative values he used in governing addressed the issues I was concerned about? Let him run his personal life into the ground if he wants. I care only about how he governs and how that affects the lives of the American people.

In this respect, I admire Canada. Now, there are not many things I admire about the Canadian government. Their socialist ways, for instance, make my hair stand on end. But they have a general approach to their politicians that Americans need to think a little bit more about. Consider a comment by the late Canadian prime minister Pierre Trudeau: "There's no place for the state in the bedrooms of the nation." [12] For Trudeau, the politics and the personal were two different spheres. And to this day it holds relatively true for Canadians, who have the tenacity to question the political decisions of their government while overlooking the personal actions of each and every politician. And it makes me ask, why can't this be our approach to politics, too?

Why don't we focus on a candidate's political actions rather than his or her personal actions? Why can't we find a candidate who focuses on the true values of the free-market economy rather than one who wants to impose his or her values or religion on hardworking Americans? We need to separate our social beliefs, whatever they may be, from our economic beliefs—for the good governance of the nation.

And you know I'm more right than Right about that.

— 4 —

Where the Right Went Wrong

President George W. Bush gave us huge, bloated government and intolerance. The entire conservative movement was badly damaged by George W. Bush, because there was no truth in advertising. Under him the party of supposedly small government became a lie.

In December 2008, after the near–financial collapse of the economy, President George W. Bush said, "I obviously have made a decision to make sure the economy doesn't collapse. I've abandoned free-market principles to save the free-market system."[1]

From that statement, you might think Bush was a true believer in the free markets. Hardly. He advocated more regulation, exorbitant spending, massive federal intervention into education, the expansion of home ownership among those who could not afford it, and protectionism, none of which is a conservative principle. With policies like that, you could have voted for a Democrat who would have come with a bonus: at least the Democrats don't hate gays and immigrants.

I don't think President Bush personally hates gays or immigrants. But you might have thought so after watching him sign a law that okayed a 750-mile fence along the southern border and advocate a constitutional amendment to define marriage as a union between a man and woman. As Bush critic Bruce Bartlett has rightly observed, Bush fooled people into thinking he was a conservative by endorsing family-value policies and by taking the nation into war. He intervened in the Terri Schiavo case and removed federal funding for stem-cell research.

But when it came to *fiscal* issues Bush was nothing but a dyed-in-the-wool liberal. Although he inherited one of the largest budget surpluses in history, he returned the country to deficit spending. Then he pulled some financial shenanigans by keeping the cost of the war off budget, as if by doing so, people would believe the war didn't cost any money. And because the GOP abandoned what they supposedly believed in, he poured fuel on the fire by endorsing the home ownership policies that would later bring Wall Street and America to their knees. He wholeheartedly encouraged the explosion in home ownership that began under President Clinton.

His supporters will say that such huge increases in spending were required in the aftermath of September 11—we had to pay to ratchet up homeland security. But that doesn't explain the massive increase in spending in the departments of labor and education and the expansion of entitlements, just to name a few.

Spending

Sure, Bush made tax cuts early on in his administration. But tax cuts are worthless, even damaging, if they aren't accompanied by cuts in spending as well. If you cut taxes without cutting spending, you are borrowing from future generations rather than taking the money from the current generation.

By the end of his first term, the budget had grown by 7 percent a year, double the rate of President Clinton, under whom it grew by only 3.5 percent.[2] When one adjusts for inflation, he was the biggest spender since Jimmy Carter (until President Obama came along). Just take a look at the most important measure of spending when it comes to a president's ability to control himself and Congress: nondefense discretionary spending. This is the only area of the budget the president can really do something about. It excludes programs such as Medicare and Social Security, which essentially run on autopilot. To change Medicare and Medicaid it literally takes an act of Congress. Three years into Bush's first term, nondefense discretionary spending was up 21 percent. Compare that to Ronald Reagan, who by the third year of his first term in the White House had reduced the dollars spent in that category by 14 percent. Even Bill Clinton has a better record when it comes to spending. By his third year in office, nondefense discretionary spending was down by 0.7 percent.[3]

The departments of education and labor, which Reagan hoped to abolish? Bush upped their budgets by 70 and 65 percent, respectively, between 2001 and 2005.[4] Which is what makes Bush's "I'm like Reagan" campaign rhetoric ridiculous. He was no Reagan, not by a long shot. In fact, Citizens Against Government Waste reported there was more pork barrel spending under Bush than at any other time in history, both by dollar volume and project number. In 2001, $18.5 billion was spent for 6,333 projects. By 2005 that number was up to 13,999 projects, at a cost of more than $27 billion. According to the group's website, this included $469,000 for the National Wild Turkey Federation, $200,000 for the (world-renowned) National Student/Parent Mock Election in Tucson, Arizona, and of course, $100,000 for the Punxsutawney Weather Discovery Center Museum.[5] (Yes, indeed, that is the home of the groundhog Punxsutawney Phil.)

Bush's handling of the 2005 transportation bill was emblematic of his inability to control Congress and spending. Never before had there been so many earmarks in a bill: 6,373 of them, worth a total of $24.2 billion. The list is disgusting: New York City got $4 million for elimination of graffiti, and $2.95 million went to Alaska, not for state roads, but for a *movie* about state roads. Was Scorsese directing with that budget? The Erie Canal Museum got $400,000. The National Packard Museum in Warren, Ohio, got $2.75 million.[6] The president protested mildly, but he signed it.

In fact, there wasn't a spending bill Bush didn't like. He didn't use the veto once in his entire first term in office. You'd have to go back to John Quincy Adams to find a president who didn't veto something in his first term. Compare that to Reagan, who used the veto twenty-two times in his first term, three times when it came to the budget. On average by 2009, Bush had spent $900 billion more than originally planned each year.[7] Afghanistan and Iraq were only a fifth of that amount.

All of this spending took place in the years leading up to the financial collapse. Bush was spending when he should have been saving. It wasn't until Bush had to face a Democratic Congress after a bruising 2006 election that he started fighting back on spending. In 2007, he threatened to veto ten of eleven appropriations bills.[8] So when the crisis hit, we should have been in a much better position financially to weather the storm, but we were financially hobbled by his credit-card mentality.

The really infuriating part is to listen to President Bush's team criticize President Obama. To hear them now, you'd think they had been models of fiscal restraint. Karl Rove, Bush's top advisor, has written a book and several op-eds in the *Wall Street Journal* in which he has complained about Obama's spending. True fiscal conservatives were infuriated. Chris Edwards of the Cato Institute followed up with a letter to the editor that rightly pointed out that even if you exclude Bush's last year, which included the Troubled Asset Relief Program, "nominal spending jumped 60 percent during that period, or more than twice the 27 percent increase under Democrat Bill Clinton."[9]

All this spending did not cause the financial crisis, but did handcuff us when we had to respond to it. The cause itself lay in another Bush policy.

The Ownership Society

One of my few criticisms of President Clinton earlier concerned his push to get Fannie and Freddie (as well as the Department of Housing and Urban Development) to lend more money to more people to buy homes when in fact they shouldn't have. I'll forgive Clinton for that, because at least it was true to Democratic Party principles, however misguided.

But President Bush should have been different. The Republican Party claims to be about personal responsibility, but they went right along with a big-government "solution" to a nonexistent problem. We were already at a very high home ownership rate of nearly 70 percent, and yet President Bush pushed for more.[10]

In 2002, Bush said, "The goal is, everybody who wants to own a home has got a shot of doing so,"[11] and he specifically set out to get 5.5 million more homeowners by 2010—a million of them minorities. He pushed Congress to spend $200 million a year on the American Dream Downpayment Initiative, which provided the down payment, closing costs, and the money to renovate to people whose income did not exceed 80 percent of the area median income. Each could receive up to $10,000 or 6 percent of the home's value, whichever was greater. His team believed forty thousand families would be able to get homes that they previously couldn't afford.[12] In the end, those new homeowners had almost no equity.

When someone has no equity in a home, when they've put none of their own money into it, it is much, much easier to walk away when the value of the home falls below what they owe on it, or when the economy turns and they can't pay their bills. We've learned this the hard way. In the same speech announcing the initiative, Bush said another thing that prevents homeownership is "that the rules are too complex. People get discouraged by the fine print on the contracts. They take a look and say, well, I'm not sure so sure I want to sign this. There are too many words. There are too many pitfalls. So one of the things that the Secretary [of Housing and Urban Development] is going to do is he's going to simplify the closing documents, and all the documents that have to deal with homeownership. It is essential that we make it easier for people to buy a home, not harder."[13]

Bush forced Fannie Mae and Freddie Mac to go along with it. He believed there wasn't enough demand in the private capital markets for these types of loans, so he got them to agree to spend $440 billion buying up these first-time, low-income-buyer loans.[14]

Bush rounded out his speech that fateful day in 2002 by saying, "I want people to see the deep compassion of America. I want the world to see the other side of our character, which is the soft side, the decent side, the loving side." [15]

How soft, decent, and loving did President Bush's initiative to get families into homes turn out to be? Not very. In 2007, foreclosures jumped 225 percent; a further 81 percent increase followed in 2008.[16] Millions of homeowners packed up their stuff and left the keys on the kitchen floor or mailed them to the bank.

The pain was horrendous and the effects on the overall economy were devastating.

Prescription Drug Reform

In the name of "compassionate conservatism," Bush enacted one of the worst pieces of legislation ever: the prescription drug benefit for the elderly called the Medicare Modernization Act of 2003, better known as Medicare Part D. No one wants the elderly crippled by drug costs, or worse, by being unable to even get the drugs they need to survive. But what is so infuriating about Medicare Part D is that it gave benefits to all seniors, even those who didn't even need the financial help. What could have been a compassionate piece of legislation for low-income seniors became a spending boondoggle that will saddle future generations with higher taxes. There is nothing compassionate about forcing working families to pay for the prescription drug benefits of baby boomers, the wealthiest retiring generation in American history (even with the collapse in stocks in 2008).

When this bill was being debated, 50 percent of seniors already had prescription drug coverage through their previous employers. For those who didn't, their average annual out-of-pocket prescription drug expenses were less than $650. Fewer than 10 percent of Medicare beneficiaries faced more than $2,000 a year for their medications.[17]

Let's look at it another way: percentage of income spent on medications. At the time, 55 percent of elderly people who used prescription drugs spent 1 percent or less of their income on those drugs. Seven percent of the elderly spent at least 10 percent of their income on drugs, and 1 percent spent over 25 percent on drugs.[18]

Those last two categories of individuals indeed deserved some help. They are likely to be poor and have some kind of chronic condition that forces them to buy medications on a protracted basis. So how about subsidized vouchers to buy private insurance? Or extending Medicaid benefits through the states, another lower-cost option directed at the poor? Or just a program aimed at low-income seniors? But Bush and Congress weren't satisfied with that. They decided they wanted to do something big, and now we are all stuck with Medicare Part D. This extends benefits to all seniors regardless of need.

What's happened as a result? Some employers stopped covering drug benefits for their retirees. The Congressional Budget Office estimated that former employers would have provided every fourth enrollee with adequate coverage.[19] But why should the employer keep providing it if they know the government is going to pick up the tab? To try to prevent this, Congress started paying employers fees so they wouldn't cut coverage. General Motors was estimated to get $4 billion of taxpayer dollars to simply keep paying for what they had already planned to pay for. Verizon planned on getting more than $1 billion back from the government.[20] That's taxpayer money being spent on something that those companies were going to pay for voluntarily. So guess what: this turned out to be a big giveaway to private corporations. If they dropped retiree drug benefits they saved money. If they didn't drop retiree drug benefits, they got a fat check from the government.

The costs started exploding from day one. The original estimate of the program from 2003 through 2013 was $400 billion.[21] But the *Washington Post* uncovered documents showing that the Bush White House knew the cost would be at least $500 billion, and that the guy drawing up the official estimate was told he'd be fired if he didn't come up with the "right" number.

When the president put out his budget in February 2004 for fiscal 2005, lo and behold, there it was: $534 billion in estimated costs through 2013. To add insult to injury, one month later the Medicare trustee said that, actually, it's likely to be at least $690 billion. Six months later the president's budget office put out yet another estimate: $732 billion through 2014. That's a jump from $400 billion to $732 billion in just two years. Where do you think it goes from there? Right now costs are soaring, and the baby boomers haven't even begun to retire en masse. The unfunded liabilities of Medicare Part D stand at $15.5 trillion.[22]

No one should have been surprised. When Medicare was enacted in 1965, official government projections said it would cost $9 billion in 1990. What was the actual cost in 1990? It was $66 billion. The Medicare payroll tax is now double what the original writers of the bill thought would be necessary and it is still not enough to cover the costs.[23]

I am all for the poor getting the drugs they need, but by extending the benefit to all, politicians did not act compassionately—they acted politically. They pandered to a vociferous voting block that wanted everything regardless of whether it might eventually deny the same benefits to future generations due to spiraling cost. And so future generations will have to put more and more of their money toward someone else's health care. That means those who are young today will have less money to pay for their children's education, their own health-care needs, their homes, and their lives. There is nothing compassionate about that kind of government interference.

Medicare Part D is, in fact, not just an unpaid-for benefit to people who didn't really need it, it is a bribe to today's voters at the expense of future generations.

Protectionism

If George Bush wasn't focused on the budget, what did we get from him? Protectionism in the form of steel tariffs. In March 2002, President Bush slapped tariffs of 8 percent to 30 percent on several types of imported steel: tin-mill steel (30 percent), coated sheet steel (30 percent), circular-welded tubular products (15 percent), and stainless steel wire (8 percent).[24] What's so special about, say, tin-mill steel, to use just one example? Maybe that one of the biggest producers in the United States was Weirton Steel in West Virginia. This was payback to the state of West Virginia for voting for Bush rather than

Gore in 2000. Bush campaigned on the promise of protecting the steel industry.

What were the costs of raising tariffs on steel? A $30,000 car likely went up by another $50. Doesn't sound like a lot? That's from just one tariff and for just one industry. You start adding tariffs for every industry that wants protection, say glass producers, parts producers, plastics producers, and the price of a car can rise by $1,000. It is a death spiral that leads to higher prices on goods and hurts the poor most of all.

In 2002, for every employee in America who worked in the steel-producing industry there were fifty-nine people who worked in the steel-using industry.[25] So to benefit one person, fifty-nine other people suffered.

Domestic companies that use imported steel were understandably furious, and if they were powerful enough, they demanded and got exemptions. Caterpillar, one of the biggest manufacturing employers in the United States, was suddenly going to have to pay more for steel parts, but it is so powerful that it lobbied for and got an exemption. I don't criticize them for that. But it does go to show that the little guy, the smaller company with no such power, has no leverage and is stuck paying higher prices.

Even worse, economists believe it cost 52,000 steel-using jobs in the United States.[26] American jobs were lost even though steel tariffs were put in place to protect American jobs. Why? One year later, the U.S. International Trade Commission reported that 25 percent of steel users said they had lost business to overseas customers who had access to cheaper, nontariff steel. A third of them reported that long-term contracts had been broken or modified by steel suppliers who could suddenly obtain higher prices because of the tariffs.

And 40 percent of steel users told the trade commission that employment would be higher if the tariffs were eliminated.

At the time there were 150,000 steel workers in a U.S. population of 275 million.[27] Why did we all have to pay more for cars, and anything else that uses steel, for the sake of one industry? Why did auto workers have to subsidize steel workers? The auto industry had plenty of trouble of its own; it didn't need Washington making things worse. Bush rescinded the tariffs one year later, but the harm was already done. His reputation as a free-trader was gone forever. Although he went on to champion free-trade agreements with countries like Colombia, his and the nation's credibility on free trade was destroyed.

There were plenty of critics from the left, and more importantly from the right, pointing out all of these issues about President Bush. Early on, the Cato Institute took Bush to task for his spending and his invasive social policies. The same can be said for the Heritage Foundation and the Ayn Rand Institute. Unfortunately, these aren't household names for the average American. The right-wing media failed the Right by being consistently supportive of the president regardless of what he did. They chose to support a person rather than a set of principles.

I think Yaron Brook from the Ayn Rand Institute summed up Bush's impact best in his response to a November 2008 speech Bush made about Wall Street: "If Bush is a friend of the free market, who needs enemies? By praising the free market while systematically undermining it, Bush has done more to discredit capitalism than any open critic could. Like a con artist who undercuts the reputation of Mercedes, by selling lemon look-alikes, Bush now led people to associate his failed policies with capitalism. The association needs to be erased. We must make it clear: Bush is no friend to the free markets." [28]

Where Social Conservatives Went Wrong

Not only did Bush support big-government intervention into *fiscal* issues, he also supported big-government intervention into *social* issues.

In 2004, Bush's right-hand man, Karl Rove, orchestrated an anti-gay-marriage movement to inspire the socially conservative base to get out and reelect the president. They were voting for president by way of an amendment banning gay marriage.

From a market-share perspective, I get it. Americans who call themselves "born again" or "evangelical" represent some 34 percent of the population. By comparison, the next-largest group, Catholics, comes in at 25 percent. In fact, 76 percent of all Americans self-identify as Christian. Non-Christians come in at a tiny 3.9 percent. [29]

That is why Karl Rove's strategy worked so well. Social conservatives came out and voted and Bush won a second term.

But here's the problem: pushing social values as a platform runs counter to conservative values. Conservative values are about liberty, freedom, and small government. Advocating constitutional amendments to define marriage is about making government bigger, not smaller. We can't only give freedom to those with whom we agree. We should also give freedom to those who are different, provided that when they exercise their rights they don't infringe on anyone else's freedom.

The full-fledged embrace of family values as part of a political platform is also politically perilous. It repeatedly leaves
members of the Republican Party open to charges of hypocrisy. How many holier-than-thou members of the GOP have
suddenly ended up on the front page for getting involved in a
scandal that went against the platform they campaigned on?

All of this hypocrisy is totally avoidable if government
would stop going places it shouldn't. The gay-marriage debate
would basically go away if states would just stop giving out
marriage licenses—for anyone, straight or gay. Government's
role is to defend private contracts—not decide who should
enter into one. Why does a state get involved in this at all?
Why do I have to go to the courthouse if I am also going to
go to my church, synagogue, or whatever house of worship to
which I belong? There are witnesses you can sign a contract in
front of; it will hold up in a court of law later if you want to
get divorced. In the end marriage could and should be a private contract between two people, regardless of sexual orien-
tation. If gays and lesbians want to marry, they could do it at
an institution that welcomes them. Think of it like privatizing
marriage. Why is government going to places it shouldn't go?
(My guess is that it wants the license fees, but that's another
issue.)

If states didn't issue marriage licenses at all, then states
wouldn't have to worry about defining marriage in the first
place and then could avoid all the moral meddling that comes
along. This would allow various members of state legislatures
to focus on the bread-and-butter issues facing American families and stop wasting money advocating for or against a constitutional amendment to define the state of wedlock.

Unfortunately, because government has gotten involved
in way too many parts of our lives, marriage is no longer just

a social issue, but also a financial one. Marriage determines access to a spouse's Social Security benefits, and sometimes to pensions, and health-care benefits, not to mention immigration status. The answer is to reduce government involvement in all those areas as well. When you reduce or remove government involvement, you also remove the connection between taxpayer dollars and social policy. This is an essential component of freedom. No one else can tell you how you can use your money if they aren't footing the bill. And no taxpayer has to worry that their money is supporting a lifestyle they find unacceptable.

The Stem-Cell Debate

President Bush also took a strong stand against government funds being used for stem-cell research. I agree that no federal money be spent on stem-cell research, but that's because the government shouldn't be funding any research at all. Let private industry define the needs of science, and leave research decisions to universities, venture capitalists, and corporations. Otherwise politics drives the scholarly agenda, and priorities and outcomes get distorted. When politicians decide where research money goes, they are far more likely to send it to big donors, rather than the most promising studies. Let me emphasize that this has nothing to do with my view on stem-cell research. We are simply wasting our money by letting government decide what we should and should not study.

President Bush got in on the school debate as well. In 2005, he told reporters that the theory of intelligent design, or in other words creationism, should be taught along with evolution in the nation's public schools "so people can understand what the debate is about."[30] But here's the problem: the federal government shouldn't have a role in education, period. I am an advocate of school choice and putting power in the hands of parents—rich or poor. The concept of school choice eliminates all the controversies surrounding these issues. You want to be sure that your kid is taught about evolution? Then pick a school that teaches evolution. You want your kid to study creationism? Send him to a school that teaches creationism. And to those of you who are opposed to kids being taught creationism because you think it's bad science—get over it. Lots of kids are already taught that. For example, if they are homeschooled, their parents can teach them whatever they want. A student at a private Catholic school is taught that God made the earth in seven days. Creationism is the least of our worries. If you get freaked out about creationism, remember that some who believe in creationism get just as freaked out about evolution. In the end, I believe the issue of creationism has become a straw-man argument. I firmly believe that, if given the choice, parents will choose a school that is best at teaching their kids to read, write, and do arithmetic, and getting them into a college or a trade within which they can prosper. Bottom line: Parents should decide.

It Didn't Start with Bush

Although this move to cater to social mores rose dramatically under President Bush, I acknowledge it did not start with him. Both President Nixon and President Reagan were guilty of pandering to social values. Remember Pat Buchanan's infamous 1992 Republican convention speech? He railed against "the raw sewage of pornography that so terribly pollutes our popular culture." And he argued, "We stand with George H. W. Bush against the amoral idea that gay and lesbian couples should have the same standing in law as married men and women." But from my view, the most absurd thing he said that night was that "there is a religious war going on in the country. It is a culture war as critical to the kind of nation we shall be as the cold war itself." Think about that. He was saying gays who want to live together and get married are as dangerous to our country as Russian nuclear weapons. And to this day we still have politicians going to the Value Voters Summit each year to thump on social issues over and over and over.

This does nothing but open the door to accusations of hypocrisy. All too often, the same politicians who are busy trying to legislate social values are also getting busy on the side. Unfortunately for the Republican Party, using family values as a test of an individual's ability to lead is mostly a Republican problem. How many times has Newt Gingrich been married? Three. That's doesn't make him the poster child for family values, but he's a Republican and has spent a lot of energy lambasting Clinton for his shortcomings as a human being. Representatives Henry Hyde and Bob Livingston, both Republicans, led the charge against Clinton but have no moral high ground to claim when it comes to adultery. Senator Larry Craig lobbied hard against gay rights for years—and then pleaded guilty to lewd behavior in a men's room.

Here's the bottom line: in the last election we learned that what really matters is economic performance. People will always vote their pocketbook. Embracing the politics of social values did nothing for the GOP last time round. John McCain, whether you adore him or not, made a fatal error. He didn't address the economy enough and when he did, he stumbled badly, telling people the "economy is fundamentally sound" even though we were on the brink of collapse. Mc-Cain, once a voice of reason on a number of issues, moved sharply to the right on social issues to court the far-right Christian vote that he thought he needed to win the 2008 presidential primaries. He chose Sarah Palin as his running mate in an effort to get a more socially conservative voter. She is truly a phenomenon, but I'm not sure it helped him get any votes. Or if it did, it lost him many others. The most conservative elements of the party are going to vote Republican regardless. The key is to go after independents. The socially conservative vote simply couldn't save the Republican Party.

Unlike France or Japan, each of which has a dominant ethnicity, Americans are bound together by a dominant economic philosophy. In this way we are unique. I am the daughter of a Cuban exile and an Italian-American. I grew up in suburban New England. On its face, it would appear that I have nothing in common with a Korean-American Buddhist from Los Angeles. But we share something that I think is far more important than a similar ethnic or religious background: we are all from families that want to have a better life, give our children opportunities, enhance our social mobility, and build our own lives and successes based on our own values. As long as we all play by the same basic rules, we can all pursue our dreams with little interference in our private decisions.

And let's face it, if we followed the moral compass of some of our political leaders—left or right—we'd get lost pretty quickly. Alexander Hamilton had a scandalous affair and was blackmailed, and Thomas Jefferson was a notorious womanizer—but should their antics have prevented them from being Founding Fathers?

So let's take morality out of the political process. Let's leave the personal lives of everyone in the personal category, not the public one. The hypocrisy infuriates me and other hardworking Americans who would rather see their government focus on bread-and-butter issues, not decide what should or shouldn't go on in someone's bedroom.

Only the Economy, Stupid

Here's a basic test for any policy proposal put forth by a conservative leader: does this policy advance the national security or economic prosperity of the United States? It's hard to see where a policy involving social issues would meet that criterion. If it doesn't, then the government has no business getting involved in it. It's absurd that our government uses its resources on things like telling doctors what they may or may not discuss with patients, or deciding who can marry, or dictating to television stations what words may not be uttered before 9 P.M. In fact, the list of such absurdities is almost endless.

People aren't stupid. To believe this, you must have an underlying faith in the American people. People know what is good for them. They know how they want to raise their children. They know if they want to adhere to religious rituals. They know that their doctor is a source of medical advice and treatment and they choose their doctor accordingly. They know which life partner will make them happiest. They know how they want to live privately. They know how to find information that they need to make decisions. Why does anyone think that someone in a state legislature or Congress knows better than you what will make you happy or prosperous?

How is it possible that some senator who's never met you knows how to organize your life or your family better than you do? And when was the last time you felt like the government did you a favor and gave you a leg up?

The amount of time, energy, and attention that conservative politicians spend criticizing other politicians for their personal failings does the conservative movement a disservice. Conservatives talk about getting government out of people's lives but often decide that the best way to beat opponents is to smear them for their personal choices.

We're obsessed with hypocrites. We're obsessed with private lives. But we should leave those obsessions to *US Weekly*. Unless it harms the innocent, we shouldn't make personal issues a focus of our government or a measure for politicians. The role of government should be simple: entrench the principles of freedom and liberty, provide law and order, ensure the protection of property rights, and defend this great nation.

I don't care what you do in your personal life, but I know I'm right when I say let's leave it out of politics.

— 5 —

Fixing Unions

If you didn't know better, you might think that the unions are really running the White House and that President Obama is a mere puppet.

If you want some insight into how angry some right-wing bloggers really are in their views about conservatism and the economy, just Google "Obama" and "unions." You'll find a lot of ranting. Blogger after blogger calls the president out because in his book *The Audacity of Hope* he noted that he "owes" some unions. Many of these bloggers then provide a long list of initiatives that the president has adopted that favor so-called Big Labor. These same bloggers often cite a comment made by Andy Stern, the former leader of the powerful Service Employees International Union (SEIU). In an interview with the *Las Vegas Sun*, Stern was quoted as saying, "We spent a fortune to elect President Barack Obama—$60.7 million to be exact."[1] And according to these conservative blogs, Stern was a frequent visitor to the White House.

There's a comparison to be made: the unions are to the Democrats what the religious right is to the Republicans. They both have too much control over their respective parties. The unions are strangling the left and forcing the government to make bad choices.

I have no problem with unions trying to form in the private sector, but public-sector unions are choking our state and local governments, reducing the services that citizens have access to while at the same time ensuring that taxes are raised to pay for overly generous benefits that those in the private sector can only dream about.

Unions used to be about representing the downtrodden and the weak. Now they are far more likely to represent "haves" rather than "have-nots." They have overwhelming influence on the political process, and it is likely that that influence has come from the spending of your tax dollars. Your taxes end up in the treasuries of the strong and well-off teachers' unions while your children get larger class sizes and fewer resources, resulting in mediocre education. Unionized state workers are often allowed to retire with full benefits at much younger ages than in the private sector.

Government workers should not be allowed to unionize at all.

This approach to public-sector administration would help make sure that your tax dollars are used in improving services in your area and prevent state budgets from being held hostage by powerful state employee unions. Frankly, the idea that any workforce thinks it's entitled to a raise, a long list of antiquated perks, and a job regardless of performance, the state of the economy, or the bottom line of a company (does General Motors come to mind?) makes my blood boil.

So, understand that I have no problem with the existence of private-sector unions. Corporate abuse of employees is kept in check by the mere threat of possible unionization. Just a whiff of unionization can lead to better work conditions and higher salaries. In those instances I actually see their value. More importantly, the free market provides a natural check on the power of unions. CATO's Chris Edwards makes a great point. If a union drives up the cost of a product, consumers will buy that product from a competitor. If a private-sector union chokes a company, the company fails and the union goes away.

But public-sector unions are an entirely different story. Governments almost never fail, so there is no natural check on the power of the government union workers. They just grow and grow and grow in both size and power. They never have to worry about asking for more, because they don't have to worry about the company going broke. Instead the government can just raise taxes to pay them off. As a consumer you can't choose a different, more efficient police or fire department, public school system, or post office. You are stuck with the ones in your area. A government doesn't have to worry about its product becoming more expensive than someone else's product, because it is the only provider— a real monopoly. It doesn't have to worry about turning a profit, and it has the option to borrow and deficit-spend. As a result, unions have worked hard to expand into government. In fact, in 2009, for the first time in history, the majority of union members were government workers. Fifty-two percent of all union members in the United States are working for the federal, state, or local government. In the private sector only 7 percent of employees are unionized.

In state and local governments, 39 percent of employees are unionized.[2]

Three times more union members work for the U.S. Postal Service than in the auto industry.[3] Three times.

Union workers are well paid, too, far better than private-sector employees. They are also likely to have far more generous benefits. The Bureau of Labor Statistics reports that weekly earnings by union members in 2009 were $908, nearly $200 more than nonunion workers. When you include benefits, the average hourly wage for a state or local union member is $39.81 an hour (wage and benefit) versus just $27.73 for private sector.[4] Despite those salaries, there is no incentive for them to do anything but punch a clock until they collect their fat pension, because it's often nearly impossible to fire them.

More than 90 percent of all public-sector employees have a defined benefit plan, meaning they have a guaranteed payout in retirement. Only 20 percent of private-sector employees have a defined benefit plan. The rest of us have defined contribution plans, usually a 401(k).[5] In other words, the only thing that is defined is how much the company puts in originally, not how much it has to pay out later. The median pension of private-sector employees who still have them is only $7,692, while public-sector employees receive on average $17,640. More than 80 percent of public-sector employees have retirement benefits of any kind, compared to only 33 percent in the private sector.[6]

In state after state, the benefits for unionized public-sector workers are ridiculously generous. In Illinois, for example, state workers can retire with full benefits at age fifty-five. They get an automatic 3 percent raise every year even if there is no inflation. Get this: workers can get retirement benefits while they are still working full-time. Does that make any sense? National Taxpayers United of Illinois discovered that some 3,500 state workers had annual pensions of more than $100,000, with some getting as much as $391,000. Finally, in spring 2010 the state got smart and changed the law for new hires. New state employees have to work until they are sixty-seven to get full benefits and they cannot double-dip. And their yearly pensions are maxed out at $106,800.[7]

The previous employees are grandfathered in.

Illinois is not alone. Many state retirees still don't have to pay anything for their health-care benefits, which of course have been skyrocketing. How did they manage to have such generous benefits? Unions. The Cato Institute did an analysis of state debt loads versus the percentage of unionized state and local workers. A state tends to have a higher government debt load when there are a larger number of unionized public-sector employees.[8]

And what do we get for our generosity? Are you happy with the service you get from that larger group of union-ized U.S. postal workers? How many times have you been met with glares, anger, and miserable customer service when you went to mail a package? I face that experience with dread every time I am forced to use their service. And guess what? I actually go elsewhere whenever I can now. That 260,000-strong union is tanking its business even as the Inter-net makes them less and less useful.[9]

The teachers' unions are even worse. Look at the devas-tating chokehold that unions have on California. From an economic standpoint the state is about to fall off a cliff and a large portion of the blame goes to government worker pensions. The pension costs rose 2,000 percent in just the last ten years. But what happened to state revenues? They increased just 24 percent.[10] How does a state make up for such a massive shortfall? It cuts funding for "little" programs such as college education. In fact, the repercussions cannot be overstated. The shortfall in government funding forced the University of California to jack up tuition by more than 30 percent in January 2010. And the unfunded liabilities for the state are expected to skyrocket even further: more than $122 billion.[11]

Like the postal service, teachers in California can get really bad grades and still keep their jobs, because their union will protect them and ensure they have a job for life. An investigation by the *Los Angeles Times* in December 2009 found that tenure, which ensures a job for life, is so easy to get that it's shameful. Teachers there can be let go only during their first two years on the job. After that they get tenure if they pass review. The investigation found that less than 2 percent failed the reviews, which are almost meaningless. The yardstick isn't whether kids are learning or getting solid grades. Teachers often get tenure after a thirty-minute class observation by the principal. The *Times* reported that some teachers refer to the evaluation as a "drive-by."[12] With tenure these teachers become part of a strong union whose rich benefits are covered at the expense of many other state programs.

And they are the first ones to holler about how the government is cutting education spending.

In New Jersey, Governor Chris Christie is cracking down on government unions. He is making tough cuts to avoid a projected $11 billion budget deficit in 2011. In the process he is effectively waging war with the teachers' union.[13] To meet the state's unfunded liabilities, Christie is making a major push that will affect the pension fund for current teachers. He has been able to get bipartisan support to reduce the state workers' pension program and upped new workers' medical costs from zero to 1.5 percent.

Did you catch that? New workers have to pay only a measly 1.5 percent of their own medical costs, and current workers still get their medical benefits for free.[14]

If you work in the private sector, I'll bet you've seen your premiums raised year after year by your employer—if you receive health-care benefits at all. But New Jersey state workers get a free ride on the back of the taxpayer.

Here's what is truly infuriating: your taxpayer dollars are used to lobby for rules and legislation that go against your interests and are only designed to cost you more money. How? Most of these unionized government workers pay union dues from their taxpayer-funded salaries. The National Education Association and the American Federation of Teachers collect about $2 billion a year in dues.[15] Public-sector unions spent $165 million in 2007 and 2008 to support campaigns and ballot initiatives. Over the last twenty years, the American Federation of State, County and Municipal Employees (AFSCME) was the second-largest contributor to campaigns.[16]

And as Andy Stern said, the SEIU spent $60 million getting Barack Obama elected. In fact, since 1989, unions have contributed half a billion dollars to political campaigns.[17]

In 2008 alone, the numbers were astounding. One out of every five dollars spent by the SEIU in 2008 went to support politicians, for a whopping total of $85 million.[18] What did they use all that money for? Not just campaigns, but paying the salaries of union employees while they worked on Democratic campaigns. AFSCME spent $63 million. The International Brotherhood of Teamsters spent $13 million, and the United Auto Workers (UAW) spent $11 million. Of the top one hundred donors, six out of the top ten are unions, with another eighteen further down the list.[19]

Ninety-four percent of union political spending went to Democrats.[20] This explains why unions have such a stranglehold on the Democratic Party—they have the money, your money. Even though union workers are only 12 percent of the entire population, they represented 25 percent of the delegates at the 2008 Democratic convention in Denver.[21] Only about 20 percent of Democrats are union members, but they are far more likely to vote and they have a lot more money to throw around than the other 80 percent.[22]

This level of lobbying power and clout is scary, especially as a changing economy renders more and more unions irrelevant, a ball and chain for businesses and the government.

The world is a different place than it used to be. Unions were formed to protect exploited workers. In the midst of the Industrial Revolution in the 1800s, trade unions representing skilled and unskilled laborers began to organize to represent workers in coal mines or mills or on the railways. They existed to ensure safety measures, to fight for better work conditions, and to obtain fair wages. They thrived because they were there to prevent child labor, prevent exploitation, and ensure a safe workplace.

Looking back, I of course appreciate their efforts, but unions should have died a natural death as our economy evolved.

Arguably, unions would have come to a natural demise but for President Kennedy's Executive Order 10988, issued in 1962, which allowed unionism in the federal bureaucracy. It was a pivotal step and led to widespread unionization among government workers. The statistics tell the whole story: Back in 1960, there were 900,000 union members working for government, and by 2009 there were 7.9 million. Nearly 50 percent of them are teachers.[23] Unions want bigger government because it leads to more members. That's why unions are bad for taxpayers, bad for the economy, and bad for the political process.

In a Labor Day speech in 2009, President Obama said, "It was the American worker—union men and women—who returned from World War II to make our economy the envy of the world. . . . It was labor that helped build the largest middle class in history. So even if you're not a union member, every American owes something to America's labor movement."[24] I understand how this nation was built and appreciate the sacrifices workers made in the past. But now it's not just the higher costs in terms of salaries and benefits: unions make us anticompetitive and actually hurt our workers and our country.

Union organizers love public-sector workers because they've learned you can only get so much out of a private company before it goes belly up and the goose that laid the golden egg is dead. Look no further than General Motors: When GM went bankrupt, it was no longer an automaker. It had become a supplier of health care that only made cars on the side, with three times as many retirees as active workers. In 2007 alone it spent $4.6 billion on health-care costs.[25] As a result of incredibly generous retiree benefits to the auto workers, Detroit automakers lost market share compared to their nonunion counterparts.

The only way to break the stranglehold was bankruptcy.

UAW workers earned seventy-five dollars an hour in wages and benefits—almost triple the earnings of the average private-sector worker.[26] I did extensive reporting on the financials of GM as they were heading into bankruptcy. The company's retirees had substantially more benefits than most other American workers. For example, no monthly health-care premiums, extremely low co-pays, and coverage of nearly everything. When I was covering the story for CNBC, my sources told me GM was one of the biggest, if not the biggest, buyer of Viagra in the country. Also, UAW workers had something wonderful called a jobs bank: it paid them nearly full wages to not work.[27] If an employee was laid off, he or she collected almost full salary. This benefit was suspended in 2008, but in 2005, some reports say, twelve thousand UAW members enjoyed the jobs bank payout.[28] Salaried employees and the administrative support staff were forced to pay higher health-care premiums year after year while they watched the unionized line workers live off contracts that reflected much more robust times. Don't get me wrong: I don't absolve the spineless management that over the years agreed to these contracts. They should have been like Reagan, who, bless his soul, broke the Air Traffic Controllers in 1981.

Many described those benefits as gold-plated. But they were causing GM to rot and rust from the inside out. It put the company, and in fact all the Detroit Big Three, at a terrible disadvantage compared to competitors. For example, the UAW's lavish health benefits added $1,200 to the cost of each vehicle produced in the United States. The Japanese automakers, located in states far less friendly to labor, are able to provide standard employee benefits. As a result, Toyota only spent $215 per vehicle in health care in 2006.[29] Every American buying an auto made in Detroit paid an extra $700–$1,000 to support health benefits far more generous than most of the Americans buying cars receive themselves.[30]

As a result, American auto manufacturers saw dramatic

declines in market share in the United States. To keep prices competitive, they skimped on the extras. When consumers went to showrooms, they chose the foreign cars.

During the auto crisis, the financial situation grew so bad that even the Obama administration saw bankruptcy as the only way out. And even then the administration made sure the unions got more than they deserved. When I covered the GM bankruptcy, every source I had, regardless of which side of the aisle they sat on or which side they represented, told me that when the carcass of the company was divided up, the union was going to get special treatment. And it did. Although they were owed less than the lenders, they were given much more of the company. The lenders were owed $27 billion, but given 10 percent of GM's stock. The unions were owed $20 billion, but given 17.5 percent in stock.

Take a look at the airline industry for another example of labor killing the very company that feeds them. After September 11, 2001, airlines like United, US Airways, and Delta had to file for bankruptcy to end the stranglehold the unions had on their bottom lines. United remained in bankruptcy for three years, as it had to get out of the old way of doing business by slashing pension and staff costs, laying off thousands of workers, and changing its business model. Flight attendants couldn't clean a plane for turnaround. They could work less than half the month and still make almost $80,000.[31] Like GM, the unions had and still have a serious negative influence on the bottom line of the airlines. Union-free JetBlue thrives because the company can turn planes around faster, sell cheaper tickets, and meet customers' needs. Have you ever sat on JetBlue and heard the flight attendants ask you to pick up papers and trash to clean the plane quickly for the next set of travelers? Traditional airlines can't always do that, because unions prohibit flight attendants from doing cleanup—another union, of cleaners, does that.

JetBlue revolutionized an industry and grew at a time when the sector in general was on life support.

Now the unions and Democrats want to make it even easier for unions to form, with something called the Employee Free Choice Act. It does two things. First, it removes the secret ballot in favor of an open time period during which unions can push employees to sign a card in favor of a union. Consider what that says about how the balance of power has shifted from employers to laborers. The unions fought so hard for the secret ballot because they didn't want corporations to bully employees who voted in favor of unions. Now the unions aren't worried about that at all. In fact, they are the ones who want to be able to bully employees to join a union. Second, it subjects arbitration of disputes to much more government involvement. If this becomes law, it will only give unions even more incentives to donate to politicians in Washington to make sure that when future decisions are made, those decisions favor unions.

Kowtowing to the unions is bad for the Democrats in the same way that pandering to the religious right has hurt the Republicans. State employees have no business unionizing. Instead of fighting for antiquated benefits that haven't made sense in decades, union leaders should stop and look at the debt load the states are carrying. So guess what? When cuts are made we can blame the unions for fewer garbage pick-ups, failing city infrastructure, and backlogged courts.

The world has changed. While I understand that unions can work in the private sector, it breaks my heart to see good companies and our very governments crippled by organized labor. The economy sat on the verge of the abyss in 2008 and the massive decline in state tax revenues exposed just how much unions are costing America.

It's time for Big Labor to adjust to the new world.

And you know I'm right about that, too.

— 6 —

Fixing Health Care

Fixing health care is easy: we buy our own car insurance, we buy our own life insurance, we should buy our own health insurance.

Neither employer-based health insurance nor government-based health insurance will lead to lower costs, higher satisfaction, or better health for its users—all presumed goals of health-care reform.

It's become painfully obvious during the financial crisis that things need to change: waves of people worry about losing health coverage when they lose their jobs; retirees worry about losing benefits because their former employer has gone bankrupt; the government decides to cut the number of adult diapers they pay for because of declines in tax revenues; and thousands can't afford to buy an individual health insurance policy even if they are employed.

Believe it or not, most of these issues would be fixed if we were buying our own health insurance.

Stick with me. It's time to get smart about the problem, assume some personal responsibility, and let the free-market system prevail in this sector. I know this may be hard to believe, but if we all bought our own insurance, we would all have lower, not higher, health-care costs.

The debate in Washington is between those who favor employer-based health insurance and those who favor government-based health insurance. They're starting the debate in the wrong place. Neither provides the right answer. In both scenarios you're not the customer, since you have no control over your health insurance. That is the crux of the problem.

Employer-Based Insurance

If you are under sixty-five and have health insurance, you likely get it through your employer. Nearly 90 percent of insured working Americans receive coverage as a benefit of their job.[1] If you work in the private sector you likely pay a monthly premium that is automatically deducted from your paycheck, and you get the plan they give you.

But the big problem with this approach: if you get your health insurance through your employer, your employer is the customer. The health insurance provider wants to please its customer. Your employer wants one thing: as low a cost as possible. The insurance company's goal is to keep costs low as well, and so they fight as many claims as they can and strive to pay for as few services as they can. If the costs go up too much or too fast, the insurance company fears their customer, your employer, will walk away and go find another insurer to provide coverage for its employees.

But what if you were the direct buyer of your health insurance? You, the actual customer? What if you could just walk away like you do when your cell phone provider overcharges you or fails to provide you with adequate service? What if choices in health insurance were as plentiful as the choices you have for mobile phones? If we were able to walk away and choose a different company, the health insurance companies would behave very differently. They'd be advertising their "network coverage," just like Verizon: "No matter where you get sick, we've got you covered." They'd brag about their retention rate of customers: "We have the lowest drop rate in the industry."

The variety of products would be endless if the consumer had the ability to pick and choose, as we do with car insurance. Health insurers could offer products geared toward women, for example, so my specific choices on my insurance plan wouldn't necessarily cover a prostate exam I'll never be getting. A man's plan might not cover mammograms. There could be low-cost, high-deductible, catastrophic-only plans for the young so they could get affordable coverage for things like car accidents and cancer. There could be plans designed to change with your needs as you age.

But if you get your health insurance through your employer, you are stuck with a plan that benefits them, not you. In general, everybody pays the same price for the same level of coverage. Maybe it covers acupuncture, and you don't use acupuncture, but your premium is higher anyway simply because you might use it. Or maybe you'd be willing to pay a higher premium to have acupuncture covered but your employer has decided against it. Either way, the choice is not yours to make.

I've got a friend who receives acupuncture. And what

makes me steam is that it's covered by her employer plan. Her coworkers pay a higher premium so that a few people can get acupuncture. I bet the majority of the employees at her company don't even know it's an option for them, nor would they want to pay for it if it were. If you could check off "skip the acupuncture" in a box on your purchasing form, that would be great, but when it's your employer's plan, you can't.

In my alternate universe of health insurance choice, you'd have the ability to lower your costs if you lead a healthy lifestyle, or if you take steps to improve your health. Some car insurance companies offer cash incentives for "no accident" drivers—the longer you go without one, the cheaper your car insurance. With homeowner's insurance you can pay a lower premium if you have hurricane-proof windows. There would likely be parallel situations with health insurance. They might lower your premium if you prove you see the doctor for a complete physical every year. If you don't smoke, you would pay less for health insurance. If you're a smoker, you could lower your premium by quitting. If you're obese and doing nothing about it, you would pay more for your health insurance, but if you go to the gym three times a week and can prove it to your provider, you could get cash back or a lower annual premium. If you lose weight from one year to the next, they might give you a premium rebate.

If we put the purchasing power for health insurance in the hands of the consumers, I believe we'll see a reduction in some of the things we find most troublesome about the insurance companies, because they would be forced to improve their customer service. First, they would be less likely to drop customers once they got sick. Information about drop rates would be available from places like *Consumer Reports*. Word of mouth from our doctors, families, neighbors—one of the most powerful information networks out there—would quickly inform of us of which health insurance providers were notorious for fighting claims, and which weren't. What if it made providers hesitant to drop sick people for fear their reputation would be so damaged they would lose healthy and therefore good customers?

Another advantage of buying your own health insurance: you wouldn't lose it if you got laid off or quit your job. Auto insurers don't cancel your policy if you get laid off. Why should consumers face the same threat when it comes to health insurance?

There's a reason why most of us get our health insurance through our employer. It's the unintended consequence of bad government policies from World War II. During the war, in the 1940s, there was a severe labor shortage. The government thought it was doing everyone a favor by instituting wage controls and declaring that no company could pay more than any other company for workers. The government didn't want stronger companies taking advantage of weaker companies by paying more for employees. So what did stronger companies do to attract workers they desperately needed? Industries and businesses that needed workers and had the financial resources began offering nonwage benefits such as health insurance. We've been stuck with it ever since. The strong companies ended up being able to attract employees anyway, which makes the entire concept of employer-based insurance a perfect example of well-intentioned government intervention that fails to achieve the desired effect and in fact has horrible long-term financial consequences.

Look what that one ill-informed government policy from more than sixty years ago has wrought. Perhaps the worst example was the near destruction of the auto companies . . .

which ended up becoming health insurance providers who only happened to make cars on the side. On the other side of the coin, some retirees who thought they would be taken care of by their employers now have to worry about what will happen if their employer goes out of business.

You don't even have to say it. I know what you are thinking: "If I had to buy my own health insurance, I could never afford it, because it would be so expensive." My response: you're using what I call "static analysis" in your thinking. Yes, right now it is way too expensive for most individuals to buy individual polices. Here's why—and how to fix it.

Why Individual Plans Are So Expensive

There are three things that make health insurance plans that people buy on their own much more expensive:

First, there is no national market for health insurance. You can't buy health insurance across state lines. You must buy it in the state in which you live. This prevents the creation of a national market, which, if it existed, would enlarge the size of the risk pool for an insurer. The larger and more diverse the risk pool, the easier it is to keep costs lower, because you have more people paying for premiums to cover the costs of those in the pool who get sick.

Second, every year state legislators pass more laws raising the number of "mandates" on insurance companies that are selling individual policies in their state. Mandates are "must-cover" requirements: "If you sell a plan in our state you must cover this, and this, and this too." It could be anything from mammograms to wigs. Back in the 1960s there were relatively few mandates. Now there are nearly two thousand across the country.[2]

You may be saying to yourself, well that's a good thing, because insurers should cover all those things. But think of it this way: a state legislature would never pass a law mandating auto dealers to sell only Rolls-Royce and Cadillac cars; then only people who could afford Rolls-Royce and Cadillac could buy cars. Yet state legislatures are essentially doing that to health insurance companies by insisting they sell the Rolls-Royce or Cadillac equivalent of a health insurance plan. And guess what? Only upper-income people end up being able to afford individual plans. The Council for Affordable Health Insurance says that each mandate generally adds less than 1 percent to the cost of a policy. But when a state has forty or fifty mandates, then the cost of your policy is up 30 percent at least.[3]

Here's another thing that state legislatures do that drives up the cost of individual policies: forcing companies to cover people with preexisting conditions and then passing laws that restrict prices or limit a company's ability to raise rates. You may like those two measures, but they are leading to fewer people having insurance, not more.

Forcing companies to cover everyone is called "guaranteed issue." In other words, it is guaranteed they will issue a policy. When state legislatures pass price caps it is called "community rating." In other words, you aren't allowed to charge based on an individual's likely costs; you have to just give everyone in that "community" the same price.

So what happens in states like New York, which has both "guaranteed issue" and "community pricing"? Individual insurance premiums are the highest in the nation. If New

Yorkers want to buy a policy independent of their employer, the average annual premium is $6,630 for individuals and a whopping $13,296 for a family policy. Compare that to the national average of $2,985 for individuals and $6,328 for families. It is not because the Northeast is generally more expensive or less healthy than other parts of the country. In nearby Connecticut, where the cost of living is comparable, they don't have guaranteed issue or community pricing, and premiums are only $3,503 for individuals and $8,477 for families.[4]

"Guaranteed issue" leads people to not buy insurance unless they absolutely need it. Think about it: why pay a monthly premium for years and years if you know that if and when you do get sick, they have to sell a policy to you anyway? Just wait until you are diagnosed with cancer or need some kind of operation. And since pricing is capped by the state, you don't have to worry about paying more even though you are going to cost the insurance company more. Sound great? Think again.

Here's what actually happens: Guaranteed issue means only the only sickest people end up buying insurance. That makes the pool of insured the costliest to cover. Young people, who are the healthiest and least likely to file claims, abandon the market, especially because with "community pricing" they have to pay the same price as older individuals who are likely to cost a lot more money. The pool of insured becomes less representative of the overall population and filled with only the sickest individuals. If companies can't raise premiums enough, they abandon the state altogether. Costs go up, and fewer individuals can afford insurance. These are the unintended negative consequences of well-intentioned government intervention.

The state legislatures are trying to solve the problem of health insurance access for the 1 percent to 2 percent of the population that is uninsurable, but what they do is destroy the health insurance market for the other 98 percent.

Third, you have to buy individual policies with after-tax dollars. As the Council for Affordable Health Insurance points out, workers with employer-based health care, or the self-employed, get an unlimited federal tax break for money spent on health coverage because it's an untaxed benefit. Workers whose employers do not provide coverage get no such tax break. That is completely unfair to those workers, who tend to be the most vulnerable because they are in low-paying jobs, often in the service sector, where employers are less likely to provide health insurance as a benefit.

A lot of us like the fact that our health insurance premiums are taken out of our pay before taxes, but I urge you to consider the other possibilities. What if you didn't get your health insurance through your employer, and instead you just got paid more? Under the current structure, your employer is encouraged to offer more coverage rather than more money, because they don't have to pay your Social Security and Medicare taxes on those benefits. The federal government allows the health-care benefits to be given out tax-free.

And what if buying health insurance was actually cheaper if you bought it on its own? That would mean more money in your household budget.

With a couple of fixes we could get to affordable individual policies.

First and foremost, we should be able to buy insurance across state lines, as we can with nearly every other product out there. If you live in a state like New Jersey that has many mandates and requirements but you don't want to pay for them, then you could buy a policy from a company based in Connecticut, or as far away as Nevada. Essentially the states would be forced to compete with each other. Consumers would make clear what level of coverage they want at what price. Somehow the insurance companies have convinced Congress they should be exempt from the interstate commerce rules.

If I can buy a car in any state I want, why can't I buy insurance in any state?

I've interviewed members of Congress who are against buying insurance across state lines because it would lead to a "race toward the bottom." In other words, state after state would reduce the requirements on health insurance companies making each state more competitive.

Exactly! That's the point!

We should be able to buy a bare-bones policy that covers us only for catastrophic events, or if we want to spend more, to buy a policy that covers every single sniffle. The key is that it would be our choice, not some government decree from above that decides our coverage.

Here's another comparison that might seem a bit odd . . . but stick with me for a minute. Mobile phones were once a luxury, for only the rich. Now third-world and poor countries have great access and very high usage of cell phones among their citizens. Have you been to a construction site lately here in the United States? You might be shocked to learn that at least a quarter of those workers are likely to be illegal immigrants, poor and sending money home to their families. Yet 100 percent of those same poor immigrants are likely to own a mobile phone. Intense competition in the industry has forced mobile phone operators to provide different levels of service and pricing for every income level. Intense competition has led to a huge decrease in costs.

We can and should do exactly the same when it comes to health insurance.

Now, as for taxation levels, there are two options. Congress could choose to tax a health insurance policy like any other benefit. Or it could give a tax break to those who are buying it on the open market. Either way is fine with me. Normally I would be against tax increases, but in this case I think if the employer-based policies were taxed, companies would be less likely to offer them, and individuals would be less likely to want them because they wouldn't want to pay such high taxes on what are very expensive plans, loaded with things they don't want. It would enlarge the market of people looking to buy individual plans, leading to a more robust market.

The insurance companies naturally are opposed to the idea of a national market with individuals buying their own policies. They prefer dealing with employers because then they have to negotiate with only one customer rather than hundreds of thousands or rather millions. Throughout this entire health-care debate, the insurance companies have fought for one thing: the status quo. Why? Because it's working for them and if it's working for them, that means it's likely not working for you, the consumer.

Why Not Just Have the Government Do It?

Every other industrialized nation has some form of socialized medicine. Doesn't that mean we should, too?

No.

Not having socialized medicine is one of our greatest strengths. First, let's talk about what happens when "everyone" is paying for "everyone else." That's what happens when health care is run by the government. Everyone pays taxes into a big pot of money, and then everyone gets benefits from that same pot of money, divided up by the government. You know what happens under that scenario: "everyone" thinks they can tell "everyone else" how to lead their lives. "Hey you, put that cookie down, you are overweight and you are costing me money!" There will be all kinds of government intervention into what we eat and what we do, all justified because it's taxpayer money that they are spending.

We've already seen examples of this. In Los Angeles, the city council voted for a moratorium on new fast-food restaurants in certain zip codes where a large percentage of the population is on Medicaid, the government health plan for the poor, and where there is a high rate of obesity. In an attempt to stop spending taxpayer dollars on obesity-related diseases, they targeted what they perceived to be one of the causes of the problem. I have the same issue with the soda tax we've been hearing about. That is pure "nanny state."

If you are supportive of the move by the Los Angeles City Council, I caution you to think about how far this kind of thinking can go: no more motorcycles, no more skydivers, no more football—it leads to higher levels of Parkinson's disease as an adult. It could go on and on, limiting our freedoms.

We are a nation based on an ideal of freedom. And maybe we don't like what some people do with their freedom, but that is their right, and we accept it, knowing that we have the same benefits.

Next, government-provided health care doesn't lower costs,

which is supposed to be the reason why we should want it. On the contrary. It raises health-care spending dramatically—often higher than it would otherwise be. We already have an example of national universal government health insurance: Once you turn sixty-five, you are eligible to get your health insurance benefits through Medicare. You've been paying 1.5 percent in every paycheck in anticipation of the very day when you could get it all back in the form of health-care coverage.

And the costs of Medicare are skyrocketing, choking the federal budget and threatening the financial stability of our country. Over the last thirty years, federal spending on Medicare and Medicaid has roughly tripled as a share of gross domestic product, rising from about 1 percent in 1970 to more than 5 percent in 2009.[5] According to the Congressional Budget Office's projections, if we keep our current policies in place, our spending on Medicare and Medicaid will be 6.6 percent of the GDP in 2020, 10 percent by 2035, and 17 percent by 2080.[6] Think about that when members of the government insist that they will lower health-care costs. Or when President Obama says eliminating "waste, fraud, and abuse" is going to control costs—if it were that easy, wouldn't we have eliminated "waste, fraud, and abuse" a long time ago?

Medicare and employer-based coverage have something in common: You still don't have any control or choice. The government is going to decide what it covers and what it doesn't. Again, you have no power, no choice, and zero control over a product you're using. The government is the only provider, so you can't go anywhere else. You can't walk away.

What happens when the government decides it doesn't want to pay more? It doesn't. So every day, more and more doctors decide they are no longer going to accept older patients, because the government doesn't cover the costs of caring for those patients. So once again your level of care is decided by someone else.

Wouldn't it have been so much better if you had put aside that money yourself and could use it in your old age? Instead of handing it over to someone else for poor coverage in old age, you could have bought better coverage elsewhere.

Instead of putting that 1.5 percent into the government coffers, the money could go into a Health Savings Account that you control but can't touch until retirement.

How about Massachusetts?

In April 2006, Massachusetts became the first state in the nation to make health insurance compulsory. If you live in Massachusetts, it was decided, you must buy health insurance coverage if you don't get it from your employer. If you don't buy it, your penalty runs as high as $912 per year. You lose a tax exemption as well. However, depending on your income level, you receive a subsidy to cover your premiums. Employers with more than eleven employees must provide health insurance or pay a penalty of $295 per employee.[7] The concept is very similar to the health-care reform that just passed in Congress.

But Massachusetts, after its much-heralded reform, hasn't controlled costs. Proponents of health insurance reform for Massachusetts said it would save money because it would solve the problem of the uninsured going to the emergency room for nonemergencies, which ends up costing all of us a ton of money. The argument is that if all those people would just go see a doctor early to get preventive care, there would be lower costs because preventive care is so much cheaper than emergency care. The savings never emerged. All the newly insured started going to more doctors, upping primary care wait times to as long as one hundred days.[8] Guess what?

More people poured back into the emergency room because their doctor was booked.[9]

The overall increase in spending: more than $1 billion when you add up the subsidies for the poor to help them buy insurance, the fees imposed on employers who either had to add coverage or pay a penalty, and new or higher premiums that citizens of Massachusetts faced as a result.[10]

Yes, you read that right, higher premiums, because along with mandating that you had to buy insurance, the state legislature also mandated all kinds of coverage, often higher than what individuals had been paying for before the requirement. And by the way, the Massachusetts legislature is considering even more things that must be covered by health insurance, and which their citizens will pay for as a result. If you live in Massachusetts, you'd have been better off if they had just raised enough taxes to cover the $250 million the hospitals were spending on the uninsured. Instead private individuals and businesses ended up spending more than a $1 billion from their pockets because of the imposed mandate.

And keep in mind that this is after Massachusetts already raised taxes on everything under the sun: tobacco, hospitals, insurers, and employers . . . and still it wasn't enough. So they arbitrarily decided to cut subsidies to legal immigrants. That's right—legal immigrants, not illegal immigrants. So much for the worthy goal of universal coverage to reduce the number of people using the emergency room. I guess the government figures legal immigrants weren't using—and won't use—the emergency room.

Don't get me wrong. I think it's great that more people are getting in to see doctors in Massachusetts. But when people in favor of universal coverage say it's going to lower costs due to less emergency room use, they are wrong. The corresponding increase in the number of people going to see a doctor is much higher and so are the costs. As a result of the changes in Massachusetts, the wait time to see a primary-care physician has climbed sharply. Compared to other cities, Boston has the highest wait times on average in the country. Some staggering statistics: the wait time to see an OB-GYN is seventy days, a family physician sixty-three days, and a cardiologist twenty-one days.

This is despite the fact that Massachusetts has more physicians per capita than any other state.

A Little Personal Responsibility

The emergency room argument plays into the myth that we are underinsured in America. The fact is that Americans are overinsured, and that is the primary driver of higher costs. Back in the 1960s, 40 percent of our health-care costs were paid for out of our own pockets. We paid doctors directly in cash and the insurance companies covered the other 60 percent. Now Americans' out-of-pocket costs have dropped to only 15 percent.[11] Consequently, we as individuals have no idea how much our doctors, prescriptions, or medical procedures cost, because we never directly pay for them.

Back to my friend who gets acupuncture: She recently switched jobs, and while deciding on a health-care plan for her prescriptions, she discovered her allergy medicine would cost her out-of-pocket more than one hundred dollars per month if she didn't have insurance. She said, "Wow, I had no idea because I only pay a co-pay of ten dollars." That is precisely the problem, especially when it is spread across the entire population. It's not that her medication was so expensive or even that it was covered on her insurance, but that she has no understanding of the real cost of medicine or medical care. None of us do. Could she survive without her allergy medicine? No, and I'm not suggesting anyone go without medication they need.

But if we were more aware of how much things cost, we would be much better at deciding what level of coverage we want. There's one way to achieve this, and it requires a higher degree of personal responsibility. If we all bore a higher percentage of our health-care costs directly, we would all be paying less for health care.

We are already seeing this where employers have switched their employees to Health Savings Accounts (HSAs) or Health Reimbursement Accounts (HRAs). Here's how it works: The employer gives you, say, $1,000 at the start of the year and you get to spend it as you see fit over the next year. In the case of HSAs, if you don't use it all, you get to keep it, roll it over to the next year, and even take it with you if you leave. Once you get through that first round of money, the company foots the bill for 80 percent of your costs and you foot the bill for 20 percent of your costs. When you hit a certain level of outlays, say $5,000 or $10,000 depending on your employer, they pick up the rest. This gives the employee peace of mind, knowing that if they or someone in their family gets a catastrophic illness, their outlays won't be more than $5,000 or $10,000. Yes, that's a lot of money, but it is not as insurmountable as a $1 million bill you would face if you didn't have insurance.

In the insurance world, they call this "consumer-driven plans." I like the sound of it already. The consumer having control of that first $1,000 is crucial because the minute people have to make choices about how they are going to spend their own money, they get a lot more choosy, especially if they know that once they surpass that $1,000 they are going to have to foot part of the bill.

The evidence is overwhelming that this is the way to lower health-care costs. The Kaiser Foundation found that under a health maintenance organization (HMO), a family cost an employer $13,100. For a preferred provider organization (PPO), $11,600, and only $9,100 for an HSA. Aetna says that over a six-year period, employers saved $21 million for every 10,000 employees using consumer-driven plans. The Mercer consultancy did a survey of employers in 2007 and found that spending on employees with PPOs averaged $7,400; for employees with HMOs, $7,100; for HRAs, $6,200; and for HSAs, $5,700.[12]

Regence Blue Shield found that people decreased their use of hospital emergency services by 32 percent when they switched from traditional insurance to insurance driven by the consumer with an HSA.[13]

There is a lesson here: we need to bear more of the burden of our health-care costs directly. We will make much better choices and we will all have lower costs.[14] A key question to ask when suggesting that people should bear more of their health-care costs: Will their health suffer if they cannot or do not access care? The study of record on this issue comes from a ten-year report from the Rand Institute in which they compared health-care outcomes between those who got free unlimited health care and those who paid for a share of the costs.

Here's the crucial outcome: In general, cost sharing had no *adverse* effect on participants' health, even though it encouraged people to consume less health care. There were some exceptions, which should help guide us as to whom we should subsidize when it comes to care. The poorest and sickest saw an improvement in several areas if they had completely free care, including better control of hypertension and marginally improved vision. They were also more likely to get dental care. The study shows it is key for the government to lend a hand *only* to the poorest or the sickest, not to *everyone*, like it did when even the wealthy got Medicare. There was and still is greater consumption but not necessarily improved health.

Frankly, I'm a little frustrated about the way Americans have come to think about health insurance versus other kinds of insurance. For some reason we've come to think that health insurance is about paying for everything, even the expected. But hold on a second. As AHIP points out, car insurance doesn't cover oil changes, it covers accidents. Homeowner's insurance doesn't cover painting your house; it covers your expenses in case a tree falls on it. Insurance is about covering the unforeseen and the unpreventable. But for some reason we seem to think that health insurance should pay for everything—like acupuncture.

This doesn't mean insurance companies shouldn't cover preventive care. In fact, they might insist that you get preventive care, and even cover it, because it would make their eventual outlays cheaper if the doctor catches something early. They might even threaten to drop you if you don't get in to see the doctor once a year. But in the end, you know yourself that you should go to the doctor once a year for a physical. That is your responsibility. You know you will have to spend a certain amount, the same way you know you will have to spend a certain amount on your rent or your mortgage. Why do you expect someone else to foot that bill for you?

"But wait," you say. "That is so cruel. The poor can't afford to pay cash. And just because you are poor doesn't mean you shouldn't be able to get the best care." I agree 100 percent that access to quality health care should not be limited to the wealthy and the middle class. But that's how it works right now, because jobs that require more high school and college degrees are far more likely to provide insurance than those that don't. The concern about the poor is worthy, but it is based on an erroneous underlying assumption that reflects static analysis. If we had more options, more supply, we would have more affordable insurance for the greatest number of people. There would be affordable options for catastrophic insurance: again think cancer and car accidents.

And for the poorest—subsidize them. I have no problem with subsidizing the poor—with a voucher for health insurance. They get a certain amount to spend on the kind of plan they want. The same goes for people with preexisting conditions. Another option for those found to have catastrophic conditions and don't have insurance: they could be put into a high-risk pool, which then gets randomly assigned to health-insurance companies. Their premiums could be based on their levels of income before they got sick. If they made a lot of money but chose not to get health insurance, guess what— they would pay a large premium for that health insurance. If they were poor, the price would be far lower.

Ultimately, doing a targeted subsidy for the poor or those with preexisting conditions is a lot cheaper than putting everyone, regardless of income, on some kind of government insurance plan that only leads to individuals making bad choices. That's what we have with Medicare and the costs keep going higher and higher.

Unfortunately, the New Health Care Reform Law is anything but reform. When the process began, the White House said the intent was to increase coverage and control soaring costs. They got the coverage part right, but not the cost-controls part.

I am fully supportive of increased access to care. What I do not support is the duplicitous way in which this law was sold to us. The American public was told over and over again that this law would lower the deficit because that's what the Congressional Budget Office told legislators.

What we weren't told was that that CBO report says government spending on health care will actually go up $210 billion over the next ten years as a result of this law.[15]

Huh? Talk about double-speak. How can the government be spending substantially more under this new law, and yet still have a lower deficit?

Two answers: it cuts Medicare spending and raises taxes. There is a new 3.8 percent tax on unearned income, which includes dividends, rents, capital gains, interest, and a host of other investment incomes. Government will tax investment. That means we will get less investment as a result. When you raise taxes on something, you get less of it. That's how higher taxes on cigarettes are justified by politicians.

Figuring out how to get health care to people who don't have it is an absolutely worthy discussion to have. And if the government had said from the beginning, "We want to achieve this goal, let's figure out how we are all going to pay for it," that would have been fine.

Instead, the White House and congressional Democrats sold it as a money-saver.

It could have been worse. Thankfully, there was no public option, which would have been government-supplied insurance, which would have likely led to the government's squeezing out private providers. That's because when you don't have to worry about profitability or return on investment, you can price things more cheaply than a private insurer can. That means cheaper in price to the buyer, but more expensive to the taxpayer, because it is taxpayer money subsidizing that lower price. More and more people would have chosen the government option based on price, and eventually, private insurers would have left the market. I firmly believe it would have led to a slow, creeping takeover of the entire insurance market by the government.

Another slight positive, the new law did establish regional exchanges, which will have several states grouping together to create a regional market for health insurance. That's a baby step toward being able to buy insurance across state lines. They should have gone even further.

But that does not outweigh all the negatives.

The worst part of the bill is that businesses with more than fifty employees will be required to provide coverage or pay a fine. That is a job killer. It raises the cost of hiring an employee. Before any business hires an additional worker, the business owner must believe that the additional worker will bring in enough revenue to cover costs. Now, for an employer the hurdle to hiring has gone up sharply. We've already seen that in Massachusetts, where Governor Deval Patrick finally admits that small businesses in his state aren't hiring because of the added health-insurance premiums.

Another major failing of Obamacare is that it will not tax the so-called Cadillac health plans until 2018. At that point, employers will pay a 40 percent excise tax on premiums that exceed $10,200 for individuals or $27,500 for families. This is the one thing that would have lowered health-care costs. It would have led employers to stop providing so much health insurance and instead shift more of their employees to consumer-based plans.

But the unions fought this tooth and nail, because so many of their members have extremely generous health plans. The White House gave in and they got the Cadillac-tax provision delayed until far into the future. I'll bet it's not delayed. I bet the unions get their way and it never even comes to pass.

Unfortunately, I think I'm going to be right about that, too.

— 7 —

Fixing Immigration

Here are four reasons why you should embrace immigration to the United States: eBay, Yahoo, Google, and Sun Microsystems. All were founded by immigrants.[1]

Nearly eighty thousand people have jobs thanks to these companies. You, the taxpayer, have received the benefits of millions and millions of dollars in tax revenue paid by these companies. Not to mention how much better they make our lives. Can you even imagine a life without Google or Yahoo? Can you imagine the world of business functioning without servers? I think it's fair to say, if you believe in progress, that life with these high-tech advancements is truly better. They've all changed our lives in a very dramatic fashion. I have to say, as jingoistic as it sounds, that I am proud to call those companies American. And if their creators hadn't been here to do it, would they have been founded at all?

Google could have easily been a non-American product. Sergey Brin, a Jewish kid born in Moscow, came to the United

States in 1979 when he was six years old because his father couldn't get into graduate school. The Communist Party wasn't about to allow Jews to get advanced degrees in mathematics. So the Brin family packed up and left. The dad went on to become a distinguished professor of mathematics at the University of Maryland. His son went on to cofound Google while he was studying at Stanford. Google—a company that has had a profound impact on the lives of many Americans. If Brin the father had stayed in Moscow, would son Sergey ever have had the opportunities he found in the United States? It's unlikely.

Russia's loss was our incredible gain.

Yahoo was cofounded by Jerry Yang, who came to the United States from Taiwan when he was a kid. eBay was founded by Pierre Omidyar, who was born in France to Iranian immigrants. Pierre's father did his residency at Johns Hopkins University, so he brought the family to the United States. Sun Microsystems counts two immigrants among its founders: Andy Bechtolsheim from Germany and Vinod Khosla from India. Both Bechtolsheim and Khosla came here to study and fortunately never left.

I just picked four household names, but there are many companies founded by immigrants in the United States. A study done by researchers at Duke, Harvard, and the University of California at Berkeley found that 25 percent of all technology companies started in the United States between 1995 and 2005 had at least one foreign-born founder.[2] These companies were responsible for an estimated $52 billion in sales, and 450,000 jobs. The immigrants came from India, the United Kingdom, China, Taiwan, Japan, and Germany. More than half of those founders came to the United States to study and only later decided to start companies here, after they'd been here on average for thirteen years.

There's something very critical to be learned: We win when we embrace the best and the brightest from all over the world. We win when we let people study and stay in America. We win when we encourage the creation of companies that provide Americans with jobs. We win when a foreign genius stays here and creates something that generates tax revenue.

Immigration can mean prosperity.

You know when we don't win? We don't win when we don't embrace immigration. We lose talent when we put a cap on the number of educated immigrants who can come to the United States every year. We currently only allow 65,000 a year into the country.[3] There are an additional 20,000 we allow to stay after they've gotten an advanced degree at a U.S. university.[4]

The annual H-1B visa application ritual is one that technology companies know well, and one they find extremely frustrating. Every year companies can begin applying for those 65,000 slots on April 1, for use starting on October 1 of that same year. In 2007, by April 2, all the visas were gone. Nearly half the companies who sought a visa that day did not get one.[5]

What do companies do when there are no more visa slots but there is a demand for labor? They are forced to send those jobs overseas. When Bill Gates testified in front of Congress in March of 2008 he told members of Congress: "Many U.S. firms, including Microsoft, have been forced to locate staff in countries that welcome skilled foreign workers to do work that could otherwise have been done in the United States, if it were not for our counterproductive immigration policies. Last year, for example, Microsoft was unable to obtain H-1B visas for one-third of the highly qualified foreign-born job candidates that we wanted to hire." [6]

I think we would be better off as a nation if skilled workers could come here. Those immigrants would pay taxes here, buy homes here, and ultimately spend money here. In fact, Gates testified that Microsoft had found that for every H-1B employee the company brought in, it added an additional four employees in the United States in support roles to the payroll.

But we shouldn't allow open immigration just for the educated. In some ways we need uneducated immigrants even more than educated immigrants. Back in 1940, only 25 percent of the entire U.S. working population had a high school degree. Even in 1970, that number had only reached 52 percent. Think of that. Just forty years ago, half of the U.S. working population was made up of high school dropouts.[7]

Today, 85 percent of those over the age of twenty-five have a high school diploma.[8]

Someone with a high school diploma doesn't want and doesn't need to spend eight hours a day in the basement of a restaurant cutting onions, or, as often happens with female immigrants, cleaning houses. They can, should, and do expect more.

Businesses that rely on low-skilled labor need these immigrants just to survive. That uneducated chunk of the labor force helps make our economy stronger, not weaker. Anyone who tells you otherwise is simply wrong. Think of it this way: If someone wants to open a restaurant, they need employees with varying skill sets, including low-skilled workers who can help with the cleaning, dishwashing, and cooking. If those workers cost too much money, a potential entrepreneur won't be able to open a restaurant. If there are plenty of immigrants available, they will. If that restaurant opens, there will be new jobs for waitresses, there's a job for the owner's accountant, and new business for the local liquor distributor who supplies the restaurant. The availability of low-cost labor for low-skilled jobs leads directly to more hiring of skilled-labor jobs—the kind educated Americans want.

Yes, I know there are Americans who have seen their jobs go to immigrants. And evidence shows that the small percentage of Americans who don't have a high school diploma likely have lower wages overall as a result of immigration. But on the flip side, those same individuals benefit from much lower costs when they go to the grocery store, or when they try to buy a home, because lower-cost labor leads to lower-cost products.

The answer to helping unskilled Americans is not restricting immigration; it's improving education. By limiting immigration in an effort to help residents, once again government is attempting to solve a problem for a very small part of the population to the detriment of the vast majority.

This isn't just theory. Economists have done cost-benefit analysis of immigration, which shows we are net winners. And guess what? Legal or illegal—it doesn't make a difference. Our economy benefits from both.

Many critics of illegal immigration cite the costs when it comes to the burden immigrants place on American society in terms of educating their children, emergency health care, and incarceration costs. Yes, we do bear some costs, but economists have shown that the monetary benefits they bring to the United States far outweigh the monetary costs.

Last year the Cato Institute did some insightful cost-benefit analysis on what would happen if we 1) did nothing and kept the status quo, 2) restricted illegal immigration through even tougher border enforcement or employer enforcement, 3) allowed a more open, visa-based immigration system, such as a guest-worker program.

In scenario 2 they assume we manage to sharply slow the flow of illegal immigrants crossing the border. As a result, the illegal immigrants who are already here get a big wage boost because once the economy starts growing again, they are needed but in short supply. As the wages in those low-skilled jobs move higher, though, it changes the occupational mix of working Americans. That's because those higher wages draw more highly skilled U.S. workers into those low-skilled jobs. That is terrible for an economy because it is equal to a sharp drop in productivity of U.S. workers. That means lower real wages.

Or say there is stricter enforcement, but not at the border. Instead it happens at the employer level. Under that scenario, the number of illegal immigrants coming into the county grows as the economy grows, but their wages don't rise, because the demand/supply curve balance remains the same. In theory that's good news for employers, because they can hire employees at a lower cost than they could otherwise. However, all those cost savings get eaten up by what the researchers call "prosecution mitigating activities." Meaning: hiring undocumented workers, but not getting caught. Translation: more lawyers!

Here's what they find under the stricter-enforcement scenarios: Yes, you get savings in public expenditures (such as educating children and paying for emergency health-care costs), but those savings are far less than the revenue we get from increased economic output and more job opportunities for more skilled Americans. If you kept the number of illegal immigrants static, the authors of this study find, we would see a drop in U.S. household welfare of $80 billion.

Under scenario 3, in which you legalize all the illegal immigrants, charge them a visa fee, and allow open borders, you
get a gain in U.S. household wealth of $180 billion. That's
more than 1 percent of GDP.[9]

There are, of course, some caveats. If we have open immigration we should have very strong restrictions on welfare.
There would be no welfare, and no subsidized health care, for
those who come here. If they couldn't make it, they'd have
to go back home. They could not live off of the government.
They could obviously get help in an emergency, for example
for a car accident. But it's crucial that we don't attract people
to this country through welfare or because they are sick and
looking for health care. I have deep sympathy for them but
we cannot be everything to everyone. England did this with
immigrants coming from Eastern Europe. They welcomed
them but said you won't get welfare if you come. They
achieved successful immigration and a labor force but didn't
get hit with higher costs.

Whenever we discuss immigrants, the issue of amnesty always arises. There are some groups out there that are not critical of immigration per se but are critical of amnesty for those
who are here illegally. The ten-point litmus test proposed by
the Republican Party for potential GOP candidates includes a
requirement that the possible contenders oppose amnesty for
those who are here illegally.

At first glance I can see how that position would make
a lot of sense to a lot of people. Instinctively, we all want to
say, "No, you can't break the law, and we are not going to
reward you for breaking the law." But I counter that with this
idea: maybe any law that turns millions of otherwise decent
and hardworking people into criminals isn't such a good law.
Think Prohibition. When drinking was deemed illegal, we

basically turned the nation into a bunch of criminals engaging in underground black-market activity. Law-biding citizens became outlaws for no reason other than they wanted a drink. Those who don't believe in amnesty but believe in deportation make the estimated 12–20 million illegal immigrants in this country criminals. But I contend that the vast majority of immigrants in America, legal or illegal, are genuinely good and decent people. They are here because they want to work. There is nothing inherently criminal about wanting to work. As researcher Dan Griswold from Cato points out, robbery and rape are inherently criminal activities.[10] Getting up in the predawn hours to be at a construction site is not.

And under a program that would legalize those who are already here, you could charge them a fine, make them pay back taxes, submit them to background checks to eliminate security risks, and tell them they only have a temporary visa. If they want to become U.S. citizens they have to get to the back of the line.

Legalizing previously illegal immigrants is not without precedent. It happened back in 1986, when my favorite president, Ronald Reagan, signed a bill that eventually gave nearly two million illegal immigrants a path to legalization.[11]

So what do we do now? Frankly, Washington is looking at this issue of amnesty all wrong. If you ever listen to the policy wonks talk about immigration, you'll hear them use the phrase "three-legged stool." They are usually talking about 1) enforcement against illegal immigration at the border and, since 1986, via employers; 2) improving the flow of legal immigration, although the definition of "improving" depends on where you stand on the issue; and 3) deciding what to do about all the people who are already here illegally: Send them back? Legalize them? Maintain the status quo? That's the three-legged stool.

Janet Napolitano, the current secretary of homeland security, uses the phrase,[12] as did the two authors of the immigration reform law back in 1986, Representative Romano Mazzoli and Senator Alan Simpson.[13]

I actually think the premise of the three-legged stool is completely wrong. We should be as welcoming and as open to immigrants as possible, so skip the enforcement or simply put the resources that currently go into keeping people out into checking the backgrounds of those we let in instead. I wholeheartedly agree we need to make sure we aren't allowing in suspected terrorists. But when it comes to immigration, I call for an open-door policy. No quotas. None. Whoever wants to come is allowed to come. If you pose no security threat to our nation, you are welcome to pursue the American dream.

The fact that I advocate open immigration doesn't mean I'm oblivious to the need for strong security. You can document every individual coming across our borders and actually know who they are. In fact, I think a process that allows for documentation and free entry would actually increase our national security. It would bring people out of the shadows. Everyone coming and going would use legitimate entry points. Sneaking across would be for criminals only. Instead of wasting money building fences and tracking the hordes sneaking across the border in the middle of the night through the Rio Grande or in the trunks of cars, we could more carefully track those who hate our way of life. Rather than chase away those who want our way of life, we'd have more money to defend against suspected terrorists.

Some people aren't just concerned about terrorists entering the country—they're worried the entire country will be overrun by immigrants. I disagree. The number of people who want to come here would eventually slow down once wage levels fall enough to make it not worth the trip.

We've actually already seen this exact thing happen, during the recent recession. The flow of illegal immigrants across the border slowed dramatically. Even the flow of legal immigrants dropped. Companies were not spending money, so they weren't hiring people. In 2009 there was actually a glut of H-1B visas—they couldn't fill them.[14]

The Pew Hispanic Center estimates that there are 11.9 million unauthorized immigrants living in the United States. That hasn't changed since 2006, when the slowdown in the economy began. If there's no money to be made here, fewer people are going to clamor to get into the country to earn. Most immigrants are coming here to earn money for themselves and their families, to buy homes and to build lives. They are not trying to live off the government, as so many irrationally fear is the case.

Right now, undocumented immigrants make up only 4 percent of the nation's population and only 5.4 percent of the workforce. There are 154 million workers in America. Almost 8.5 million of them are unauthorized immigrants. They work in jobs that require very little education because only half have high school diplomas (compared to the 85 percent of the American population that does).[15]

As a result, you are far more likely to find them, rather than Americans, working in agriculture, construction, and in the hospitality services, such as restaurants. They are one of the reasons that the amount of money Americans spend on food has gone from 23 percent of our disposable income to only 10 percent of our disposable income and why we instead have extra income to use for something else.[16]

In the construction trades, they are 17 percent of the workers. They are 28 percent of the landscaping workers. They are 23 percent of what's called "private household employment," better known as nannies and maids. They are 20 percent of workers in the dry-cleaning and laundry business. That's up from 10 percent back in 2003.[17] Our massive housing boom is what drew them north. The massive decline in housing is what's slowed them from coming in the last two years.

They don't make a ton of money. According to Pew, the 2007 median household income of unauthorized immigrants was $36,000. Compare that to the median household income of U.S.-born residents: $50,000.[18]

One of the ironic and unintended consequences of making immigration extremely difficult is that illegal immigrants who can't find work here are reluctant to go home to wait out the recession because it was so hard to get into the country to begin with. If the flow of labor were more liberal, when times got tough here many would be more willing to go back home and wait out the recession. We're essentially forcing unemployed illegal immigrant workers to stay. Some have paid smugglers, known as "coyotes," thousands of dollars to help sneak them across the border. They've ridden thousands of miles, packed in a trunk. The cost of getting to the United States was so high, they'd rather stick it out here through tough times and wait for things to get better.

So here's what we do: We establish a temporary worker program for those who are here already and for those who want to come here to work. It is crucial that the visa go to the worker, and not the employer, so that everyone has more mobility. That is also the best way to avoid abusive tactics by employers. The government should also eliminate the distinction between highly skilled workers and low-skilled workers. Demand from American companies and the free-market-based occupational mix of the United States should be the drivers of supply.

Free and open immigration is part of our history. It is in the American DNA. Remember the Pilgrims? With the exception of the Chinese in 1882, we didn't restrict immigration at all until the 1920s. Then we got paranoid and started putting in new restrictions and quotas geared toward keeping the immigrant flow mostly Western European in nature. We established very high quotas for people from countries like England and Germany but severely limited southern and eastern Europe, countries like Italy, Greece, and Poland. Asian people were simply not allowed. Those laws made no mention of Canada and Mexico, and people from those countries could, at that time, come and go as they pleased.[19]

The next big change came in 1965 under President Lyndon B. Johnson. The country-specific quota system went away and we began allowing immigration based on family connections and limited work visas. Within five years the number of Asian immigrants had climbed by 400 percent, many of them refugees from the wars in Southeast Asia. They made up roughly half the eight million immigrants who came over in that period. The others were mostly from Mexico.[20]

In 1986, under Reagan, we legalized immigrants who had been living here illegally since 1982. It was also the first time we moved enforcement in from the physical borders and put the onus on employers to not hire illegal immigrants. In 1990, we set annual limits on the number of immigrants who could come in: 700,000 from 1990 to 1993, and then 675,000 thereafter.[21]

I'm not sure what everyone is so afraid of. America was built on the backs of immigrants. Nearly all of us came from somewhere and we should be proud of this heritage. But this particular issue divides conservatives, probably more than any other. If you are truly conservative you believe in the free movement of labor, capital, and goods. Immigration should be subject to the free market as everything else is.

Americans are always focused on the exceptionalism of their country. We believe that we are the most ambitious, best educated, most creative, most economically free people in the world. If we have that self-assessment correct, we should be able to compete with anyone and win. So let's put our money where our mouths are and be prepared to compete. I believe when Americans measure up, we'll continue to get the jobs we want and start the businesses we want to start. Having to compete will only make us better.

For anyone out there who has a grandfather or great-grandfather who came to this country from another to make a better life for his family, you know I'm right.

Fixing Education

Whom do you trust more—the government or your mom? No doubt about it, I trust my mom. And my guess is that you do, too. So let me ask this: why do we let the government control children's education instead of parents? Why is some political appointee from Washington given the responsibility for shaping the minds and futures of our kids?

By making education a government-run program, Washington has stripped parents of their rights to decide what is best for their families. And frankly, the moms and dads of middle America know a lot more about their children's interests and needs than some middle-management bureaucrat located in the nation's capital. Why don't we fix the system and equip parents with the ability to be actively involved in their children's education?

The main problem with education in our country is that it is a monopoly. There is no competition among schools. There is no incentive or reward for high-quality programs and teachers. Monopolies allow the poorest and weakest programs not only to continue but also to soak up our resources and ensure weaker schools. And let's face it, there is one undeniable fact about monopolies: they harm the public. They keep prices higher than they otherwise would be in a competitive world and lead to fewer, lower-quality choices because no one is given an option. With monopolies, you pay (and pay and pay) because you have no other choice.

Remember what it was like when telephone service was a monopoly? We all had the same costly dial phone with no features. And remember when the lines were down or didn't work? The phone company simply ignored you when you complained. Now look at the system: We have landlines, cell phones, and video phones. They come in all shapes and sizes. We get to pick and choose from a range of features like call waiting and caller ID. And using a phone now is cheap—do you remember when a twenty-minute call to Europe meant that you had to cut back on your groceries that week? Competition leads to innovation and efficiencies. If our phone provider doesn't respond to our complaints or needs, we just switch to one that will. When Americans have a choice in products and services, we all win. In fact, there is a reason U.S. lawmakers have adopted antitrust laws and tasked the U.S. Department of Justice to enforce them. Monopolies are bad for businesses and consumers alike and those that operate them need to be charged and prosecuted.

And yet we still have one huge monopoly in America: the education system run by the U.S. government. When it comes down to which school a child will attend, parents have almost no choice. School boards divide up the districts among themselves and children go to the school to which they are assigned. What happens if the parents or children don't like the school? What happens if the school has failing test scores? What happens if it has violent crime? Or what happens if the school doesn't provide the programs your child needs or is interested in? Nothing. Nothing happens. Parents don't have a choice. If a child would do better at a school that encouraged sports over music, or if a child needs a freethinking format to reach his or her full potential, there is little to nothing that can be done. Imagine today's Beethoven having to attend a school with a large sports program but no band or music course offerings. Too bad—it's zip-code schooling or nothing.

That is, unless you have money. Wealthy people have a choice about what schools their children attend. They can pay for private school or they can move to a neighborhood with better schools. Rich children who excel in sports attend a school with a sports program. Or gifted kids attend schools where they are fast-tracked for college programs. In fact, when choosing where to live, many high-income parents make the determination simply based on the quality of the local schools.

Who loses out? Children from poor and middle-class families. They're stuck. Their families can't afford to move or pay for private school. They have no choice. It is zip-code schooling for them. Children are assigned to schools regardless of their needs, interests, or priorities.

The solution to this problem is to give all parents, regardless of income, the freedom to choose which school their children attend. The American education system needs to adopt a free-market approach to education. As often happens with a monopoly that has no competition, the provider has gotten lazy. The administrators of public schools know that they've got customers coming through the door no matter what, so they don't have to improve. In fact, they don't even have to provide good quality education.

Give parents a choice. That way, when they see poor service and poor results, they can reject a school and choose another one. Poorly performing schools will either get better or shut down.

If parents could choose where they send their children to school, we would know quickly which schools are fulfilling their mission and which schools are failing. It's a much better option than the massive federal intervention schools have to endure as a result of the No Child Left Behind (NCLB) law, which was championed by President George W. Bush in 2001. NCLB forces schools to waste money on all kinds of testing to demonstrate they are improving test scores. Many schools just manipulate the system to make it look like they aren't failing.

NCLB has turned out to be yet another bloated government program. It is an unnecessary squandering of millions of our tax dollars on schools that don't prioritize the interests of children. If the parents, the actual users of the educational system, could reject failing schools directly (rather than waiting around for the federal government to decide which ones don't work), the system would improve itself in a cost-effective and innovative manner. Children would get the skills and training they need to go on to be productive Americans.

Would you pay your monthly cell phone bill if the phone wasn't working? No. Wouldn't you switch to a phone company that worked and gave you great service? Yes. Why is education any different?

Fixing the educational system requires a simple change in the way school funding works. A locality should give a cash equivalent to the parents, rather than the cash to zip-code schools. The parents of each child should get a voucher equivalent to the dollar amount the system was spending on the child, and parents can use the voucher for any school system they want. They can send their kids to a public school, a private school, or even a religious school.

A voucher system is the major tenet of a movement known as "school choice," which aims to bring free-market competition to the education system. Just as competition has led to more and better products at lower costs in nearly every aspect of our lives, school competition can lead to better schools, and at lower cost.

I'll get into more detail about exactly how it would work, but first let's debunk some myths surrounding education. To start with, it isn't true that America needs to spend more on education to get better academic results from its students. We've done that and it hasn't worked. Back in 1960, we spent $2,670 per student in America. By 2005, the number had grown to $9,391. Adjusted for inflation, it is an increase of 250 percent.[1]

Even more recently, when you look at per student spending in terms of percentages, the growth is startling. Dollars spent per student in public schools went up 37 percent from the 1980–81 year to 1990–91. Though it slowed in the early 1990s with an increase of less than 1 percent from 1990–91 to 1994–95, it shot up again by 25 percent from the 1994–95 school year to 2005–2006. In fact, that $9,666 spent per student in the 2006–2007 school year is an all-time high. This number includes local, state, and federal spending.[2]

And yet student test scores in the United States have remained the same. The Department of Education has a tremendous database where you can view decades and decades' worth of scores among American students of varying ages.[3]

On a scale of 0 to 500, the reading scores for seventeen-year-olds in America back in 1971 was 285. By 2008 that number had increased to only 286. For thirteen-year-olds the score went from 255 to 260 over the same period of time. For nine-year-olds, there was a bit more improvement, from a score of 208 in 1971 to 220 in 2008. That is a gain of just under 6 percent. But spending per pupil during that same time period climbed a whopping 117 percent.[4] How does the United States compare to the other most industrialized nations of the world, such as those in the G8? When it comes to spending on a per student basis, the United States is higher than all of them. In total dollars as a percentage of GDP, the United States spent 3.8 percent of its GDP on primary and secondary education, more than any other country in the G8. In terms of dollars per student, we spend more than every other industrialized nation.[5]

The U.S. government uses the G8 as a comparison group because of the similarities in their economic development and because the other G8 countries are among the major economic partners of the United States. The leaders of these countries meet regularly to discuss economic and other policies.

And yet our students are middling. Whether it is science proficiency, reading literacy, or mathematics, our students don't outperform at any age, in any subject.[6] We're never at the bottom, either, but considering our spending levels versus our GDP, we ought to be getting more for our money.

Another myth: we don't pay teachers enough. According to the American Federation of Teachers (AFT), a division of the AFL-CIO, the average teacher salary in 2009 was $51,271, excluding benefits.[7] That salary puts them, as individuals, above 54 percent of all households in America when it comes to income.[8] During the worst recession since the Great Depression, teachers' salaries did not suffer. According to the AFT annual compensation survey, U.S. teachers saw an increase in their salaries of 5.6 percent from 2008 to 2009.[9]

When it comes to international comparisons for teachers' salaries, we do just fine as well. We are second only to Germany in starting salaries for elementary and high school teachers: $34,900, and $33,700, respectively. Japan, where students perform far better, only pays its starting teachers $26,300 on average. (All these numbers have been adjusted by the Department of Education to take into account what economists call purchasing-power parity. In other words, you are getting apples-to-apples comparison.[10])

When it comes to hours of instruction, Americans are at the very top of the list among countries that submit the data (which is most of them). The average number of hours a teacher spends in the classroom each year in the United States is 1,080, more than in France, Germany, Russia, Italy, and Scotland. So there is no excuse. The data tells us we need to do something different.

A voucher system is the answer. Currently each town or city has a big pot of taxpayer money dedicated to education. They dole it out to schools based on the number of students in that school. A locality can easily calculate how much they are spending per student in any school district. But instead of doling out that money to each school, a school board could dole it out to the parents in the form of a voucher for each child in a family. Note that this does not raise the amount of taxpayer money being spent: the dollar amount remains the same under either scenario.

If parents choose to send their child to one of the public schools, fine. The voucher covers it. If they choose to send their child to a local private school, and the tuition is equal to or less than the amount of the voucher, again it is covered. However, if the tuition at the private school is more than the face value of the voucher, parents have to make up the difference.

In an ideal voucher system as envisioned by the Milton Friedman Foundation, participating schools must follow only a few rules. If a school has more applicants than spaces, they must hold a random lottery to fill the slots. This ensures they don't cherry-pick the students with the best grades, or disallow students with poor academic records. Participating schools must have a uniform, simple application process. The minute there are "extra" requirements such as parent interviews, poor and working parents are at a disadvantage. And, finally, they must meet certain safety standards and financial standards. Any school that wants to participate in the system must agree to these rules. But that's it. No other restrictions about what must be taught, or what curriculum must be followed, or how long or little the teachers can work. Schools have the freedom to evolve and try different things. Schools that have high enrollments would then be eligible to apply for infrastructure funding such as sports facilities and more classrooms.

The Knowledge Is Power Program, known as KIPP, is a great example and new standard for educating our students. Even President Obama has endorsed KIPP schools as a model for education reform. KIPP schools are charter schools. They essentially began as an experiment in Houston's inner city. The school is run like a business, with the ability to hire and fire staff at a fair-market rate—not at a mandated government wage. KIPP schools have a much longer school day than the standard school does. They are open from early in the morning to early in the evening and even some half Saturdays—like a business that is meeting its customers' needs. If teachers don't advance their students' interests, they don't work there.

The result is success, expansion, and a great education for those students who have chosen to attend. KIPP schools now operate like franchises across the country. They are run like businesses and are efficient and effective. The free-market system prevails and students win.[11]

I think there should be an expansion of for-profit schools. Why do schools have to be not-for-profit? Some people are just aghast at the idea of a profit motive in schools. Why? Financial incentive drives so many wonderful products and innovations in our lives. How many times have you bribed your kids to get them to do their homework or do well on a test? We willingly pay Apple for an iPad, an iPod, or an iPhone, knowing that Apple makes a handsome profit on those products when we buy them. Lifesaving drugs are invented by companies trying to make a profit. Why are we so appalled at the idea that an entrepreneur who comes up with a school that does a phenomenal job of educating children should make money doing it?

If, as a parent, you were faced with the choice of a for-profit school that you knew increased your kid's chances of getting into Harvard, or a not-for-profit school of equal cost that didn't increase your kid's chances of getting in, which would you pick?

A real-life example of free-market choice in education with positive results is happening right now in New Orleans. There has been revolutionary change in the way the city's children are educated.

Before Hurricane Katrina struck in 2005, the public schools of New Orleans were an abysmal failure. Of the 128 public schools, almost 75 percent were labeled as failing by the state. On more than one occasion, the Louisiana state government had threatened to take them over, and after Katrina struck, the state did.

Louisiana did something radical and embraced a system based on choice. It allowed parents to choose any school in the system, and it allowed entrepreneurs to come in and start schools with public funding but very few restrictions. Education innovators descended on the region. A KIPP school opened, as did numerous other types of experimental schools. Dollars dedicated to education followed children to their schools of choice. Now there are thirty-three traditional schools and thirty-seven charter schools educating the nearly 25,000 students that remained in or returned to New Orleans after Katrina. Student performance has improved dramatically.[12]

Test data from the fall of 2009 shows incredible improvement in school achievement. For example, school performance scores for Orleans Parish increased from 56.9 in 2005 to 70.6 in 2009. Below 60 is considered failing.[13] Overall, the percentage of failing schools in New Orleans dropped by over 20 percent from 2005 to 2009.[14]

Yes, there are still some problems with the New Orleans system. The application process for attending a school is not uniform. Some of the more popular schools have requirements such as interviews and additional questionnaires. Critics rightly argue that rigorous application processes favor families with greater resources. For example, if you have a car it is easier to drop off applications at more than one school or attend entrance interviews if they are required. If a parent cannot take time off from work during the day, it is difficult to meet with principals or attend informational sessions.

But the program is still young. And there is increasing demand for these schools. Most educational systems experimenting with school choice don't start out with anything nearly as dramatic as New Orleans. They often begin with "charter schools." Charter schools are what I think of as school choice lite. They are what I hope will be the precursor to a full voucher system. A charter school is publicly funded but freed from much of the bureaucracy, rules, and regulations that burden many traditional public schools. When states pass laws allowing charter schools, individuals— whether parents, teachers, or entrepreneurs—can start new schools. When a student chooses to attend a charter school rather than the traditional local public school, the taxpayer money that would have gone to the public school to pay for that child's education instead goes to the charter school.

New York City is one of the biggest innovators in America when it comes to charter schools. Back in 1998, the state authorized the establishment of charter schools. Within ten years there were seventy-eight of them in New York City and another twenty-six scheduled to open in the next two years.[15] The demand for spaces in these charter schools is so strong that nearly all of them have to conduct random lotteries to fill their places.

A study funded by the U.S. Department of Education looked at the scores of all the students who attempted to get into those charter schools and compared those who got spots with those who didn't and instead attended the traditional public school for their district. On average, students who attended New York City charter schools from kindergarten to eighth grade outperformed students who did not get to attend charter schools.[16]

Even more impressive, those who attended charter schools

dramatically closed the gap between students in the city and in its affluent suburbs, or what they call the "Scarsdale-Harlem achievement gap." Scarsdale, in Westchester County, is one of the most affluent cities in New York state, Harlem one of the poorest communities.

The kids in Scarsdale far outperform the kids from Harlem. On New York state exams, a score of 650 means a student is proficient, whether it is the state's math or English test. Scarsdale students routinely score in the area of 685, which is thirty-five to forty points higher than the kids in Harlem. However, kids in Harlem attending charter schools rather than local public schools score an additional twenty-three points higher when it comes to English, thirty points higher when it comes to math.[17]

One of the arguments made against charter schools is they skim the best students from the public school system, so of course they are going to have better results. But the New York City system demonstrates that that is completely untrue. It uses a lottery system that prevents school administrators from cherry-picking only the best students.

The greatest concentration of New York City charter schools is in Harlem and the South Bronx, some of the poorest and toughest neighborhoods in the country. Some of them are converted public schools. Most are new schools, either for-profit or not-for-profit. One factor is consistent: the vast majority of the students are black or Hispanic, poor, and come from families with less education than the city average.

While black students make up 34 percent of public school students in New York, they are 64 percent of the charter school population. Hispanics make up 15 percent of public school students, but 29 percent of the city charter school students. Compare that to white students, who are 15 percent of the public school students but only 4 percent of the city's charter school rolls.[18] These numbers counter the argument that poor minority parents don't take the time to focus on their kids' education. If parents have moved a child into one of these charter schools, they've given their child's future some thought. The numbers also fly in the face of charter school critics who say only connected white parents can get in. Minority kids are getting in. And if our biggest failing as a nation is not educating poor minority kids, these numbers suggest a step in the right direction.

There is abundant statistical evidence that charter schools are providing choice to those who couldn't otherwise afford it. The average household income in charter schools' census tracts is $37,639, while it is $59,743 for New York City overall. Nearly 44 percent of households in charter schools' neighborhoods have incomes less than $20,000, while only 28.4 percent of New York City households have such a low income. Also, 41 percent of the adults in the same census tracts have no high school diploma or GED, compared to only 28 percent of New York City adults overall. And 57 percent of families in charter school areas are headed by single parents, while only 39 percent of families in New York City as a whole have single parents.[19]

Any student in the five boroughs of New York City can apply to its charter schools, regardless of income. The application process is minimal: name, date of birth, parents' contact information, etc. The charter schools do not ask for transcripts, nor do students have to write an essay or demonstrate their academic performance. New York City charter schools are required to take all applicants if they have space for them. If a charter school does not have enough space for all those who apply, it must hold a random lottery. Almost

94 percent of the students who apply to New York City charter schools are put into these lotteries.[20] As a result, cherry-picking of top students is nearly impossible.

Charter schools are enormously popular, yet numerous states have laws that bar or limit their operations. Legislators have often caved when faced with the demands of unions that prioritize teachers' jobs over kids' education. Some states simply don't allow them, many states put an arbitrary cap on the number allowed, and some simply make the requirements so onerous that entrepreneurs don't even bother to try to develop them.[21]

If I haven't convinced you yet that choice is the answer with education, let me give you one more example of great success that isn't zip-code-based. You don't think more charter schools or the voucher system will work in America? The concept has already been tried, and it is very successful. It's the GI Bill. It grants military personnel an education voucher for use at any college or university in America. Under the rules for the new GI Bill, if you serve for just ninety days you get a stipend for housing and books and your tuition is paid directly to the state. And guess what—you get choice. You don't get sent to a school based on your zip code. You get a voucher of sorts and you choose where you want your dollars to go.

Choice has made our university system the best in the world. The university system is based on competition and succeeds because attendance isn't determined by zip codes. We are the envy of the world when it comes to higher education, and yet we offer some of the weakest programs in elementary and high schools.

Critics of school choice say that many parents don't know enough about education to choose a good school for their children. That is ridiculous. Parents know their children best and what's best for their children. This criticism is in fact often a veiled way of saying that poor or uneducated parents don't know what is best for their children at all. That is elitist. Many of us had parents or grandparents who arrived in America poor and uneducated. Look how well they did. And New York City's charter school results demonstrate that the most avid users of them are the children of poor or less-educated parents. You don't need to be rich and armed with a degree from Harvard to know the importance of a good education and have an interest in seeing your child succeed.

Yes, there are some parents who simply don't care. Maybe they are addicted to drugs, or maybe they had a child at far too young an age. But no system will ever make up for a parent who just doesn't want to parent. And certainly today's school systems are ill-equipped to help the children of those kinds of parents. You can never create a system that catches every single kid, and if you try, you end up hurting the majority by focusing your efforts on a very small minority.

Critics of school choice also say it will hurt public schools. True, but only the bad ones, and that's the idea. Bad public schools will fail and go away as their customers leave for better service. That's why entrepreneurs start new schools in places where the public schools are the worst. They know they'll find demand if they supply quality education. Good public schools have nothing to fear; they will be able to keep their customers.

We're supposed to accept leaving education in the hands of the government and public education, yet a study by the Heritage Foundation from April 2009 suggests that one in four members of Congress doesn't. Private school was the choice of 38 percent of the members of the 111th Congress.[22]

People say, "We need public education in America!" Yes, we do. But that doesn't mean we need bad public schools and it doesn't mean we have to get education from a monopolist government provider.

President Obama is taking his own crack at trying to fix education in America. With more than $4 billion in prize money, his administration is running a Race-to-the-Top competition among the states. The states win big grants if they make big changes that Education Secretary Arne Duncan believes would improve student results.

These changes include allowing for more charter schools and tying teacher compensation to student performance.[23] Frankly, I am pleasantly surprised, because these two goals are anathema to the teachers' unions and yet President Obama is clearly willing to take them on in this arena.

The first two winners were Delaware and Tennessee, getting $100 million and $500 million, respectively. Delaware won after passing a law that allowed for teachers to be removed from the classroom if they were rated ineffective after three years even if they had tenure. I know what you are thinking—you need a law to get rid of someone who's been doing a bad job for three years? It just goes to show how much control teachers' unions have had when it comes to fighting off anything that keeps their members from getting fired, even if they are bad teachers.[24]

Tennessee won that half billion dollars after passing a law that factors student performance into the teacher evaluation process. Again, isn't it amazing that you need a new law to permit connecting a teacher's evaluation to how his or her students perform? To the rest of us, the concept is completely intuitive—but not to the teachers' unions.

When the first round of winners was announced there

were critics who felt the administration gave too much sway to whether or not the states' teachers' unions had supported the changes. In fact, when the first two awards were announced, Secretary Duncan pointed to the fact that in both states the unions had backed the reforms. There were other states with much more aggressive measures in place, but they didn't have the backing of the unions and thus didn't get the money—Florida and Louisiana, for example.[25] Not a surprise to me, considering how union-friendly this White House is.

Still, the mere competition has had a big impact on state education laws already. Many states, in an attempt to win Race-to-the-Top money, passed laws increasing the allowable number of charter schools and tying teacher pay directly to student performance.

In an effort to be a winner in the second round of awards, New York State passed two laws in late May that raised the cap on the number of charter schools in the state to nearly double what it was before—it would be better if there were no cap whatsoever, but let's take what we can get at this point—*and* allowed for teachers' evaluations to be tied to students' performance on standardized tests.[26]

Could Secretary Duncan have been more aggressive? Yes. Do I wish he had been more aggressive? Yes. Still, many states, in an effort to win the money, have faced down the teachers' unions and pushed for changes that they resisted for so long. I see it as a very wily move by Secretary Duncan to get what he wanted: more charter schools and more student performance–teacher pay connection, without having to go to the mat with the unions.

I'll bet if we asked him, even my fourth grade teacher, Mr. Maloney, would say I'm right.

— 9 —

Shrinking the Budget

For those of you who object to the size of the federal deficit: get over it.

Yes, it is too big. Yes, it is scary. And don't get me wrong—the deficit isn't an insignificant matter. But this country has a much bigger issue to be concerned with. The far more serious problem is the enormous size of the federal budget itself. It's way too big and it's getting even bigger at one of the fastest rates in our history.

The size of the budget threatens both our long-term stability and our economic liberty. Think of it this way: the size of the federal budget is the size of the government's claim on our money. Whether the government borrows or increases taxes, it's ultimately sucking money out of the private economy— meaning my money and your money. Eventually you and I, or future generations, are going to have to pay for all the spending that's going on right now.

Back in 1995, Milton Friedman wrote in the *Wall Street*

Journal, "Our country would be far better off with a federal budget of $1 trillion, and a deficit of $300 billion, than with a fully balanced budget of $2 trillion."[1] Today his words continue to hold true, but we have far exceeded the $2 trillion level to which he referred. Spending has grown so much that in 2010 the federal budget reached $3.7 trillion and was headed for $3.8 trillion in 2011.

Every dollar that the government spends must be taken from someone. At the rate we are spending, everyone, in every single tax bracket from the poor to the wealthy, will end up paying much more in the future.

Here are some terms you should understand as we go through this.

The deficit: the difference between what the government brings in via taxes, versus what it spends each year. Our deficit in 2010 is expected to be $1.5 trillion and in 2011, $1.3 trillion.[2] To give you some idea of how big that gap is, the Tax Foundation calculates the federal government will spend $33,000 per household, but will raise only $19,000 from each household through taxation.[3]

Deficit as a percent of GDP (economists love to focus on this one): compares the size of a country's deficit to the size of its economy. In 2010, the president's budget predicts that our deficit will be 10.6 percent of our GDP. This is the highest level since World War II. It will still be historically very high in 2011 at 8.3 percent.[4] And over the next decade, the president's own predictions indicate that it will never fall below 3.6 percent. To give you some context, if a country is a member of the European Union, it is not allowed to have a deficit as a percent of GDP greater than 3 percent. Great rule. If only they'd followed it—Greece wouldn't be on the brink of disaster.

Total debt: the accumulation of previous years' deficits. For years the government has been spending more money than it collects. When you add it all up, as of May 31, 2010, we were in debt to the tune of $12.9 trillion.[5]

Total debt can be divided into two categories and the difference between them matters. First, there is debt held by the public. This is money the government has borrowed from other people. If you own government bonds or Treasury bills, you are in this category, right alongside the Chinese government. Right now, total debt held by the public stands at $7.7 trillion.[6]

Then there is intragovernmental debt. These are promises and commitments made to people, say when it comes to future Social Security or Medicare payments. It's essentially a future IOU. That stands at $4.5 trillion.[7]

Economists tend to focus on debt held by the public rather than intragovernmental debt. The reason is simple. Public debt has to be paid back, but intragovernmental debt does not. When push comes to shove and a government is in dire straits, it can tell its citizens, "Sorry, you aren't going to get what we promised you," or "You're going to have to work longer before we give you this money," or "We just aren't going to cover as many medical procedures as we originally thought we could." Greece did this in the spring of 2010. California did it last year. The state cut services for residents and offered IOUs to state contractors to pay bills and pay their debt holders. It's terribly painful and infuriating, which is why a government should never overpromise in the first place. But as harsh and callous as it may sound, the consequences of not paying back constituents are less dire than of not paying back public debt.

If a government doesn't pay back its public debt, the

costs are enormous. A government's future ability to borrow is hampered. It's just too devastating, and will be even more painful for a nation's or states' people. Look again at Greece in 2010, and California, whose treasurer constantly repeated during their various budget crises that no matter what, California would do everything and anything to make sure its bondholders got paid. And they met these obligations, although that necessitated laying people off, hiking student tuition, cutting back on Medicaid, and even issuing IOUs. But mission one for any sovereign borrower (as states and countries are called) is to pay back money borrowed in the public markets.

It's like the difference between owing money to your family and owing money to a bank. If you don't pay back the bank, your ability to get a loan in the future falls dramatically, or at a minimum you are going to pay much higher interest rates if you want to buy a car or a home. If you don't pay back your brother, the holidays may be extremely uncomfortable, and maybe he never talks to you again, and maybe your mother gets mad at you, but your credit rating remains intact. But let's get back to definitions.

The debt-to-GDP ratio: how much total money we owe compared to the size of our economy. This number is growing astronomically. According to the president's own budget analysis, our public debt-to-GDP ratio is going to hit 63 percent in 2010, then 68 percent next year, and will be in the 70-plus percent range through 2020.[8] This number hasn't been so high since the early 1950s, and that was a result of World War II.

Historically, the debt-to-GDP ratio has always looked its worst during recessions, because tax revenues take a big hit. But if we grow the economy, the number can improve dramatically, provided we don't keep the spending accelerator pedal pushed to the floor.

Government spending as a percentage of GDP: by far the most important measure of our nation's fiscal health. Based on President Obama's 2011 budget, government spending is going to be 25 percent of the GDP. The historical average is 20.5 percent (which is still too high, in my opinion). And even though White House forecasters expect strong economic growth starting in 2011, the president's spending levels still represent 23 percent of the economy all the way through 2020. That's if the Obama team is right and the economy rebounds sharply as they predict. Their fingers may be crossed, but many economists are skeptical. Even the Congressional Budget Office pointed out in the 2010 budget that the White House forecast was pretty optimistic.

Throughout this crisis we keep hearing "we have to spend our way out." But in its future budgets, the White House also plans to keep spending and spending even after the economy is expected to improve. If we stay on this path we will look more and more like Europe, where governments frequently have budgets at least 50 percent of GDP. They face slower growth and stagnant economies because of such mismanagement.

Pimco economist Tony Crescenzi said that at the rate we are borrowing, our interest payments alone will exceed all discretionary spending by 2020.[9] It's no different than an individual who has spent years and years racking up credit-card debt and so is paying more interest every month than all other monthly expenses combined.

The Tax Foundation did a great analysis of what level of taxation would have to be imposed on every tax bracket if we wanted to balance the budget. Those in the lowest tax bracket would have to pay out 24.3 percent of their income, rather than the current level of 10 percent. The 15 percent bracket would have to become the 36.4 percent bracket. Those currently in the 25 percent bracket would pay out 60.6 percent of their income. The 28 percent bracket becomes the 67.9 percent bracket. The 33 percent bracket skyrockets to 89.8 percent. And the 35 percent bracket becomes 80 percent.[10] In fact, after you include the payroll tax, local taxes, and state taxes (which average 8 percent), earners in the top bracket would have a tax rate above 100 percent. They'd have to give back some money from last year, not just this year, when doing their taxes. And by the way, why would any high earner bother to work anymore? The income from the tax bracket would fall steadily.

The solution is not to raise taxes. The solution is to spend less. The budget has to get smaller, and the government should focus its energy on a few key areas. When it comes right down to it, there are only five departments that we absolutely need: Defense ($636 billion in 2009), Homeland Security ($51 billion), Treasury ($701 billion), State ($21 billion), and Justice ($27 billion). Most others could be eliminated.[11]

Eliminate these five departments completely: Education. Yes, you read correctly. First eliminate the Department of Education. What if I tell you that the very existence of the Department of Education is why college gets more and more unaffordable each year? Then let's get rid of Commerce, Energy, Transportation, and Housing and Urban Development.

Let's go through these one by one.

Nearly everything the Department of Transportation does could be devolved to the state and local governments, particularly the program called the Highway Trust Fund. In 2009 it was 72 percent of the department's budget, or $53 billion.

(Devolve simply means transferring the responsibility to states or local governments, away from the federal level.)

You might think the highway program is about highways and maintaining the nation's roads. If only it were so, but it's not. Your federal gasoline taxes have paid for movies about highways, graffiti cleanup, museums, bike paths, pedestrian trails, river walks, sidewalks, horse trails, and a lovely $150,000 stoplight in Briarcliff Manor, New York.[12]

Here's how the Highway Trust Fund works. When you buy a gallon of gasoline, the federal government imposes an 18.4-cents tax, and then the state tacks on its own tax, the average total being 21.72 cents. For most consumers, at least 40 cents of the price of a gallon of gasoline is taxes. It could be as high as 50 cents' worth in some states. That 18.4 cents of federal tax goes directly into the Highway Trust Fund, a program established back in 1956 supposedly for building highways.[13]

But now it is just a bucket of money for politically motivated projects for members of Congress, the so-called earmarks. President Bush signed a $268 billion highway bill back in 2005 that set a record for the number of earmarks—more than six thousand. Long gone are the days when Ronald Reagan vetoed a 1987 highway bill because it had a whopping 152 earmarks.[14]

There is no restraint anymore. And there is no shame. I don't exaggerate when I say the implications are deadly. More than a quarter of the nation's bridges are structurally deficient. People die when they collapse. But at least the National Packard Museum in Warren, Ohio, got $2.75 million for its expansion.[15]

Two-point-seven-five million.

The federal government should stop collecting the gas tax. Let state governments tax gasoline as they see fit. Let them keep the money themselves for the projects that they need in the state or eliminate it altogether so that consumers can decide how to spend their own money. Moreover, dollars will be saved in administrative costs. There is so much waste just in the cost of the money being collected and sent to Washington, where Congress tacks on an administrative fee and then sends it back again to fund state and local pet projects.

Another, more important effect of letting states decide if and when to impose a gas tax is that they would no longer be vulnerable if their congressional representatives were weak, low-ranking, or too principled to obtain the appropriations for needed projects. It also would prevent extremely powerful senior members of Congress from getting more than their fair share. Alaska used to get huge appropriations from the transportation bill—due in large part to the clout of Senator Ted Stevens, who was in Congress from 1968 to 2009.

Shifting the spending to the state would realign incentives and end states' get-my-share-of-that-money approach. Currently there is a big pot to which each state has contributed, and therefore every state has an incentive to get as much of that money back as it can. Those that are better at the game get more than others. Remove that federal pot and the thinking changes. (By the way, this could be said for many other parts of the federal budget.)

When politicians are fighting it out at the state or local level, the battles over money are that much closer to the people who are actually going to foot the bill. If Alaskans want a bridge to nowhere, Alaskans can put up the money. Ask yourself if the $500,000 Alaskans received in 2005 for the Big Lake to Wasilla Pedestrian Trails would have been built if Alaskans had to use local dollars to do it. If no one in Ohio is willing to pony up $2.75 million for a museum dedicated to the history of the Packard car, why on earth should somebody in Alabama or California be paying for it with their federal taxes? I'll bet state officials would get a lot more stingy if their spending projects came straight out of their pocket and not some murky pit of D.C. money.

Moving power from the federal to the state and local realm is something I believe in when it comes to most government spending. Much of what's being done at the federal level should be devolved to the states.

Milton Friedman advocated this type of devolution because it meant dispersion of power. He generally felt there should be as little concentration of power in Washington as possible, because if people didn't like the policies in one state or town, they could move to another. When a state chooses to spend money, it adds directly to its own tax burden. It forces the state government to weigh the benefit of a project versus having to pay for it, knowing that if their taxes rise too high they will lose their population and businesses to other states.

I realize that when programs or missions are devolved to the state level, it doesn't necessarily guarantee lower taxes. Rather, it is a shift from your federal tax bill to your state and local tax bill. But that's the idea. Because when most taxation happens at the state and local level, people have the power to vote with their feet. If they don't like something done by the state, they can pack up and simply move somewhere else. If everything happens at the federal level, people are stuck, unless they want to move to another country.

And I sure don't.

If a state keeps raising taxes at a faster rate than other states, and to a much higher degree than other states, people can and do leave. A state loses tax revenue for every taxpayer who leaves and isn't replaced by a new one. States like Cali-

fornia and New Jersey with high tax burdens have been losing population for years, making the departure rate a natural
check on the state legislature.

We should also get rid of the Department of Agriculture.
First of all, farm subsidies are harmful. They're bad for small
farmers, bad for consumers, and bad for poor countries. We
spend tens of billions of dollars a year on subsidies, and even
though President Obama has talked about slashing payments,
the farm lobby is raising strong opposition.

There are a number of subsidy programs but perhaps the
most destructive is the price-guarantee program. The government guarantees a farmer that he or she will get paid a certain
price for a crop if the price falls below a certain level on the
open market.

One of the justifications for farm subsidies is that farming
is risky, because of weather, natural disasters, and lack of cer-
tainty about pricing. Oh yeah? That's true of the oil industry,
and the natural gas industry. Yet we the taxpayer don't guarantee the price on their products. Exxon Mobil, Royal Dutch
Shell, and Chevron took a bath on refining gasoline last year.
Feel bad for them? Didn't think so.

Technology CEOs might argue their business is extremely
risky, too. Remember all those failed dot-coms? Risk is a part
of doing business. When there is risk, there is the potential
for reward. But farmers want to be rewarded no matter what.
And don't kid yourself—farming is a business. Farm subsidies
turn out to be corporate subsidies, because the vast majority
of the recipients are big corporate farms, not small family
farms.

Most of the subsidies go to five crops: cotton, wheat, soybeans, rice, and corn. So how do citrus farmers survive with
all this uncertainty? What about avocado growers? Simply

put, they rely on supply and demand. There was a shortage of avocadoes in 2009 and prices went up to the benefit of farmers. Florida tomato growers got slammed in the winter of 2009–2010 because of cold weather. Nearly 70 percent of Florida's domestic crop was destroyed. The consumer is paying for that in high prices. Again, supply and demand. And where does it end? If the farmer is covered, should the Wendy's fast-food chain get a subsidy, since tomatoes are more expensive? Maybe Congress should pass an Italian Restaurant Protection Act for these kinds of occurrences?

Subsidies also set up perverse incentives. They induce farmers to produce more of the crops they know will guarantee a payment, which means there will be a greater supply of them. This means the price will go even lower. Subsidies therefore increase the likelihood more subsidies will be needed, since oversupply pushes down prices.

Our farm subsidies punish poorer countries that have economies that rely on agriculture to a far greater extent than ours. Since subsidies induce more production in the United States than would normally occur, overseas farmers get a lower price for their product and are unable to sell into the U.S. market.

While farm subsidies are the most heinous of the Agriculture Department's programs, an even bigger part of its budget is dedicated to food stamps. The food stamp program would work better if it were devolved to the states. Now, I don't advocate getting rid of food stamps. Each and every state could run its own food stamp program as it sees fit. There is precedent for this in President Clinton's decision to shift welfare from being a federal program to fifty different state-run programs. It worked phenomenally well in reducing the number of people on welfare. At the time, the big catchphrase was "fifty laboratories of democracy." When it comes to any kind of welfare, aid, or subsidy, this should be the model.

Subsidies or welfare assistance administered at the federal level cannot be tailored to the needs of local communities. It becomes a one-size-fits-all solution that often turns out to be no solution at all. It becomes much easier for the receivers of the aid to not be accountable for what they receive.

Translation: fraud.

And there are so many different branches of the federal government doing this kind of thing. For example, the Department of Labor administers all kinds of reeducation program for workers. Great idea. Let the states do it. Michigan's needs are very different from Arizona's.

The United States government subsidizes too many groups. Nearly all subsidies should get axed. Corporations shouldn't get them; builders shouldn't get them; farmers shouldn't get them; wind turbine producers shouldn't get them; Alaskans shouldn't get them. The only group that should ever receive subsidies: the poor and the disabled.

Now on to education, which I know gets some people fired up. I can't even suggest modifying the Department of Education. It should just go away completely. There is nothing it does that couldn't be done at the state and local level. About the only thing it has succeeded in doing is raising the cost of college for middle-class families.

The Department of Education does two things. First, it helps fund various education initiatives across the country. Devolve that job to the states. It's a waste to send those taxpayer dollars all the way to Washington, have the feds skim to pay administrative costs, and then send it back to the states or municipalities. This kind of federal intervention into education is relatively new in our history.

The second thing the department does is subsidize higher education through grants and loan guarantees. Again, the intentions were good, but the reality is that the government has achieved the opposite of what it was hoping to do. I completely understand the desire to have high levels of education. But there is already a huge inducement to get an education: higher future salaries. A college graduate will earn double in his or her lifetime what someone with only a high school education will earn. Let's say in a given year a college graduate makes $25,000–$50,000 more than someone with just a high school diploma. Over a lifetime, that's a million-dollar difference. Parents know this and that's why they work so hard to save and why they take on staggering loans to pay for college.

When you subsidize a product that is already so highly coveted, it drives up the price. Colleges, which are a business like any other, raise prices to capture that extra money. The end result is that the poor get subsidies that still aren't enough, the rich always have the money to attend, and the middle class gets screwed because they are squeezed between the two.

College is about to get a lot more expensive, because under President Obama and as part of the new health-care legislation federal tuition grants have become entitlements just like Social Security. In other words, it's a program that goes on automatic pilot no longer subject to an appropriation from Congress. And as part of the new program, Pell Grants will automatically increase at the rate of inflation plus an additional percentage point.[16]

This will be yet another effort driven by good intentions that will have the opposite effect. Ten years from now everyone will be shocked at how expensive education has gotten. Congress will chastise colleges and universities for overcharging. When you subsidize demand for something that already has plenty of demand, you drive the price higher.

Get rid of the Department of Energy. It was created by President Jimmy Carter in the 1970s to help reduce the nation's reliance on foreign oil—that's worked out really well, hasn't it? The current government suggests spending $8 billion in energy research in its stimulus package. The total the U.S. government has funneled to energy research since Jimmy Carter—a whopping one-hundred and fifty-eight billion dollars.[17]

I am not against money being spent on research for alternative energy, but it should be private capital, not taxpayer dollars, making those research investments. There is so much potential profit out there for anyone who comes up with a solution to the energy issue that there is already plenty of financial inducement in the private sector for research. Government funding of research is inefficient and is far more likely to be steered to political constituencies.

The Energy Department also manages the Strategic Petroleum Reserve. That is a useful and necessary function. Hand that over to Homeland Security or the Defense Department or give it to the private sector to run.

Now, even if we wipe out all of these departments I've mentioned, we still have a problem with the budget because of entitlements. Entitlements are things you're supposedly entitled to regardless of your fiscal condition. Take a look at the overall budget and you'll see what I mean:

In 2010, we are going to spend $2 trillion, 58 percent, or roughly two-thirds of the budget on entitlement programs. This component of the budget includes programs like Social Security and Medicare. This spending is also called "mandatory spending" because the programs run on cruise-control.

The other third of the budget is discretionary spending. This includes defense spending and buckets of money for things like the departments of energy and education. Spending on defense is the largest discretionary chunk of the budget. We are going to spend $708 billion on national defense in 2010, or 22 percent of the budget. The rest of the departments *combined* account for 15 percent of the budget.

The irony is that discretionary spending is what causes all the screaming and yelling every year: the accusations of pork-barrel spending and congressional earmarks to please the constituencies back home. And while I certainly don't endorse it, it's not our biggest problem.

I might sound like a broken record, but we need to shrink, shrink, and shrink government. It's too big, and so is the budget—overwhelmingly huge. Want to know where I'd cut first? It's time to take on the third rail of politics. I realize it might not be popular to say, but I am going to do it anyway.

Let's get rid of Social Security and Medicare altogether.

In 2016, for the first time in history, it is projected that we will spend more on Social Security than we do on defense spending: $927 billion versus $749 billion.[18] That's startling, if you ask me. I think the solution to this insane spending is to simply eliminate both departments entirely as well. But that conversation deserves a chapter of its own . . .

After you read it, you'll know I'm right about that, too.

— 10 —

Good-Bye, Social Security; Farewell, Medicare

The U.S. government runs the country's biggest pyramid schemes: Medicare and Social Security. They are going to put us in the poorhouse if the government continues to run them. As long as the point at the top of the pyramid is the older generation, the collecting crowd, and the base of the pyramid is the younger contributing crowd, these Ponzi schemes will continue to chug along. But if the pyramid gets inverted, it simply doesn't work. Look at what is going on in Germany right now: The government can't keep its commitments to its elderly because the size of its working-age population has shrunk. We are fast approaching just such a scenario in the United States with a huge wave of baby boomers about to retire.

The most fair and just way to fix this mess is to stop it altogether.

Before you accuse me of not caring about old people, give me an opportunity to explain. I care about the elderly, not only the ones living right now, but also the ones living two hundred years from now. If you think things should stay on the same path as they are on now, you are saying you only care about old people for the next thirty years or so, and after that, forget it, because the system will be bankrupt by then. You and your parents will have support, but your kids won't. And worse, they will be stuck paying for the debts you incurred for them.

If we keep both programs going, we're going to create a nation crippled by intergenerational warfare. The younger you are, the angrier you should be about this mess. You'll be funding the retirement of baby boomers, the wealthiest generation in American history, many of whom raised single-income families but expect to lead double-income retirements.

To understand the problem, here's a term you should get to know, because you are going to hear it more and more: unfunded liabilities. This is how much we've promised to pay out in benefits in the future, versus how much money we are actually going to bring in to pay for those benefits. The grand total of the shortfall facing the American public for its biggest social welfare programs: $100 trillion.[1] That means we owe future generations $100 trillion more in benefits than we are scheduled to bring in via taxes.

Social Security, a program started in 1935 to provide financial support to the elderly, is in the red to the tune of $15.1 trillion.[2] Every paycheck, you give the government more than 6 percent (until you reach the cap), and your employer matches your contribution to support Social Security. If you are self-employed, you foot the whole bill yourself.

But while Social Security is worrisome, Medicare is worse. It is decimating the federal budget and it wants to eat more and more of your paycheck every year. According to the

Medicare Board of Trustees' own accounting and annual report, its unfunded liabilities total $88.9 trillion.[3]

Medicare is the program that pays for hospital care for the disabled or citizens over the age of sixty-five. It also covers some doctor's visits, home health services, and prescription drug benefits. We all pay a 1.45 percent tax of our paychecks supposedly to cover Medicare, and our employers add on another 1.45 percent, totaling 2.9 percent. The self-employed pay 2.9 percent of their wages in a Medicare tax. But those taxes don't even come close to paying for the overall costs. That's a huge problem.[4]

In fact, Medicare taxes only cover 86 percent of Medicare spending. In 2017 these dedicated taxes are only going to cover 81 percent of what we are expected to pay for Medicare. The rest will come from general revenues—that's our income taxes. By 2050 the Medicare tax will only cover 39 percent of what we anticipate we are going to spend on it.

When you add up the future liabilities of both Social Security and Medicare, you see that the two monsters are eating into more and more of general tax revenue. By 2020, 25 percent of federal income taxes will have to go to cover those two programs, and by 2030 that number will reach 50 percent of our income taxes. It gets worse, though, because by 2060, 75 percent of federal income taxes will have to go to cover Medicare costs.[5]

Here's a third way to look at it: from the perspective of your personal tax return. The National Center for Policy Analysis estimates that when today's college students reach retirement in about 2054, working individuals will have to hand over 37 percent of their paychecks simply to fund Social Security and Medicare. No, that is not a typo—37 percent of their earnings will be used to fund just those two programs, never mind national defense, or building bridges or highways. That 37 percent is just the cost of supporting retirees.

We cannot and we should not tax people to such a high degree. It is both unfair and unethical to burden America's youth with such a high tax rate because politicians couldn't say no to a group of voters who were eager to palm off their expenses to their children, grandchildren, and great-grandchildren.

People over sixty-five years old have had all their lives to work and save. The young are just starting out. Why should they be so burdened? Think of it this way: would your parents or your grandparents ever come to you and demand you hand over nearly 40 percent of every paycheck to them to fund their retirement? If you're elderly, would you ever go to your grandchildren and insist they give you 40 percent of their income? This is what is happening right now. This country is taking from the young to pay for the old, and unless politicians make some sound but hard choices, we're going to cripple our future generations.

Raising taxes isn't the only choice. As the Medicare Board of Trustees said in its 2010 report, another, less appetizing option is a cut to benefits. They are sounding a dire warning, but if Congress doesn't heed their advice and do something soon, that is exactly what will happen. I firmly believe Medicare and Social Security benefits will be cut, and the programs will become "means-tested." In other words, you will qualify to receive benefits only if your assets and income fall below a certain level. It wasn't originally designed to be that way, but that's how it's going to have to be. It will become a program designed to assist those living below the poverty line, even though many people paying into it assumed they would benefit as well.

In other words, the government will break its promise

to a portion of the population and not pay them the benefits they have contributed toward and were expecting to use in retirement. Exactly when we will reach that breaking point is difficult to pinpoint, but it will arrive. The end result will look familiar: It will look no different than what happened to GM and Chrysler retirees and the citizens of Greece. The auto giants had to say, sorry, we just can't do it anymore. You are going to have to foot more of the bill for your retirement benefits than you originally thought. Do you really want that message when you are in your eighties? Wouldn't you rather hear it now, when you can still do something about it?

Think that Washington insiders won't break their promises to workers? Think again. Governments do it all the time. Many European countries did it to their public employees earlier this year. We did it ourselves to Civil War soldiers, who had to march on Washington to get paid. State governments are starting to do it with pensions in the coming decade. Already state officials are breaking their promises on Medicaid, which is the health insurance provided to people living at or below the poverty level. Arizona has frozen enrollment in its Children's Health Insurance Program and they are thinking about shutting it down altogether. Nevada made big headlines in 2010 because they wanted to cut the number of adult diapers they give to Medicaid recipients. Such moves will happen with Medicare and Social Security, too.

Here is the key point: why did we ever think that as Americans we should rely on the government to take care of us? For your sake, don't assume the government is going take care of you. We would all be better off if we stopped believing that the government is going to fund our retirement, because there is an ever-growing chance it won't.

So, you'll have given up all this money over time for nothing. You will have been forced to hand over part of your paycheck to buy a poorly performing annuity from a monopoly provider who doesn't guarantee a rate of return. Wouldn't it have been so much better all along to just get that money yourself and make choices for yourself about how it would be saved, invested, or spent?

A better way is for us to move toward personal accounts. Your Social Security taxes would go to a personal retirement savings account, not to the government. Here is the single-biggest advantage to a personal account: you own the money in it. That means you can leave it to your children or your grandchildren. Right now you don't own your Social Security benefits. If you die, the checks stop. This is extremely unfair to low-income families. Actuarial tables bear out the sad fact that if you are poor, you die at a younger age. The poorer you are, the less likely you are to ever see a single Social Security check. If that money were yours, at least you could pass it on to your children. For the poorest, it could be the only inheritance they have to pass on.

Another advantage to personal accounts: you are far more likely to be aware of just how much you have available for retirement and what kind of lifestyle you can afford. You know when you need to start making larger contributions and at what age you can settle back and relax because your retirement fund is secure. Imagine trying to predetermine how much you are going to get from Social Security in twenty-five years—you can't do it. It isn't just the complicated mathematical calculations: the whole program hinges on uncertainty and can be junked simply with a vote from Congress. It would be like trying to predict when there will be another earthquake on American soil.

Ending Social Security and relying on personal savings

accounts would naturally lead people to work longer. Today people can retire at sixty-seven. Sure, they can work longer if they want to, but the incremental increase they will ultimately see in their Social Security check is very low, so there isn't much incentive to stay in the workforce. If they were putting aside their own money, their retirement reserve would get comparatively bigger for every extra day they worked. There would be much higher incentives to stay on the job and off the government rolls.

The argument against personal accounts is that they are too dangerous; you will be subject to the vagaries of the stock market. Okay—so is being subject to the decisions of some unknown future members of Congress safer? They've already reneged once, on the ultimate retirement age. What's next? Remember, you have no legal rights with regard to those benefits, and Congress can change them at any time. So with Social Security, you are not subject to market risk, but you *are* subject to political risk and the changing whims of Washington. The only thing that could save you from the whims of the future members of Congress is personal ownership and control of that money.

That of course requires some personal responsibility. Critics of privatization say most people don't know enough to invest or simply won't. I find that hard to believe. When Social Security was started, very few people owned any kind of stocks or mutual funds. But now owning stocks or funds is much more mainstream. To me, "the people aren't smart enough" is a nanny-state argument.

I concede that one of the greatest hurdles to Social Security reform is the belief that the average person simply won't save. I don't want to create a system that forces anyone to have to do anything, but in Chile, for example, people are forced to save for retirement into their own accounts—not the government's. A modification of this could work here. All we need to do is shift the taxes people pay in Social Security over to personal retirement accounts that we can't touch until retirement. That way money goes into productive investment instead of into congressional coffers for later misuse.

The American Enterprise Institute has an idea for helping people invest when they don't know how: have them invest in life-cycle accounts. Most mutual fund companies offer them. Here's how they work: If I'm twenty-five years old in 2010 and I want to retire when I'm sixty-five, in forty years, I invest in a fund that I can't tap into until 2050. So my investment adjusts with my age. When I'm young, I am more heavily weighted in stocks, perhaps 75 percent of my investment. As I age that number shifts, weighting me more in bonds. Just think of how many near retirees would have been saved in 2008 if they'd had their money invested like this, instead of loading up in stocks at the age of sixty. Some people nearly got wiped out but it could have been easily avoided.

Several studies have compared what would happen if you had invested in the stock market rather than in Social Security. The American Enterprise Institute has done an analysis that suggests people would be much better off.[6] The well-known economist Robert Shiller has done a study that says people would come out about the same.[7] Coming out even and having control of your money sounds a heck of a lot better than just hoping the government will be solvent by the time you get to retirement. And it doesn't imprison the future of your children and grandkids.

The biggest hurdle in moving toward private accounts is the transition cost. Today's workers are paying for today's retirees, which means any decline in current revenues has to be made up elsewhere. But that would only be a short-term effect, because you are reducing the future liabilities, and it is better than the other alternatives. Michael Tanner of the Cato Institute explains it this way: "Think of your own credit card debts. Rather than making the minimum payments for the rest of your life, it would be much more fiscally responsible to pay them off today. And doing so would save a lot of money in the long run." [8]

I'm not saying it is going to be easy, but if we start paying for the transition now, it will be much cheaper than paying for it later. The time frame depends on how much you want to allow people to shift. I'm not suggesting you touch the incomes of those within ten years of retirement. But you could start with people under thirty right now, and give them the option to invest 2 percent or 4 percent of their Social Security taxes in a personal account. The bigger the number, the tougher it will be in the near term on the budget, but we will get to solvency that much more quickly and dramatically improve our deficit outlook. Milton Friedman described it as making implicit costs explicit. [9]

People would be more responsible with their earnings if they were forced to be. If you think Social Security is going to be there, you have a lot less incentive to save. If we start now and get young people used to the idea of saving on their own, as many already do with their 401(k)s, they'll be prepared for old age without needing the help of the government.

Finally, you could still have a social safety net. Subsidies could still exist for the poor. But currently we have the young, some of whom are not well off, paying for many elderly people who actually are quite well off. Seniors versus children versus working people. Who is more worthy of support?

We should follow the same approach with Medicare. Start allowing people to save for themselves. Medicare is another pay-as-you-go Ponzi scheme that always requires today's workers to pay for today's retirees. And just like Social Security, the early beneficiaries are far more likely to reap the benefits than the later beneficiaries. Look at how most corporations in America have canceled pensions and moved to 401(k)s. Employees save their own money, self-manage it, and take it with them when they leave. We need to shift Medicare in the same way, from being a defined benefit to being a defined contribution plan.

Martin Feldstein of Harvard has argued that current workers should be allowed to set aside a portion of their payroll tax into personal accounts that would be used to buy health insurance upon retirement. Again, the transition would be the most costly part.[10]

The remedy for exploding Medicare costs is the same one the nation should use for health care in general: let the consumer choose the plan. Let the end user drive the coverage choices. Medicare users could choose a high-deductible catastrophic plan or one that covers things like physicals. Anything left over in the account could be used to pay out-of-pocket expenses. It could be similar to Health Savings Account plans, where the government could agree to give seniors $1,000, or $2,000 a year to start. After that, individuals would have to pick up 20 percent of further costs. After a certain amount, if you get a catastrophic illness, the government could step back in to foot the rest. Or maybe it could be structured so that if you pick up 30 percent of the cost, the government agrees to step in at a lower price threshold.

It's uncomfortable, but it's time to make some tough choices about Social Security and Medicare. We can't afford to keep waiting. Just because we've been doing something for years, doesn't mean it's right. Right?

11

The Tragedy of Fannie and Freddie

If you have a hate on for Wall Street, and if you're someone who seethes at the thought of bankers making millions, I've got two institutions that should make you even angrier: Fannie Mae and Freddie Mac, the monsters of the housing industry. They didn't prevent the housing crisis, and in fact they were a major cause of it.

Fannie is the nickname for the Federal National Mortgage Association, a government-sponsored corporation created to help banks and lenders make loans available for homebuyers. Freddie Mac is short for the Federal Home Loan Mortgage Corporation. It is very similar—it keeps money flowing to banks, making it easier for homebuyers to get mortgages.

Fannie and Freddie are emblematic of two key truths about government. First, once a government institution is created, it will likely never to go away, even when it's no longer needed. It will feed off the taxpayer for as long as it can, claiming that its role is crucial to protect us from this, that, or the other thing.

Second, government's good intentions often lead to terrible consequences. Originally they were created to increase home ownership among Americans, then they were tasked with increasing home ownership among low-income Americans. Even after home ownership soared, officials justified their continued existence with the argument that they provide stability to the housing finance market.

So much for that.

The housing bust and the financial crisis proved beyond doubt that Fannie and Freddie don't provide stability. And as for all the low-income homeowners who were supposedly going to benefit from their intervention into the market—they are far more likely to be facing foreclosure right now. Where's the compassion in that?

A third point to keep in mind as you ponder Fannie and Freddie's relevance is that while there are lots of people and institutions to blame for the financial crisis, the private sector did a much better job than Fannie and Freddie did at managing its way through the mess. Everyone complains about the money spent saving the banks. There's a cost to bailing out Fannie and Freddie, too.

It's going to cost us significantly more than bailing out the banks. At a minimum, it's estimated that taxpayers are going to be on the hook for $163 billion from 2009 to 2019.[1] And that's just according to Congress's own rosier budget estimates. When you add in all the money the government forgoes when it allows Fannie and Freddie to subsidize the mortgage market at taxpayer risk, the cost climbs to $389 billion. Your $389 billion.[2]

Compare those numbers to the bank bailouts. When all

is said and done, the Congressional Budget Office (CBO) estimates, the entire financial sector bailout will total less than $53 billion, or less than one-tenth of the Fannie and Freddie bailout.

According to the CBO, the insurance and finance giant AIG, which received $180 billion and has been Congress's whipping boy for years now, will ultimately be able to pay back a large chunk of that money. The CBO thinks the final bill on AIG is only $36 billion total. Bank of America and Citigroup, the banks that received the most bailout money ($45 billion each), have paid it all back.

And yet the banks' executives have been publicly pilloried over and over again by Congress. I'm not saying they didn't deserve some of it, but when it comes to Fannie and Freddie, a much bigger and costlier problem exists. Congress hasn't been nearly as fierce in its vendetta toward these institutions. Why? Because it was Congress that created the problem. Congressional representatives would have to look in the mirror and interrogate themselves to explain this mess.

Washington doesn't want its actions or behavior to be questioned. Politicians and bureaucrats try very hard to prevent the public from identifying their mistakes. Look at the way they announced a major round of support for Fannie and Freddie. It was on Christmas Eve in 2009 that Treasury officials saw fit to put out the press release to inform the public that the government decided to give unlimited taxpayer support to prop up the two institutions. Prior to this announcement, there had been a cap of $200 billion to backstop them.[3]

Every year for the next ten years, the government anticipates handing over piles of money to Fannie and Freddie. They will get cash infusions every time they end up with what's called negative equity: when what they owe is greater than what they are worth. It's just like someone who bought at the peak of the market and now owes $250,000 on a home that will only sell for $200,000. His or her negative equity is $50,000. Fannie and Freddie, the so-called stabilizers of the housing market, bought a ton of stuff at the peak of the market, due to a combination of government pressure and their own stupid decisions.

There is a key reason why we are going to spend so much more helping out a government-backed institution than a private institution: the government allowed Fannie and Freddie to do things they never allowed a private institution to do. Fannie and Freddie were allowed to operate with a much lower capital base. Think of a capital base as just-in-case money. If everything starts going bad, financial institutions have all this capital they can use to pay off losses on bad loans. So we are making up for it now by replenishing Fannie and Freddie's capital with taxpayer money. In addition, Fannie and Freddie were allowed to leverage at higher multiples than any of the financial institutions. When Bear Stearns failed, it was leveraged 30 to 1. According to my CNBC colleague David Faber, Fannie and Freddie were leveraged more than 90 to 1. Think of it this way: for every $1 million Fannie and Freddie had in capital, they had lent $90 million.

Did I mention that Fannie and Freddie CEOs are allowed to get as much as $6 million a year in compensation thanks to the taxpayer?[4]

It all really makes me wonder why these two institutions even exist. Fannie Mae was established during the Depression to help increase home ownership among Americans. I don't doubt it was tough to get a loan back then, because the Federal Reserve made horrendous mistakes in the 1930s. Money was kept too tight, and banks were failing in vast numbers. So the federal government stepped in, but once again, good intentions sowed the seeds of future disaster.

Big gains were made in home ownership levels from the 1940s to the 1960s, rising from about 40 percent to 60 percent. The level of home ownership hovered in the 60 percentile range for the next forty years, and peaked at 69.2 percent in 2004.[5] Even in the first quarter of 2009, after the massive housing collapse, home ownership rates fell only to 67.3 percent, a relatively robust number considering the real estate market conditions.[6]

By the 1990s, the mortgage market had become incredibly robust; maybe that was because of Fannie and Freddie, or despite Fannie and Freddie. Regardless, banks were making home loans and investors were buying those loans in large quantities. But despite achieving the goals of high ownership levels and a private mortgage market, did the government declare victory and go home? No, it wanted more and more and more, even if it meant financial disaster for the taxpayer and the very homeowners it was trying to help.

Fannie and Freddie's evolution demonstrates something economists call "mission creep." They will grow their mission merely to maintain their existence. Fannie Mae came first. It was established in 1938 with the mission to buy mortgages that had been underwritten by banks but insured by the Federal Housing Administration. When Fannie bought a mortgage from a bank, it freed up capital on the bank's balance sheet so it could go out and loan more money for yet another house. This two-piece government backstop made banks more willing to write a mortgage, because banks knew that if they kept the loan and the homeowner defaulted, the Federal

Housing Administration (FHA) would cover their losses, and if they needed to raise cash for some reason, they could easily sell the loans to a willing buyer: Fannie Mae.

The first instance of mission creep came in 1949, when Fannie Mae started buying mortgages guaranteed by the Veterans Administration (now the Department of Veterans Affairs) as well. Fannie underwent explosive growth even then. Consider that in 1948 they bought 6,734 loans; two years later, they bought an eye-popping 133,032 loans.[7]

In 1968, the company had grown so much that President Johnson didn't want it on the federal budget anymore. The cost of the Vietnam War was skyrocketing and he wanted to make the deficit look smaller. So Fannie Mae was converted to a publicly traded company. Two years later the government created the Federal Home Loan Mortgage Corporation, or Freddie Mac, to serve as competition to Fannie Mae because Fannie was deemed too powerful.

More mission creep: Freddie Mac was going to buy conventional mortgages, not those insured by the FHA and VA. Another significant difference: while Fannie Mae kept most of the loans it bought, Freddie Mac repackaged them all and sold them. In 1972, Fannie Mae joined Freddie Mac and started buying mortgages that were not insured by the FHA.

The most significant mission creep came twenty years later, in 1992, when significant new legislation was imposed on the two entities. It required them to meet specific goals on the financing of *affordable* housing. Those goals would be set by the Department of Housing and Urban Development. President Clinton used the new law with gusto when he came into office a year later.

Clinton wasn't satisfied with a home ownership rate of roughly 64 percent in the country, so in the summer of 1994 he set a home ownership rate goal of 67.5 percent.[8] He ordered HUD to make it easier to buy a home in America. Clinton's first secretary of housing and urban development, Henry Cisneros, told Fannie and Freddie that 42 percent of their loans had to serve low- and moderate-income families.

Both Fannie and Freddie adopted more flexible underwriting guidelines, including lower down payment requirements, and they accepted mortgages for buyers with lower credit scores. They pioneered the 3 percent down mortgage and offered borrowers with lower credit scores an interest rate a percentage point above a conventional thirty-year fixed rate for a prime borrower.[9]

By 1999, 25 percent of the growth in Fannie Mae's portfolio was coming from the so-called nontraditional markets. Also that year, Clinton's goal was within sight: home ownership rates were touching 67 percent.[10]

Still, Clinton wasn't satisfied. In the fall of 1999, the *New York Times* reported, "Fannie Mae has been under increasing pressure from the Clinton administration to expand mortgage loans among low and moderate income people and felt pressure from stock holders to maintain its phenomenal growth in profits. In addition, banks, thrift institutions and mortgage companies have been pressing Fannie Mae to help them make more loans to so-called subprime borrowers."[11]

You can see right on HUD's website this little gem, under the highlights from 1997–99, when Andrew Cuomo was in charge of HUD (yes the same Andrew Cuomo who is now New York attorney general, and a candidate for governor). "In July 1999, Secretary Cuomo established new Affordable Housing Goals requiring Fannie Mae and Freddie Mac to buy $2.4 trillion in mortgages in the next ten years. This will mean new affordable housing for about 28.1 million low and moderate-income families. The historic action raised the required percentage of mortgage loans for low and moderate-income families that the companies must buy from the current 42 percent to a new high of 50 percent—a 19 percent increase—in 2001." [12]

So Fannie and Freddie started buying even more subprime loans. Watch the growth: In 2000, Fannie bought $1.2 billion in subprime loans. In 2001 it bought $9.2 billion in subprime. [13]

In 2001, President George W. Bush took office. Now, you might think a free-market, personal-responsibility-endorsing Republican might not like this kind of thing. But you'd be wrong. Although he came from the other end of the political spectrum, Bush loved the home-ownership-at-any-cost story even more than Bill Clinton did. He set a goal of 5 million more homeowners by 2010, including 1 million new minority homeowners. [14]

Down payments? We don't need any down payments. They were practically giving money away by this point. Bush asked Congress to fund a program that would help low-income homeowners receive $10,000 or 6 percent of the purchase price, whichever was greater, to cover down payments, closing costs—and even renovation. Bush told Fannie and Freddie they needed to help out, too. In his speech announcing the "American Dream Downpayment Initiative," as it was called, Bush said, "And I'm proud to report that Fannie Mae has heard the call and, as I understand, it's about $440 billion over a period of time. They've used their influence to create that much capital available for the type of home-buyer we're talking about here. It's in their charter; it now needs to be implemented. Freddie Mac is interested in helping. I appreciate both of those agencies providing the underpinnings of good capital." [15]

And help they did. In 2002 they bought another $15 billion of the stuff. [16]

So home ownership among low-income Americans increased. According to a 2002 HUD study, home ownership rates increased at a faster rate for low-income families when compared to all families, and they pointed specifically to areas where the two institutions had underwritten more than 30 percent of the loans. But then, in 2003, they really dived in, buying $81 billion in subprime loans, and from 2004 to 2006 they bought a staggering $434 billion in subprime loans. [17]

Don't think they were upset about this. They were making a ton of money doing it, even though they knew it was risky. Congressional investigators came up with a document from 2005: a confidential presentation to the then-CEO of Fannie Mae. The presentation said that when it came to the quality of the mortgages they should buy, the company could either "stay the course" or "meet the market where the market is."

"Stay the course" meant focusing mostly on secure, prime, and fixed-rate mortgages. That would "maintain our strong credit discipline" and "protect the quality of our book."

Ah, but the real "revenue opportunity" was subprime. That of course would mean they would "accept higher risk and higher volatility of earnings." They knew it could lead to "higher credit losses" and "increased exposure to unknown risks." [18]

Which do you think they chose? Wall Street investors loved it, too, and cheered them on. Remember even though the companies had a government mission they were publicly traded. As long as prices kept rising and homeowners who were in trouble could sell into a rising market or refinance, everything was fine.

But then it wasn't.

In 2008, when all these loans went bad, the government took over Fannie and Freddie. Here's the incredible irony. Despite the large volume of subprime mortgages that they bought, it was still a relatively small portion of their overall portfolio. Still, the stuff was so bad that a small sliver of their loans threatened their entire structure, not to mention the entire global economy, because so many people and governments all over the world held their debt—the money they had borrowed to buy all that garbage.

There's a reason for this: Congress allowed them to flout all the rules that real companies have to follow. They were exempt from paying state and local taxes, they didn't have to file documents with the Securities and Exchange Commission (SEC), and they were allowed to have far lower capital levels than any other institution. And that last reason is why, when every other bank in the system survived after a temporary loan from the U.S. government, Fannie and Freddie are still connected via a feeding tube to the government trough.

They put $5 trillion worth of taxpayer money at risk.[19] How did it get so big and why did we get stuck with the bill for these supposed "non-governmental" institutions? Again, you can point straight at the federal government. Fannie and Freddie were government-sponsored enterprises, or GSEs. What on earth does that mean? Surreal is the only way to describe the bizarre netherworld of the regulatory standing of these two companies from the 1970s to 2008.

Decade after decade, government officials always said that there was no government guarantee when it came to Fannie and Freddie's debt, even though they were GSEs. If they got in trouble, claimed the government, investors were out of luck, on their own. That's why they had turned them into private companies, after all. Every piece of paperwork the companies put out when they issued debt said the same thing: the U.S. government doesn't back us.

But no one believed them. Every other mortgage company out there had to borrow at higher rates than Fannie and Freddie and have a larger capital base. Investors would lend to the two giants at lower rates expressly because those investors believed if the two ever got into trouble, the government would bail them out. Since they could borrow more cheaply than anybody else, they did. They borrowed and borrowed and borrowed, and bought and bought and bought.

And when it all came crumbling down, the government did indeed bail them out in the fall of 2008. We have been footing the bill ever since.

I am not trying to absolve the Wall Street banks. They did many of the same stupid things that Fannie and Freddie did. But they cost us far less than these two GSEs. It is precisely because Fannie and Freddie are government sponsored that they are turning out to be so much more costly.

Government once again had the best of intentions—to make it easier for people to borrow money to buy a home—and once again its efforts had punishing consequences.

What's truly infuriating about the government's constant attempts to raise ownership levels is that we already support housing in so many ways in the United States. Besides Fannie and Freddie, the tax structure of the United States favors homeowners. Mortgage interest is deductible. In 2009, that saved homeowners $80 billion collectively on their tax bills.[20] There's also a deduction for state and local property taxes that provides a similar tax savings for homeowners. There is

an exemption for mortgage-subsidy bonds that allows investors in bonds issued by states to earn interest on those bonds
tax-free if they are invested in mortgages of first-time and
low-income home buyers.

We are one of the few countries in the world where most
mortgages are nonrecourse loans. That means if you don't
pay your mortgage, the lender can't come after your other assets, even if you have money sitting in the bank. In most other
places in the world, they can sue you for your other property.
In this country the only collateral on most mortgages is the
home itself. In addition, several arms of the government guarantee home loans, including the VA, the Department of Agriculture, the Federal Home Loan Banks, and the FHA.

Yes, I realize that the rate of minority home ownership
is lower than it is for white Americans: 50 percent versus 75
percent.[21] But we as a nation need to grapple with the underlying causes of that—lower levels of education and hence
lower income are some of the key reasons. Focus on solving
those issues and minority home ownership will be solved, too.

By the way, what is so wrong with renting? There is a
lot to be said for renting. It allows flexibility when things go
wrong. You can move to a smaller, less expensive place much
more quickly, even if it means losing a one-month deposit. At
least you haven't lost tens of thousands of dollars in equity
that you may have spent years building.

But the government never learns. In fact, it repeats the
same mistakes over and over again. That's why the government needs to get out of the housing market completely. It is
so tempting to push an institution to give loans that private
institutions would consider too risky. It's a great way to get
votes. Take, for example, the FHA. Back in 1956, the number
of mortgages they insured that had loan-to-value ratios of

more than 90 percent were only 1 percent of their portfolio. But year after year they weakened their standards. In 2008, more than 85 percent of the loans in their portfolio had loan-to-value ratios of more than 90 percent. Twenty percent of those loans are now going bad. In 2009, the FHA was insuring 6,000 mortgages a day, four times as many as in 2006.

In late 2008, when it was clear the housing market had collapsed, the *New York Times* interviewed some of the people who had just received FHA loans. One of them was Bernadine Shimon, a teacher and single mother in a Denver suburb. She had already lost one home to foreclosure, and no bank would give her a loan. But the FHA did. They helped her buy a $134,000 fixer-upper. She cashed in her retirement savings to come up with the necessary funds to get her part of the deal done. Her mortgage payment is 50 percent of her take-home pay, much higher than the 30 percent recommended under prudent lending standards.

So every dime she's got is in that house. If she loses her job and can't pay the bill, she loses it. A financial advisor would never let someone place all of their money in a single stock. But the FHA has aided and abetted Bernadine Shimon in placing everything she had into a single asset, with an income level that puts her at a much higher risk of default. Who thinks this is a good idea? She does. In the article she said, "The government is doing what it needed to do—taking a risk on people." [22]

Wrong. That is precisely what got us all into trouble in the first place.

Chaz Fullenkamp, a young automotive technician, told the *Times* how excited he was to get an FHA-insured loan to buy a $179,000 house in Columbus, Ohio. "I knew in my heart I could not really afford the house, but they gave it to me anyway. I thought, 'Wow, I'm surprised I pulled that off.' " He went on to say, "If I got unemployed, I'd be wiped out in a month or two." [23]

Are you kidding me?

Finally, in the summer of 2010, facing rising defaults, the FHA got tougher and decided that those with credit scores of less than 580 would have to have at least 10 percent to make a down payment. Instead of being able to finance up to 6 percent of the closing costs, now only 3 percent can be financed. [24] Too little, too late.

Those who defend the continued existence of Fannie and Freddie and the FHA say mortgages would be more expensive and harder to get.

Umm . . . yeah, that's the point. It should be harder to get a mortgage.

Those who defend the continued existence of Fannie and Freddie based on the belief that they boost home ownership should look at Canada, which has almost the same level of home ownership as the United States but with no institutions equivalent to Fannie, Freddie, or the FHA.

The FHA should just stop. Shut down. Fannie and Freddie should be wound down. Private mortgage insurers will step in and fill the void. Will mortgages be harder and more expensive to get? Yes. And that would be a damn good thing.

You know I'm right.

12

In Defense of Defense

I've spent a lot of time in this book saying what the government shouldn't do or shouldn't spend money on. Defending the nation, however, is a critical and essential role of government. Defense isn't just in our security interests, but in our economic interests as well. That being said, I don't advocate overspending or footing the bill for other nations, which is what we do now. We are and should be the leading superpower in the world, but we can do it for less.

U.S. defense spending should be about the United States defending its sovereign borders. Invasion and civil war should be our primary concerns.

Yes, terrorism is a huge problem, but a conventional army is not the way to combat it. Terrorism is a problem best dealt with via intelligence agencies and law enforcement.

Many defense hawks argue that the United States should, as a rule, commit to spending at least 4 percent of GDP every year on defense. That makes no sense to me. If twenty years from now our economy is five times bigger, we should be spending five times as much? Why? By that logic, we should spend less on defense in the years that we are in a recession.[1]

Instead, defense spending should be based on protecting us from whatever potential threats that we face. But we are spending at levels not seen since World War II, when we were worried about Hitler taking over all of Europe and Japan conquering Asia and the Pacific. Our spending is above the levels in the mid-1980s, when we were combating the Soviet Union in the Cold War. Why? We don't have massive enemies like Nazi Germany or imperial Japan or the Soviet Union. Nor is there any country in the world that approaches that military scale today.

Again, let me reiterate that I am not encouraging isolationism or pacifism, but I am encouraging restraint. As Benjamin Friedman has written, we tend to see foreign disorder as foreign threats. There is no reason for that. In the end, our strength comes from our economy and our ability to fund a military, not the other way around.

In 2009 the United States spent as much on defense as the rest of the world combined: $661 billion.[2] In the current fiscal year, 2010, the defense budget is $708 billion. That does not include the $16 billion or so the Department of Energy spends on maintaining our nuclear stockpiles, the Homeland Security budget of roughly $50 billion, depending on the year, the Department of Veterans Affairs, military construction, and other agencies, all of which total another $130 billion.

All in, we are spending $1 trillion a year on our defense and security.[3] For those of you who think that I shouldn't include the VA, I disagree completely. To exclude the cost of assisting the men and women who helped us is to ignore what is one of the most costly parts of preparing for and waging war.

Defending Europe

Part of the problem is that we're spending too much to defend other nations that are fully capable of defending themselves. It is time for the European Union to assume some responsibility. Ever since World War II the Europeans have chosen to spend very little money on their self-defense. They have assumed, rightly, that the United States would come to their aid in the event of any kind of threat. Yet the European economy is bigger than the American economy. There is no good reason for us to foot the bill for them.

Our generosity has enabled the Europeans to pay for their massive welfare states. They have chosen to spend their money on socialized medicine and extremely generous pension benefits for their workers. Here's the really irksome part: all the while, they turn to us and snidely say, "The United States is the only industrialized nation without socialized medicine"—as if that were a bad thing. They say it without ever acknowledging that the only reason they can (temporarily) afford their high levels of social spending is that we subsidize their defense budgets. In fact, we are their defense budgets. (And still many of them are going broke because of their social welfare programs, even without defense spending.)

Even when you combine the three biggest military spenders in Europe, they don't even come close to us. The United Kingdom spends $55 billion,[4] Germany $49 billion,[5] and France $46 billion.[6] The combined total defense spending by European allies: $280 billion compared to the U.S. defense budget this year of $708 billion.[7]

It's not like they don't have the money. In 2008, in twenty-nine different European countries, government spending was more than 38 percent of GDP and in almost half those countries it was closer to 50 percent. This is a staggering percentage particularly when compared to the United States, which is 25 percent. And yet barely any of the European governments spend even 2 percent of GDP on their respective militaries. The United States currently spends more than 4 percent of GDP on defense.[8]

In particular, the leaders of France and Germany love to throw their weight around, suggesting the United States should do this and the United States should do that. Give me a break. Ever since World War II, they and their counterparts in other European nations made very clear choices about how they were going to spend their money—on lavish social welfare programs. In doing so, analyst Max Boot points out, "they abdicated their claims to great power status." If they want more weight in the world, they can put their money where their mouth is. And they should. Their defense should be their responsibility. But we've given them an excuse to not take prudent steps to defend themselves.[9] They are far more vulnerable to threats because of their geographic location; Russia could one day threaten them again, if it so chose.[10] They are also far closer to the threats emanating from the Middle East. It is in their best interests to take the necessary steps.

I cannot fathom the way of thinking that leads them to tolerate this situation. Would we as Americans ever support the notion that we should depend on another country to defend us? Absolutely not. We understand the implication: we would be at the mercy of someone else if we did not control our destiny. Yet the Europeans do exactly that, despite having the money, despite being far more vulnerable geographically.

How do they rationalize that? Easy—they know they can rely on the United States.

Spending Less Doesn't Put Us in Danger

Some very hawkish individuals argue the United States could spend half of what it does now and still be the massive military superpower in the world.[11] That's because we outspend our enemies like crazy. North Korea, Syria, and Iran spend a little more than $10 billion combined.[12] Throw Cuba and Burma into that group and still the United States spends more than twenty-five times what those five countries spend combined.[13]

We spend way more than our frenemies: five times more than China, and ten times more than Russia.[14] In fact, we spend more on research and development of new weapons than Russia spends on its entire military.[15]

China on the Rise . . . Slowly

Let's talk about one potential future threat that gets a lot of headlines: China. Someday China could rival us because they have the size and the will and they have a giant economy. The hawks in the Pentagon would have you believe that China is a huge future threat. They throw around a lot of statistics that on the surface sound frightening.

For eighteen of the last twenty years China has increased its military spending by double-digit percentages.[16] In 2008 they upped their military budget by 18 percent compared to the previous year.[17] In 2009 they upped it by nearly 15 percent. This year they plan to slow it down, relatively speaking, to only a gain of 7.5 percent.[18] By some estimates, China's military expenditures rose 200 percent between 1999 and 2008.[19]

According to their official statistics, that brings them to $78 billion in 2010, making them second only to us in terms of official military spending. But according to experts who monitor this, all these official numbers are likely to be understated and their spending this year is probably closer to $122 billion,[20] up from $69–$78 billion in 2005.[21] The Chinese government is very secretive about its defense spending, so no one knows for sure.[22]

Should we believe what the hawkish Pentagon officials say? Even if China is spending $122 billion, it is much less than the $1 trillion that we are spending. To give you some additional context, we spend more than $2,700 for every man, woman, and child in the United States on defense. China spends less than $100 in per capita terms.[23] When it comes to percentage of GDP, they are somewhere between 2.3 percent and 2.8 percent.[24]

In addition, their capabilities and reach are still far weaker than ours. For example, their navy is much smaller and is limited to short-range missions.[25] China doesn't have an aircraft carrier yet, though there are predictions it will have one in the next decade.[26]

I'm not saying they can't get there. But the hurdles to parity with the United States are far greater than some would have you believe. Even the best military experts say it will be decades before they can even come close to matching us dollar for dollar. The RAND Corporation points out that their labor force will stagnate and then decline, because of their one-child policy; the domestic savings rate is going to decline as the

elderly use their savings; there is likely to be market satura-
tion of their exports and hence a slowdown in the money they
bring in; and the government will likely be under increased
pressure to spend on pensions and health care. (Sound familiar?) In the end, despite the projected growth of the Chinese economy, the rising demand for other things from their
population means they cannot match the United States dollar
for dollar when it comes to military spending anytime in the
foreseeable future.[27]

And here's the other crucial thing about China: they aren't
like the Soviet Union, which was both expansionist in its mission and determined to destroy capitalism, the very foundation of our way of life. Despite calling themselves communist,
the Chinese government is running the country toward capitalism at an incredibly fast rate. China's mission to grow its
economy does not contradict our beliefs; it actually confirms
them.

Defense and the Dollar

Having a strong military is in our economic interests as well,
because our unquestioned ability to defend ourselves is crucial
to the U.S. dollar. The dollar is the dominant currency in the
world and the currency most foreign governments choose to
hold in their bank accounts. This is not an accident. Near the
end of World War II, the global monetary system we know
today was set up at a conference in Bretton Woods, New
Hampshire. It was victory in World War II that ensured U.S.
economic dominance and led to the continued role of the dollar as the world's reserve currency.

Having the world's reserve currency means that other central banks keep massive amounts of U.S. dollars in vaults and bank accounts around the world, because they trust it more than any other currency to maintain its value. That belief is driven by the sheer size of our economy, our political stability, our fairly stable monetary policy (though lately that is questionable), and yes, our military ability to back it all up when push comes to shove.[28] When it comes to war the victor decides the currency.

Sixty-three percent of all official foreign exchange reserves are held in U.S. dollars. Only 27 percent of foreign exchange reserves are held in the euro. Eighty-six percent of all foreign exchange transactions involve the dollar. The International Monetary Fund says sixty-six countries peg or manage their currencies to the dollar, while only twenty-seven do the same with the euro.[29]

Oil and nearly every other commodity in the world is priced in dollars. That means if you run a business in a foreign country and you want to buy oil, you have to use U.S. dollars to do it.[30] That gives U.S. businesses an advantage all over the world because they don't have to foot the bill for exchange costs the way their foreign competitors have to.

In 2008, at the height of the financial crisis, there was a lot of talk about the dollar losing its status as the world's reserve currency because of our deep economic problems. In fact, that's still being debated. However, at the worst moments in the past two years, investors around the world actually bought the dollar and overall it rose in value against most major currencies because ultimately the United States is seen as safer, more stable, and better able to defend itself.

The dollar being the world's reserve currency also means that the United States can borrow more cheaply than any other country in the world. That translates into lower bowering costs for people buying homes or cars (for better or for worse). Because we have the world's reserve currency, we have a distinct advantage over everyone else: when our finances go to hell and the world is on the verge of crisis, our borrowing costs actually go down, because so many people want to own U.S. Treasuries, the safest investment in the world. There is no other country out there with that blessing.

Having the world's reserve currency provides an economic boost to the United States of some $40–$70 billion in a typical year, according to McKinsey Consulting. That's even after you take into account the costs that come as a result of having a strong dollar: mainly more expensive exports and lost jobs.

Some, like Representative Ron Paul, believe that the dollar's role as the world's reserve currency is actually a curse. Paul argues that the need to defend it has led to massive military spending that is unnecessary and actually destructive to the very character of our nation and people.[31] He argues that the world should go back to the gold standard and that gold should be the world's reserve currency. That would mean a country's wealth is measured by how much gold it has in storage and that each unit would be worth a certain amount of gold. And he makes the argument that because the dollar is the world's reserve currency, it gives the government an excuse to spend too much on our military in order to defend it and be the world's policeman. If gold were the measure, that wouldn't be necessary.

He also points out that we are far less disciplined by natural market forces. Our ability to borrow cheaply is not a blessing but in fact a real problem that leads us to be less productive. I acknowledge that our ability to borrow cheaply is part of what got us into trouble, but it will take a crisis far greater than the one we just went through for the dollar to lose its dominance or for us to go back to a gold standard. Given that it is not realistic anytime soon, I'd rather the United States be the dominant power in the world. It gives us flexibility and choice.

Too Much, to Too Many

All that being said, we ask our military to be too many things to too many people.

Why, for example, is our U.S. Navy policing sea lanes to protect some foreign millionaire's ships from Somali pirates?[32] Think about that. Your tax money is being used to defend the profits of a foreign shipping company. Why? Those companies should hire their own security, and if they can't afford it, they should get out of business.

Our defense spending should be about exactly that: defense. Instead our military has a long list of responsibilities that go well beyond the traditional roles of a military, which are to prevent invasions and civil wars. Now it contains China and North Korea, transforms failed states, chases terrorists, keeps oil cheap, democratizes the Middle East, protects Europe, Asia, and the Middle East from aggression, popularizes the United States via humanitarian missions, responds to natural disasters,[33] polices sea lanes, responds to genocide, and deters rogue states from aggression.[34]

Enough already. You know I'm right.

— 13 —

Rating the Ratings Agencies

This latest financial crisis taught us a whopper of a lesson: the government, its agencies, and the sponsored institutions that were developed to protect us can fail us, big-time. What's worse is that some of these institutions had given us a false sense of security and in the end just caused a massive amount of heartache for individuals and institutions. If the ratings agencies, the SEC, and the Sarbanes-Oxley Act had done what they were created to do, they would have saved us from the catastrophe that began in 2008. They didn't. They flunked, which proves my point implicitly: less is more when it comes to government. Government will nearly always fail. You must protect yourself.

Let me explain these failures by first looking at the ratings agencies Moody's, Standard & Poor's, and to a much lesser extent, Fitch. These are companies that rate bonds. Just as brokerage firms rate stocks (equity) with a buy, sell, or a hold, the ratings agencies rate a company's bonds (debt).

Their labeling system is a little different than the one used for stocks, but the idea is generally the same. If one of the ratings agencies says a company's debt is rated triple-A (the very best), then they believe it is very likely the company will pay back the money it has borrowed. If a company's debt is rated poorly, the ratings agency thinks it's far less likely to pay back its debt. Really poorly rated debt is called junk bonds or high-yield bonds. Companies with bad or risky debt have to pay very high interest rates in order to get investors to lend them money. You might remember the junk-bond king Michael Milken. He created the junk market when he discovered huge returns and made *junk bonds* a household term.

During the housing boom, the ratings agencies also started rating bundles of mortgages on a grand scale. Even though these bundles had a lot of junky mortgages in them, the agencies often assigned them a triple-A rating.[1] With all of these agencies in place to protect investors from buying exactly what these companies were peddling, how could this happen?

The ratings agencies are government-sanctioned and got very lazy. For decades now they've been allowed to act as a quasi-cartel or oligopoly, whose participants are chosen by the government.[2] They didn't have to compete because they were legislated into profitability. They had no new ratings agency breathing down their necks trying to get in on the action. They became one of many on the long road paved with government's good intentions.

One hundred years ago, in 1909, a guy named John Moody started rating railroad bonds. He analyzed the financials of the railroads and then assigned them a rating based on that analysis. Private investors paid his private business for that information. In 1916, another company, named

Poor's, got in on the business as well. In 1922, Standard Statistics began doing the same thing. (They would merge later to become Standard & Poor's, still in existence today.) Fitch started rating bonds in 1924.[3] At that time all of these companies were private businesses. No government helped them get started or supported them along the way.

Investors were hungry for their analysis because the companies they rated didn't disclose much back then. The SEC wasn't created until 1934. It is important to recognize that the buyers of the bonds, the investors, were the very same people paying for the research and the analysis of the bonds.[4]

In 1936 came the first of a series of crucial government decisions. The Office of the Comptroller of the Currency, which was in charge of regulating banks, decided that banks could only hold bonds rated investment grade. For the first time, the service of these ratings companies was required by a government mandate. Throughout the 1930s and 1940s, state insurance regulators started requiring insurance companies to do the same and carry only high-quality-rated bonds. These were the first steps in a long process that led the ratings agencies to be first regulated and then legislated into profitability.[5]

Banks were allowed to use the ratings of private companies that were already in existence and there was competition between the various companies as they tried to prove that their analysis and reliability were better than the other guys' in the business.[6]

But in 1975, a crucial step in changing the ratings game happened. The SEC decided it was officially going to sanction which ratings agencies were allowed to rate bonds. Keep in mind that some companies, such as Standard & Poor's and Moody's, were already rating debt and had been doing it for decades. But now the government was going to give them an official stamp of approval. The SEC invented a new acronym: NRSRO—nationally recognized statistical rating organization.[7] The SEC did this because it didn't want banks relying on some fly-by-night ratings firm with weak standards to rate the stuff on banks' balance sheets. As part of that process, they grandfathered in the three agencies—Moody's, Standard & Poor's, and Fitch—that they felt to be worthy.[8]

This was a bad move for competition and a bad move for investors who thought they were protected. Not only had the government decreed that these companies' services had to be used, but the government had also put up a barrier to entry by other companies who might have challenged ratings. Thus regulators inadvertently created an oligopoly.[9]

It was around this same time that a huge change occurred in the business model of the ratings agencies. Instead of getting their revenues from investors who wanted to buy bonds and were willing to pay for the analysis, the ratings agencies shifted to getting their revenues from companies that were selling the bonds.[10] There are several theories as to why that happened. Xerox's invention of the copy machine might have made the companies worry that once one investor bought a report, he or she could easily hand it off to someone else.[11] That may be so, but economists also believe that by officially designating certain ratings agencies as acceptable, the SEC essentially made the ratings agencies grantors of licenses to issue debt.[12] And as a result, companies had to go to them to get a license to issue debt.

Year after year, the ratings agencies grew more powerful and profitable because of ever more regulation and legislation requiring their ratings. Beyond the federal government, state legislatures jumped on the bandwagon and required insurance companies and pension funds to hold only investment-grade debt.[13] And the only way to know if a bond is rated triple-A is to pay a rating agency to rate it. How can you not make money when the government mandates companies to use your product? And if you're one of the few games in town, with no new competition sprouting up, you're in great shape financially and perhaps not too motivated to up your game.

But it didn't stop there. Bit by bit and in various ways, the regulations in favor of ratings agencies just kept on coming. For example, in 1991 the SEC decided that money-market funds couldn't carry more than 5 percent of their assets in lower-rated commercial paper.[14] Translation: more business for the agencies. As recently as 2001, the regulator for Fannie Mae and Freddie Mac added rules that required the use of the ratings agencies as well.[15]

Which brings us to the housing boom of the 2000s. Banks and mortgage companies wanted to sell all these junky mortgages to investors. And guess what? It sure would be a lot easier to sell them if they were rated triple-A, so they convinced the ratings agencies to give a ton of this stuff investment-grade ratings. There were piles and piles, billions and billions of dollars of this garbage. But every time the ratings agencies gave one a rating, they got paid.

The ratings agencies say there was fraud in the underwriting process and a drop in loan standards that they didn't know about.[16] They can say whatever they want, but we all know what happened. It was all just a pile of junk.[17] With their seal of approval from the federal government, they failed yet again, just as they had with Enron[18] and just as they had with WorldCom.[19]

The ratings agencies had gotten lazy because they no longer needed to work hard to get business. Customers just came to their doorstep day after day, forced to by well-intentioned government rules. This is especially worrisome in the face of another potential ticking time bomb—the municipal bond market.[20] As part of the endless investigations by Congress to nail down what went wrong, the former head of compliance at Moody's testified that his former company, once it had done its initial analysis of a municipality, sometimes never looked at the rating ever again. A bond rating could be twenty years old but an investor would never know it. Analysts who cover stocks would be fired for failing to follow a company after just a few months, but an analyst at Moody's didn't have to revisit his or her rating once. The municipal debt market is huge: a $2.7 trillion market, with two-thirds being held by individual investors.[21] So much for investor protection, huh?

The existence of the government-endorsed ratings agencies created another problem: investors got lazy about assessing the quality of the bonds they were buying themselves. They figured if a ratings agency condoned by the U.S. government says the bonds they want to buy are triple-A, well then, so it must be. In Wall Street parlance, investors outsourced risk assessment.

Unfortunately, investors should have been assessing the risk of the ratings companies that held their fortunes in hand.

Congress is considering all kinds of supposed fixes for the credit rating agencies. Fixing the regulations that contributed to this mess in the first place isn't the answer. But less regulation overall would be far more effective. The SEC should just dump the NRSRO designation and allow any companies that want to rate bonds to compete in the open marketplace. Investors should decide which agencies work and which they are most confident in. All these rules and regulations about insurance companies, and pension funds, and money markets, and banks having to hold only certain qualities of bonds? Those should go away, too.

If they did nothing to prevent the last crisis, why on earth should we assume they will do anything to prevent the next one? Right?

14

The Insecure SEC

My grandfather Salvatore Caruso started out as a farmer and then cleaned beer taps for the rest of his life. To prevent my father from wincing when he reads this, I'll only say that when my grandfather died a few years ago he had a very nice, dividend-producing portfolio.

Grandpa started investing in the market in 1932, driving his dad's Model T down to the local Kidder Peabody office and reading how much he paid for a stock in the paper the next day. That's where they used to list all the stock prices before the Internet. He had a basic rule: he bought good, solid companies. He liked Boeing, figuring there would always be a need for planes. He didn't like retail because he didn't want to have to predict which styles would sell well and which ones wouldn't. Never bought an airline. Thought they were only for trading and not for investing. He started investing before government protection and before the SEC. He worried about risk, but he never relied on any protection from the government. He did all this in the midst of the Great Depression and the losses by other investors. In fact, he lived through it all and bought stocks along the way.

The SEC itself is another example of an agency that was meant to protect us but hasn't. If the financial crisis we just lived through doesn't prove that regulations do nothing to help stave off disaster, what about some other historical failures to remind us: Enron, WorldCom, and that guy Bernard Madoff.

The Office of the Inspector General of the SEC found that "between June 1992 and December 2008 when Madoff confessed, the SEC received six substantive complaints that raised significant red flags concerning Madoff's hedge fund operations and should have led to questions about whether Madoff was actually engaged in trading. Finally, the SEC was also aware of two articles regarding Madoff's investment operations that appeared in reputable publications in 2001 and questioned Madoff's unusually consistent returns." [1]

Think about that. During a period of sixteen years, eight different opportunities arose to uncover Bernie Madoff and yet the SEC failed each time. You've probably heard about Harry Markopolos, who actually brought them the very evidence they needed to uncover Madoff's scam. He told them it was a Ponzi scheme and had done all the painstaking work to prove his case and make it easy for investigators. But according to the inspector general, the SEC "almost immediately expressed skepticism and disbelief." [2]

It doesn't end there. Bernie Madoff claimed he was using a certain financial institution to clear his trades. The SEC contacted the institution to get a list of trades, but the institution responded saying there were no such trades at all. You'd think that that alone would have been enough to get the SEC, an agency created to protect investors, to launch an investigation into Madoff's movements, but it wasn't. Here the SEC investigators had caught him in a bald-faced lie, and yet they never did any follow-up at all.[3]

Also in the report from the inspector general was this little nugget: "numerous private entities conducted basic due diligence of Madoff's operations and, without regulatory authority to compel information, came to the conclusion that an investment with Madoff was unwise."[4] So once again the private sector, without any extraordinary powers such as subpoenas and regulatory oversight, achieved for its clients what a government institution did not achieve for the investing public. Private institutions have a real incentive to uncover fraud: money. They don't like losing it. Government institutions have no such motivation. They live forever. Heck, when they fail, they usually get even more money, not less.

The SEC got a lot more money and staff after the collapse of Enron and WorldCom. In 2001 its budget was $437 million. In 2008 it got $906 million,[5] nearly twice as much.

Sarbanes-Oxley

All that new money, along with a whole lot of new regulation passed after the collapse of Enron and WorldCom, was supposed to make us safer. The Sarbanes-Oxley Act of 2002, named for the two members of Congress who shepherded it into law, required CEOs to sign off on their books so they could no longer pull a Ken Lay (the late CEO of Enron) and say they had no idea what was going on.[6]

Eight years after Sarbanes-Oxley was signed into law, the CEO of Lehman Brothers, Dick Fuld, signed off on his company's books. Later he claimed he had no idea that his chief financial officers were using a shoddy accounting trick called a Repo 105 to hide $50 billion in troubled assets.[7] Poor guy. Three different CFOs in a two-year period pulled the same trick and he had no idea, but he signed off on those financials anyway.[8]

I guess you can't blame Dick Fuld, because the 2,200-page report by the examiner assigned to investigate what happened at Lehman Brothers shows us that once again, with evidence right under their noses, government protectors failed to see or act on anything either. As columnist Antony Currie points out, regulators from the Treasury Department, the SEC, and the Federal Reserve were "crawling all over Lehman—and even had examiners embedded in the Wall Street firm during its final six months."[9] Three different government agencies all with a mission to protect the public, the investor, and the system, and they still can't get it right. Does that give you any confidence in any of these institutions to do anything for you? Does that give you any confidence in the new consumer protection agency that we will get as a result of the new financial regulatory reform?

The typical Washington response is more money, more regulation, and more inspectors—more, more, more.[10] The big problem is that it will never be enough, because some elected officials think regulation is the only way to fix problems. The opposite is true. Amusingly, only in Washington can a failed institution be rewarded with more money, more power, and more employees.

Consider the speech that former SEC commissioner Harvey Goldschmid gave in 2002, in the wake of the Enron scandal. He proudly stated, "In the wake of scandal comes reform," and proceeded to go through all the scandals of the previous century and all the subsequent reforms put in place to "restore confidence" to the markets. But he and many like him can't see the forest through the trees. He went on listing scandal after scandal, and reform after reform, and yet he never noted the obvious: we still get massive scandals, despite all the reforms. Of course, when it comes to the SEC, one way to fix it is through more financing. "We need the money," he said in the same speech.

Here's a better response: get rid of the SEC. This would stop investors from believing what always turns out to be untrue: that the SEC is going to protect them. Many believe the SEC needs to exist to prevent and prosecute insider trading and go after incredibly dangerous people like Martha Stewart. They are wrong.

The SEC is supposed to protect us against things like insider trading, right? So while we're getting rid of the SEC let's just make insider trading legal. When I interviewed Milton Friedman for CNBC, he nearly made me fall out of my chair when he said, "Insider trading should be legal." I've spent a lot of time thinking about this and researching it and I think he's actually 100 percent right. There's a growing body of thought that believes scandals such as Enron would happen less frequently if there were no prohibitions against insider trading.[11]

Prohibitions on insider trading are akin to price controls. If insiders were able to buy and sell, a stock would move quickly to the price that most accurately represents its true economic fundamentals. When insiders can't buy or sell, the price in the marketplace is less likely to reflect the economics of the business. Insiders know better than anyone else what is going on and their moves would tell us far more quickly whether the business was going to show improvement or decline.[12]

Enforcement of insider trading is also problematic because it is asymmetrical. Professor Donald Boudreaux of George Mason University uses a great example. Say an insider learns the Food and Drug Administration is going to approve a new blockbuster drug, and so he or she buys more shares. That is a move detectable by the SEC. However, what if that very same insider already owned shares and abandoned plans to sell? That kind of insider trading is undetectable. The amount of undetectable nontrading could be as high as detectable trading.

Professor Boudreaux makes the case that if the stock market is functioning well, even though there are potentially many undetectable investment decisions made on insider trading, what would be the harm of allowing the detectable ones to be legal, too?

Now, *corporations* may want to prohibit insider trading among their employees, and that could be their prerogative and in their economic interest. If a company wants to buy shares in a company and word leaks out that they are interested in doing a deal, the shares may rise in anticipation and make it more expensive to do the deal. But we should think of this as proprietary information and leave it up to the corporations to decide when it is. They can create internal prohibitions that allow them to fire and sue anyone acting on proprietary information.[13]

Supporters of the SEC say the ban on insider trading is needed so the little guy can trust the markets. Do you? Has it achieved its mission?

If you need any more proof of how well an unregulated

market can work, look no further than the currency market. It is the largest and most liquid market in the world, with daily turnover of at least $3 trillion.[14] And although it is the least regulated, it is one of the smoothest running. There's no one from the SEC trying to chase down people for insider trading because there are no laws against insider trading when it comes to the currency market. There is no central exchange and there is no central clearinghouse. And yet it functions wonderfully well and is incredibly liquid.[15]

Back to my grandfather: I'm not trying to hold him up as this perfect exemplar of investing. I'm just using him to make the point that he started investing before the SEC even existed. Before the government ever even broached this idea of an even playing field. He made his money despite the SEC, which had nothing to do with his success. He didn't even care about the government protecting him because he never believed that they would.

And rightly so: neither should you.

15

Regulation in the Air

I could go on and on about well-intentioned government regulations that failed us. But I have a few regulations I'd like to rant about that resonate with everyone, not just investors. From airlines to wireless to the greening of America, it's important to take a look at ways the government is going nanny-state on us.

Nanny-state rant, part 1: In 2005, as part of the highway bill, the federal government decided to give a refundable tax credit to companies that powered their vehicles with alternative fuels.[1] Senator Chuck Grassley of Iowa crafted this bit of legislation to benefit his home state.[2] He was hopeful it would increase the use of ethanol, made from corn hopefully grown in Iowa. Two years later, Congress tinkered with the tax credit again and extended it to alternative fuels used in things besides cars. So for example, the fish-processing businesses in Alaska that use fish oil to run boilers could claim the credit as well.[3]

The paper industry got wind of this and wanted in on the government largess, too, because they already use biofuel. Turns out that a certain kind of processing to make paper from trees produces a black sludge known in the industry as black liquor. It has tons of carbon in it, which means it is rich in energy. The paper industry has used it since the 1930s to fuel their processing plants.[4] It is without a doubt an alternative fuel.

Here's the catch: the way the law was written, companies could only get the fifty cents a gallon tax credit if they were using a blend of alternative fuel and taxable fuel.[5] No problem. The paper industry reoutfitted their processing plants and began adding taxable diesel to the system so they could get the tax credit.[6] And boy, did they. Since it was a refundable tax credit, the Internal Revenue Service was actually cutting checks to them. The industry raked in more than $8 billion in 2009 in taxpayer money.[7] International Paper, the biggest company in the industry, got $1.7 billion in refund checks from the IRS.[8] Smurfit-Stone Container Corporation got $654 million from the IRS in 2009, while their total profits for the year were only $8 million. If not for the IRS cutting them a huge check they would have lost $646 million last year.

So, the paper industry started using fossil fuel when they hadn't before, to get a clean-energy tax credit for something they were doing anyway. That is the perfect example of the law of unintended consequences.

Environmentalists went berserk because a law designed to reduce the use of fossil fuels actually increased the use of them. Of course, environmentalists tried to blame the paper industry for doing this, but they should have been blaming

Congress for trying to nanny-state us all to green by gumming up the tax code with ever more junk.

And it raises all kinds of legitimate questions about who should be rewarded. Spokespeople for the paper industry rightly counter that if the government is going to reward new users of alternative fuels, why shouldn't it reward those who have been using it all along?[9]

Oh, and did I mention that it started a trade spat with Canada, too? Our neighbors to the north were rightly infuriated because it gave our paper producers a huge advantage over their paper producers.[10] Our paper companies could sell their products at a lower cost than non-U.S. paper companies or they could keep the prices the same but just have much higher margins on those products.[11] It is completely unfair and pushed them to consider trade intervention of their own.

Don't think that the situation with the paper companies is unique. Congress and the White House (all White Houses, not just the Obama administration) love to muck up the tax code with all kinds of junky incentives and tax breaks to try to induce this or that kind of behavior. It's ridiculous and it costs us money whether they are giving people big tax breaks to buy a house or corporations big tax breaks to use so-called alternative fuel. The unintended consequences come from out of nowhere and always seem to take them by surprise.

Nanny-state rant, part 2: cell phones. We take them for granted most of the time and don't stop to think about how the government has interfered in the betterment of our cell service.

Someday our grandchildren will ask, "Was there really a time that cell phones didn't work very well?" In the meantime, government mismanagement keeps our cell phones from working as well as they should. That's because the government controls the allocation of spectrum, the invisible highway in the sky over which our radio signals, cell phone conversations, and mobile data travel.

Using an iPhone in New York is an experience so fraught with dropped calls and slow connections that it led renowned media writer Michael Wolff to pen a column with the blunt title "AT&T Sucks." [12] As of this writing, AT&T has an exclusive agreement with iPhone creator Apple to be the sole network carrier for the product. The iPhone is beloved by its users because it makes getting on the Internet so very easy compared to other smartphones on the market. So easy, in fact, that those iPhone users are known as data hogs because they use ten times the network capacity used by other smart phone users. The *New York Times* labels the iPhone "the Hummer of cell phones," and a "data guzzler." [13] That has consequences for AT&T. Their infrastructure cannot handle the amount of traffic being used by the iPhone users, so customers' calls are more likely to get dropped, and getting on the Internet becomes very slow. All this make Michael Wolff very, very angry. To combat the bottleneck, heavy users will now be charged for usage—no more unlimited data plans for new customers with AT&T.

But a better solution would have been less government intervention. The government controls a scarce resource it has no business controlling. There's a commodity in the skies known as radio spectrum and the Federal Communications Commission (FCC) decides who gets to use it. For decades the spectrum was underutilized and uncontroversial. However, over the years it has become more and more valuable as technology has advanced and scientists have figured out ways to take advantage of it, be it with garage door openers or cellular phones.[14] Some analysts have argued that the air above us is actually more valuable than the land below.[15]

However, for decades, if you were a company that had a new product that needed spectrum you couldn't buy it or even rent it. Instead, since the Radio Act of 1927, you've had to go begging to the government to get spectrum.[16] Professors Dale Hatfield and Phil Weiser explain it well. Imagine if the government decreed that 20 percent of all gasoline should be used for farming, 20 percent for manufacturing, 20 percent for home use, and 20 percent for government uses, and 20 percent for potential future government use.

What would happen under that kind of scenario? Farmers don't use nearly as much gasoline as consumers who drive cars. So farmers' gasoline would be cheap, because they would have plenty of supply, but consumers would pay exorbitant prices because their demands are so much greater. And even though farmers would likely end up with extra supply that they didn't need, they wouldn't be allowed to sell it to consumers who desperately needed it.

That may sound bizarre, but it is exactly what happens with radio spectrum. The government decided long ago to hoard a ton of it for themselves and give TV broadcasters a large chunk of it for free, not knowing that things like wireless phones would come along one day and want to use some of that spectrum, or that the advent of cable television would reduce the need for spectrum by TV broadcasters.

For those of you under thirty, when I use the term *broadcaster* I'm referring to a TV channel you used to be able to watch without subscribing to cable. You needed an antenna, often in the shape of rabbit ears, to receive it and watch it. That's how most of America and the world watched TV until the 1980s, when cable came along. For those of you over thirty, ask someone young what the difference is between broadcast and cable, and I'll bet they can't tell you.

In addition to broadcasters, the Department of Defense has huge swaths of spectrum[17] and it is unclear just how much of it they are using. The government controls lots and lots of spectrum, so much so that less than 10 percent of the spectrum the wireless industry would like to use is offered for commercial use.[18] FCC staffer Blair Levin, who wrote the broadband report for the FCC, told the *Wall Street Journal* that the "biggest wasters of spectrum are government agencies that have one third of the most valuable spectrum."

What the government should have done, and slowly but surely has started doing, is hold auctions in which various companies bid for the use of spectrum.[19] That would bring in revenue to the government and allocate the spectrum to the industries that need it the most. The winners of those auctions could buy and sell it in the future depending on their needs. And, extremely important, there should be no restrictions, as there are right now, determining what that spectrum can be used for.

The FCC's most recent broadband plan, released in the spring of 2010, calls for more "liquidity" in spectrum, in other words the buying and selling of it. This is a great idea. (There's a lot I don't like about the National Broadband Plan, which you can check out at www.broadband.gov, but this idea of spectrum marketplace is one of the few good things in it.) They need to step on it so that the myriad technological changes can occur.

All of these issues would go away if the FCC would just get out of the way. The FCC should continue to auction off nearly all the spectrum, even some of the unused space that is being hoarded by the government. I would also suggest a crucial change from what is happening now, though: that the FCC treats the winners as if they had bought property rights, giving those winning companies the right to use, lease, or even sell the spectrum to someone else.

The FCC has to stop controlling what the spectrum can be used for when it conducts these auctions. Right now it lets wireless users bid on so-called wireless spectrum. There is no such thing. There is certain spectrum that has characteristics that make it better or worse for certain kinds of technologies, but there is no official wireless spectrum.

When the government dictates which businesses can bid on spectrum, it is no different from the government picking winners and losers. This time around the winner is the wireless industry, whereas they picked the TV broadcasting industry back in the 1920s and 1930s.

The FCC is so backward and has so many antiquated rules. It still prohibits profanity on broadcast networks but has no oversight of the cable networks. Think of how absurd this is. Does a ten-year-old kid, when he picks up the remote control, distinguish at all between a broadcast network and a cable network? These outdated rules need to go away.

Over and over again, when we see government get involved in the allocation of a scarce resource, it ends up making our lives more difficult. Just like your iPhone calls not connecting, many times your plane flight doesn't connect, either.

Nanny-state rant, part 3: government controls in the sky need to go away.

The airlines were deregulated in 1978 and the result is that many more people can afford to fly.[20] In the three decades since deregulation, passenger levels have tripled. That's a much faster pace of growth than the overall population in the United States and it's driven largely by intense competition among the airlines that has driven the price of flying down sharply.

There are all kinds of ways to measure this. The price to fly one mile has dropped from 8.29 cents in 1978 to 4.17 cents in 2008—nearly 50 percent.[21] The average price of a domestic airline ticket at the end of 2009 was $301. As *Reason* magazine points out, if prices had merely kept up with inflation over the last ten years, the price would have risen to $427.[22]

Unfortunately, though the airlines were deregulated, the airports and air traffic were kept under government control and in fact are mostly government owned. So while the airlines are extremely responsive to consumers, bureaucrats who use a central-planning mentality to dole out departure and arrival slots control the infrastructure on which the airlines rely.[23] Thus we suffer horrendous delays at the nation's major airports with on-time statistics hovering near record lows.[24]

Since 2000, at least 15 percent of all domestic flights have been late by at least fifteen minutes.[25] More than 20 percent of U.S. flights were late in January 2010.[26] (Believe it or not, that's actually an improvement from the 30 percent of flights delayed at the height of the most recent economic boom. The economic recession has led airlines to cut the number of flights due to fewer passengers, and the one upside has been slightly fewer delays.) Back in 1990 the national average for all delayed flights was 40.9 minutes. Now that has increased to 56.5 minutes.[27] The number of flights that are delayed by at least two hours has gone from 4.3 percent of all late flights to 10.1 percent.

The New York area, with its three airports, is in a class all its own when it comes to travel nightmares. A whopping 31 percent of all flights arrive late. Twenty-one percent leave late. And New York averages the lengthiest delays in the country—sixty-nine minutes.[28]

Many people want to blame the airlines. That's unfortunate. They've done a great job responding to customer demand. But there is a growing imbalance between the demand for air travel and the supply of airspace.[29] And who controls the supply of that airspace? The government.

Just like radio spectrum, airspace is another scarce resource in the sky that the government won't let be allocated by price. Instead, the Federal Aviation Administration (FAA) has an arbitrary distribution system that allows some incumbents from the 1970s to keep slots and allows private jets a certain percentage of slots.

The answer is the same as with spectrum: decide on the safe number of departures and arrivals during each time period and auction the slots off to the highest bidders. The airlines will bid more for the peak time slots compared to the nonpeak slots. The FAA should not allow incumbents to be grandfathered in as they are now.[30] You should see the 2008 rule for allotting slots in high-density airports such as New York: it goes on and on, for nearly thirty pages.[31] And even if you don't live in the New York area, you are still affected, because so many flights connect through New York.

The airlines already do auctions via price with passengers. You see it all the time when you search for a flight online. If you are willing to get up at the awful hour of 3 A.M. to get to the airport for a 6 A.M. flight, you will very likely pay a lot less for that ticket, as compared to a flight that leaves at 9 A.M. Yet the FAA can't figure this out? New slots become available and it becomes a mad dash of lobbyists descending on the capital to get a piece of the action.

There are some critics of auctions who say they've never worked. That's because they've never been done properly. Governments have siphoned off some for private aviation (private jets), some for incumbent airlines, and some for foreign carriers.[32]

Instead of the government looking at itself for the problems, especially in the larger markets where more than half of all delays are due to the airport system and not the airline,[33] the government wants to blame the airlines. In fact, in the fall of 2010, the Department of Transportation announced it would fine an airline $27,500 per passenger if a plane sat on a runway for more than three hours.[34] That can easily get up to more than a $1 million a plane. The unintended consequence will be much higher cancellations. So instead of waiting a couple of hours, you may get stuck for a couple of days, until they can get you on another flight.

As a frequent flier, I can say with all honesty I'd rather take off three hours and twenty minutes late if the airline can make that determination, rather than be yanked back to the terminal because the government says so.

I'm not alone in my viewpoint. The CEO of Continental told an investor conference, "Any passengers at two hours and forty-five minutes, they really want to go to L.A. or Mumbai or wherever, but the government, by God, says 'We're going to fine you $27,500.' So guess what we're going to do? We're going to cancel the flight. And with the loads we've got today, you're not getting there for maybe days. And so the government is inconveniencing more passengers by passing what is candidly a very stupid rule."

The Department of Transportation spokesperson said in response that airlines should schedule their flights "more realistically."[35] Easy for him to say, but the vast majority of the delays don't have to do with the airlines but rather are caused by the inadequate National Aviation System.[36] In airports like New York's, nearly 65 percent of the delays are because of the National Aviation System, not the airlines, and not the weather.

So auctions would help with delays because they would allocate scarce resources effectively. However, auctions would not deal with the necessary increases in capacity that we are expected to need over the next decade. For that we need improvements in technology and upgrades to our antiquated air-traffic control system. The FAA has a plan for a satellite-based air-traffic control system called NextGen, which, "when fully implemented, will safely allow more aircraft to fly more closely together on more direct routes, reducing delays."[37] It is estimated to cost $22 billion through 2025.

But you wouldn't know that NextGen is such a priority when you look at how the new administration spent the first round of stimulus funding for airports.

The American Recovery and Reinvestment Act of 2009 allotted $1.3 billion to airports and yet only 19.9 percent of the total funding went to the twenty-six largest metropolitan areas where the congestion problems are the worst. Of the $2.6 billion of government investment doled out by the Airport Improvement Program (AIP) in 2009, only 21.8 percent went to those twenty-six airports. That means that less than 25 percent of the money went to airports serving 72.8 percent of the passengers. Wait, it gets better. If you look at the top one hundred metropolitan airport areas, they only got 37.1 percent of the funds in the AIP, even though they carry more than 80 percent of the passengers.[38]

Who did get that money? Once again, Alaska scored big. (There is a whole book to be written about how Alaska manages to get so much federal money for so few people.) Akiachak and Ouzinkie airports each received roughly $14 million to replace their airports. Akiachak has 659 residents, a seaplane base, and an airfield with a gravel runway, and is within seven miles of two other airfields, according to the Department of Transportation's inspector general, which to its credit was just as flabbergasted as you probably are reading this right now. Ouzinkie has only 167 residents and they average forty-two flights a month total.[39]

Four other airports receiving 2009 funding don't even have commercial passenger service. And according to the inspector general, at least four grant recipients have multiyear histories of grant management problems, raising doubts about their ability to ensure the funds are effectively administered. Kentucky's Owensboro, Daviess County Airport received more than $650,000 even though they've been cited for poor administration of funds for ten of the past eleven years.[40]

This happens because the government has very different motivations than the private sector. When awarding this money, the FAA decided that every state should receive at least one grant. So that's why Dover, Delaware, got more than $900,000 to design (not construct) a new runway at an airport with no commercial flights. The FAA told the inspector general's office that it was the only project in the state "ready to go."[41]

Think about the implications for your money: The government officials didn't want the best use of the money. Instead they wanted to spread it around. So if that meant compromising by giving the money to airports with a history of financial mismanagement, or to projects that do not alleviate the most pressing needs in the airport infrastructure, so be it.

The money to Alaskan airports reflects another misguided mission of the federal government: to make sure even the most rural areas of the country are served by air. On the surface it sounds oh-so-egalitarian. But when the government insists that "everyone" get something, what everyone gets is miserable service. In the effort to make something better for a tiny part of the population, the entire population suffers. We see this over and over again, whether it's education, health care, or air service.

There is an entire subsidy program called the Essential Air Service, which is taxpayer money given to private airlines so that they will fly unprofitable routes to rural places. It was created in 1978 during the deregulation process to make sure that rural areas still received air service where it was previously mandated by law.[42] Sounds moral and just, right? But because of the proliferation of discount carriers, the Government Accounting Office found, rural residents would sometimes bypass their smaller, local, subsidized airport and instead drive much farther to an airport because it was home to a discount carrier with much cheaper airfares.[43] Still, in the most recent budget, $175 million of our taxpayer money is going to subsidize these flights.[44]

The funding for airports should come via a far more direct route. The way the money is funneled to them right now is a huge part of the problem. The money for airport improvements comes from an airline ticket tax and goes straight to the coffers of Congress. The largest airports naturally generate far more in tax revenue than do small airports. But as I showed in the example above, the largest airports get far less of the money allotted compared to the money they generate. That's because the Department of Transportation still has to go to

Congress every year to get money for capital investments, and the politics poison the process, making it susceptible to corruption, earmarks, and the wrong incentives.

The airports and the air-traffic control system should be funded directly by users. All kinds of networks, such as telephone networks and utilities, are funded this way, through fees directly charged to their customers. Either privatizing both systems or running them in a similar fashion to private corporations can accomplish a better funding structure. Once this is done, they should be allowed to auction or simply raise fees on the time slots that are most sought after, and then they should be able to keep that money themselves for airport improvements.

This may all sound wonky and too much like an economist, but I highlight these issues to show how a well-meaning government often makes our lives more miserable, for no good reason. Even worse, it's not always well-meaning. Sometimes regulation is purely political—designed to help a special interest at everyone else's expense.

If you're stuck on a tarmac reading this or your iPhone won't connect, you know I'm right.

— 16 —

Private Banking

Tax receipts shriveled during the recession and money in federal coffers shrank. So the U.S. government has gone in search of ways to fill the void. Vendetta number one: chase down the undeclared, offshore accounts of U.S. residents. At first glance this may sound reasonable, but banking secrecy is good for America, it's good for the world, and it's a crucial component of freedom. The American government's efforts to draw out Swiss account holders is nothing short of hypocritical, because the United States is the largest tax haven on the planet.

I'm against tax evasion by U.S. citizens. I don't agree with the fringe element in the United States that has this crazy idea that somehow the U.S. Constitution prohibits the collection of taxes. But forcing Switzerland to reveal names and banking information (a criminal violation there) is outrageous. Freedom and democracy are best secured when banking secrecy and tax havens exist. Moreover, they keep everyone's taxes lower, too.

Don't get me wrong. I completely understand the anger demonstrated by Americans and members of Congress when wealthy people don't pay what they are legally required to pay. As Senator Max Baucus, Democrat from Montana, said earlier this year, "Tax evaders cost our country tens of billions of dollars every year in unpaid taxes, and honest, law-abiding taxpayers pay the price."[1] Yes, he's right.

But as Americans we are very lucky to have the luxury of being able to be angry about tax evasion. That is because we see it from our particular cultural context: we live in a society that is fundamentally just. Yes, we can complain a lot about government waste when it comes to tax dollars, and yes, there is some fraud. But in the end we can rightly fall back on the idea that tax dollars are being spent in ways that are generally appropriate. And more importantly, if we don't think so, we have a mechanism to change that: democracy and the vote.

Consider what life would be like if you lived outside the United States. Perhaps you are a business owner in Venezuela or a dissident in Russia. Maybe you even live in a different time in history. In the past, many governments barred women from entering contracts or owning property. Or perhaps you were a member of a Chinese minority in Indonesia in the 1960s, and you've just been banned from owning a business, or were a Jew living under Hitler.[2] You, and anyone else who lives under such circumstances, are fearful of losing nearly everything for which you've worked, because an unjust government has arbitrarily decided you have fewer rights than other residents.

Unreasonable seizure is not limited to the distant past. It happens today in countries with little or no democracy. Someone I know who lives in China discovered two years ago that there was ten thousand dollars missing from his bank account. When he asked where the money went, the bank informed him that the government had decided to impose an additional one-time tax on accounts that were larger than a certain size. The government had simply taken the money, and there was no choice in the matter. The Chinese government controls the nation's banks and can see everyone's accounts, and obviously, from this incident, it thinks it can take what it wants when it wants. Because there is no democracy in China, there is no mechanism for fighting back.

Venezuelan leader Hugo Chavez regularly announces some seizure of private property. If it is a foreign company from which he is seizing assets, he pays them off with what he claims is a market price, decided by his government, of course. If you are a Venezuelan business owner, you receive no such compensation.[3] Chavez was democratically elected in his first election but the subsequent ones have been arguably corrupt. For many in Venezuela, he is little more than a dictator.[4]

There are a number of legitimate reasons in other countries around the world why people would want to keep their financial information private and secret from the government. As Dan Mitchell of the Cato Institute points out, if a wealthy family in Mexico honestly fills out their tax returns, they could very well fall prey to local workers in the tax collection office selling that information to kidnapping gangs—rampant throughout that Latin American country. Next thing you know, a family member will be taken away and a ransom demanded.

Angry opposition to tax evasion is only justified in countries where the rule of law exists, where private property is protected, and where human rights are respected. As Americans we are lucky to be in a thriving democracy that protects our right to political speech.

In 2009 we did something to Switzerland that set the United States on a dangerous path. We forced the country, which has long prided itself on its bank secrecy laws, to hand over information related to thousands of Swiss bank accounts held by Americans. This is a criminal offense in Switzerland. The citizens of this small country have supported privacy in contractual matters whether they involved medical, legal, or financial matters. What makes this action by the U.S. so dangerous is that we have now given justification to other less just countries to demand the same.

Now any country can turn to Switzerland and argue that confidential information should be released. Say there's a minority group living in a country headed by a dictator who has demanded that the group hand over 90 percent of their property. Some may try to hide assets in Switzerland. But now that same dictator can turn to Switzerland and argue that it is helping his citizens break his laws. Since they handed over information to the United States, why shouldn't the Swiss hand it over to him?

Yes, it is wrong, and even disgusting that some Americans do not want to pay their fair share. But it is something we should accept, however infuriating, knowing that the alternative is the increased subjugation of other people around the world. This is a trade-off, pure and simple, and the choice is humanitarian. Accepting lower tax receipts in the United States preserves a path to freedom for subjugated people in other parts of the world.

We fully accept another trade-off in a key area in the United States—the criminal justice system. We set a very high bar for guilty verdicts, knowing that some criminals will go free, because we find it even more unacceptable that an in-

nocent person be jailed for a crime he or she didn't commit.
I think we should follow the same logic when it comes to tax
havens. We accept that some people will rip off the government, knowing that it allows other people to find not only a
tax haven, but a safe haven.

I feel quite strongly about this issue because I have seen
how easily a corrupt government can take anything it wants
from citizens. My grandparents left Cuba in 1962 as a result
of communist dictator Fidel Castro. Castro appropriated
every business and declared an end to private property. As
Castro's rebels were advancing, my grandparents had friends
who repeatedly took suitcases full of money out of the country and deposited them in banks in Miami. My grandparents
never did. I wish they had. Their lives would have been so
much easier when they got here.

This leads to what frustrates me most: the fact that the
United States is the largest tax haven in the world. Whether
you are part of the archlibertarian, tax-haven-loving Cato Institute, or a supporter of the left-leaning Tax Justice Network,
there is broad agreement that many foreigners keep trillions
of untaxed dollars in the United States. Why? Because they
are encouraged to do so, helped by a friendly set of federal
and state laws designed to attract their money here to the
United States, where it will live tax-free, and in secrecy.

If you are a foreigner living outside the United States and
you open a savings account here, you pay no tax on your
interest here. If you invest in stocks or bonds and later sell
them, there is no interest on your capital gains here—you just
settle up at home. This is by design. We do this on purpose
because we want that capital invested in the United States.
Foreigners looking to invest can put their money anywhere

in the world that they want to, so for us to remain competitive in attracting investing dollars, and to prevent that money from going anywhere else, we just don't tax it at all.

Foreigners have a sizable pile of money in America. The grand total in 2008 was $8 trillion, according to the U.S. Treasury. Do you realize how helpful it is to have $8 trillion worth of additional capital sitting in U.S. banks and investments? That's more capital for banks to lend to homeowners and businesses, and it's more investors in our nation's corporations.

The Tax Justice Network has created a Financial Secrecy Index, and guess which country is at the top of the list: the United States, in particular the state of Delaware. I don't agree with any of the policy prescriptions suggested by the Tax Justice Network, and in fact I think they are pretty crazy. If they are reading this, I'm sure they think I'm nuts, too, so I guess we are even. But they have done a great job of assembling data that points to the hypocrisy of legislators like Senator Carl Levin, who rails on and on about tax evaders when in fact, right here in the United States, we do many of the same things to get foreigners to put their money here.

The tiny state of Delaware is number one on the list of biggest tax havens in the world.[5] Delaware provides banking secrecy; keeps the details of trusts and the beneficial ownership of companies off the public record; doesn't maintain company ownership details in official records; and allows protected shell companies.[6]

The IRS does not collect information on foreigners' money in the United States, so if Hugo Chavez demanded the United States hand over information about all Venezuelans, we wouldn't have anything to give him. Yet we did that very thing to Switzerland.

What if Chavez turned to the United States right now and demanded that we hand over information about Venezuelans with accounts in the States? I have no doubt that the U.S. government would tell him to stuff it and he would have the right to accuse of us of being hypocritical.

This war on secrecy to me is very much akin to the war on drugs. Many people want to attack the supply of drugs when instead we should be focused on the demand for drugs. We are attacking the suppliers of bank secrecy instead of the things that lead to a demand for bank secrecy.

What is the cause of capital flight out of developing countries? Yes, sometimes it is drug money, or mob money, or someone trying to hide money from the tax assessor, but when a dictator is rushing money illegally out of the country, the cause is weak government institutions, not the banks that take the money.

Often the demand for banking secrecy is more akin to demand for banking stability. In the spring of 2010, Greeks started taking their deposits out of banks and sending their money to places like Cyprus, not because they were trying to avoid taxes, but because they were terrified the nation's banks were going to fail, due to the nation's financial crisis, brought on by government mismanagement.

Some foreigners want to put their money in the United States or Switzerland because the two countries have had very stable currencies over many decades, as opposed to horrendous inflation or devaluations that destroyed the value of their home country's currency. You don't fix that problem by outlawing banking secrecy. You fix that through reforms that lead to strong and independent central banks.

Legal tax havens aren't just about helping foreigners. They also help you directly by keeping your taxes lower than they otherwise would be. Tax havens provide tax competition. In the last thirty years, tax rates all over the world have come down as business has become more globalized and countries have had to compete for investors and business. In 1980, the average corporate tax rate was 48 percent. In 1990 it had fallen to 42 percent. In 2000 it had fallen to 34 percent. Today it stands at 28 percent. Because capital can flow all over the world much more quickly—and can seek out countries that are friendliest to capital—it has forced countries to become more competitive and to lower taxes to attract businesses and investment. They should be doing the same when it comes to taxation on individuals as well.

If you look at the countries that are the most vociferous about combating so-called tax havens, you'll notice they are the countries with the highest taxes. Countries like France, for example, want everyone in the world to suffer under the same growth-killing, debilitating tax structures so that they don't have to compete with low-tax jurisdictions. Many Asian countries have rightly scoffed at them and kept their low tax and cost structures in place, attracting more business while European countries fight a losing battle.

The Organisation for Economic Co-operation and Development (OECD) began a campaign against what they called Uncooperative Tax Havens in 2000, and sadly, they are getting more and more countries to sign on to information-sharing agreements[7] and an internationally agreed tax standard.[8] Some liken it to an OPEC for politicians.[9]

Here's what I don't understand: we, and members of Congress, get apoplectic when someone suggests that U.S. laws should be second to laws established by the United Nations. So why should we be willing to hand over our sovereignty on taxation and banking secrecy as if it's nothing?

They want to eliminate what they call "harmful tax competition." There is no such thing. We know that companies should compete, individuals should compete, and so too should governments. The Department of Justice sues companies when it believes companies are harming competition. Why shouldn't these same concepts apply to countries? The ones who call it harmful are the ones who can't make the tough decisions about spending and see their population shrinking or leaving to other places. Yes, it is harmful to them, and it should be.

Even the OECD's very own economists, after examining the forces shaping tax policy, noted that a key reason for the erosion of a country's tax base is high taxes. In a globalized world, capital is mobile. Some countries have actually lowered taxes to stem the loss of tax revenue.

The best way to reduce tax evasion is to lower taxes. The vast majority of people in the world believe they should pay something in taxes. We all understand we need roads and infrastructure. But there is a point at which taxation levels become so high they approach expropriation. We're not there yet in the United States, but many parts of Europe are. I know I'm very right when I say we can't let this happen.

A Mad Hatter's Tea Party

As Americans, we pride ourselves on our commitment to democracy and our devotion to free and fair elections. Our liberty is based on self-government and the rule of law. We have the right to express our political views, but in the end we support each and every electoral outcome even if we voted for the losing party. The Bush-Gore debacle at the U.S. Supreme Court in 2000 makes this point well. Neither Republicans nor Democrats were particularly happy with the process, but when the judges made their decision, everyone across the political spectrum rallied behind the new president.

We seem to take the existing system as a given, but maybe we don't have to. It's been around for so long, we assume that our electoral process will always be the same. We need to remind ourselves, however, that it is our American values and our steadfast resolve to uphold the principles set out in our Constitution that ensure the ongoing operation of our system. Unlike so many other nations, we don't determine the outcome of elections with the barrel of a gun.

But that doesn't mean the existing electoral system can't be improved upon. Sure, it works, but why settle for something that has so many design flaws? We can do better. And we see this now more than ever.

The election process has a bit of an Alice in Wonderland feel to it. Not only is it a bit surreal, but the rhetoric often sounds like gibberish. The multiyear event is a kind of Mad Hatter's tea party. It really is a process that goes on forever while making it seem like time stands still. It isn't great for those of us who want change, since it effectively entrenches the status quo.

What really troubles me, however, is that the current system for voting for the U.S. president embraces the two-party political system with a ferocity not seen in other democratic nations. Not only do the Republicans and Democrats dominate the election outcomes, they *are* the election process. There is virtually no room for independents. In theory, independents can run, but the deck is so stacked against them that it is not really viable.

In times like these, when there is no candidate representing the vast American middle, the system is both worrisome and troubling. As a fiscal conservative committed to individualism and the free-market economy, I want some choice in who becomes our president. If the Republicans and Democrats want to spend their time pandering to extremists on either end of the political spectrum, at least let the rest of us have the opportunity to support a candidate who really represents the American people.

Don't get me wrong. I'd be happy if the Republicans mounted a candidate who focused on less government and reduced taxes. And if the Democrats put forward a nominee who wanted to rein in those large congressional spending projects and commit himself or herself to a leaner government, I would surely take that candidate a bit more seriously. Up until the emergence of the Tea Party, the Republicans were intent on satisfying those among the religious right. And the Democrats are no better with their big spending programs and the emphasis on pleasing the unions.

I want a candidate for president who is committed to the free-market economy, but with the current two-party presidential voting system it is virtually impossible to elect candidates who represent these views.

The Primaries

The primary process is incredibly confusing. It's hard to explain and hard to understand. It varies by party and by state.

The primary elections determine who gets to represent the Democrats and the Republicans on the ballot for president. Candidates from each party compete against one another for effective control over their party's ticket. In theory, it seems reasonable. Rather than letting party insiders choose the top of the ticket, this process allows everyday Americans to have some influence over the nominations.

Each state decides how to hold its primary. Some states, like Iowa, adopt a caucus process, whereby voters registered for each party meet in small groups to vote for their candidate. It is relatively informal and there are speeches given to sway the undecided present at the meeting. Primary elections are a bit more formal: voting is done by secret ballot. So-called open primaries allow voters to vote for the candidates of either party. Closed primaries are ones that effectively restrict who can participate in them. You normally have to be registered as either a Democrat or a Republican to get a vote in these primaries. And in the closed primaries, only Democrats can vote for the Democratic slate and only Republicans can vote for the Republican slate.

The process is problematic for a number of reasons: First, it means that voters who consider themselves to be independents and don't want to be card-carrying Republicans or Democrats don't really get to participate. This is a problem because almost 40 percent of Americans consider themselves to be independents. And the numbers are growing. An April 2009 study by the prestigious Pew Research Center indicated that party alignment is in rapid decline.[1] This means that the candidates elected to run for president by primary process don't necessarily reflect the values of the nation, because almost half the population doesn't identify with either party.

Second, in order to get elected, candidates must develop platforms that please party loyalists even though these platforms may not reflect the sentiment of Americans who consider themselves to be independents. This process ensures that moderates that want to focus on national issues such as reducing government and focusing on the deficit have little chance to win the Democratic or Republican ticket anymore. To get elected, Democratic and Republican candidates must target those located in the extreme right or left of the political spectrum, rather than centrists who refuse to become card-carrying party members. Consequently Republican candidates in the primaries often focus on social issues and family values. Democratic candidates focus on things like the environment and making unionization easier in order to appeal to the party loyalists participating in the primary and caucus process. Without having an independent group of voters participating, presidential candidates who have a platform emphasizing personal responsibility and free-market capitalism over nanny-state solutions and government regulation either lose or simply don't participate.

Third, the primaries are run on a state-to-state basis over several months. Iowa and New Hampshire lead off the voting and their results are considered to be quite significant. Winning early in one of these states is virtually a necessity now to capture the nomination for either the Republican or Democratic parties. Yet these states hardly reflect the heart and soul of middle America. Why do we want potential presidential nominees to develop platforms that are designed to appeal to largely Iowan rural voters? Is this really the way to select a presidential ticket?

It's up to each state to craft a solution. In June of 2010, California made a dramatic change to the way it will conduct its primaries. No more traditional party primaries. Instead, it will be an open election with the top two vote-getters facing off in the general election.[2]

This should make it easier for independents and moderates. I'm not sure it will work, but my fingers are crossed.

Perhaps primaries should all be open to independents. Or independents could be allowed to participate in them under the umbrella of one or other of the parties. Do we need to open the process up to third parties? I don't know. I don't have the answers. But what I do know is that candidates who interest me, that is, those who advocate for free-market principles and less government in their primary election platform, do not stand a very good chance of getting on the Democratic or Republican ticket. This hardly seems like a reasonable or effective way to elect a president when so much of the population consider themselves to be independents.

The Electoral College and Election Day

While the primary process is a problem, the election day is no better. When we go to the polls every four years to elect a president, we cast the ballot in secret. But nobody is actually voting directly for the country's new leader. Rather, we are mandated to vote for "electors" who are designated on a state-by-state basis. In each election, 538 electors are selected. To get elected president, one needs to win 270 of the electoral votes.

Known as the electoral college, this process ensures that a president can be elected without receiving the most voter support. Winning the popular vote in this system means nothing. In fact, you can win the popular vote and actually lose the election because you don't win a sufficient number of electors. Al Gore, for example, won the popular vote in the 2000 election but lost the electoral college to George Bush, who then went on to become president.

In all but two states, electors are chosen in a "winner take all" manner.[3] This means that if one candidate has 51 percent of the vote, he or she gets 100 percent of the electoral votes. Because of this winner-take-all system, the electoral votes don't necessarily reflect the wishes of the American people and the results can be skewed. Only two states, Maine and Nebraska, award their votes based on a proportional voting system.[4]

Consequently, during presidential campaigns, the candidates do not design policy platforms and do not get elected based on broad appeal to voters across the country. They can't target that 40 percent of independent voters who are spread across the nation, many of whom want their government to stay focused on limiting its size and balancing the budget. Rather, they have to set policy platforms and pitch their campaigns to garner the support of states that are likely to award them a disproportionately large number of electors. And since most states have a winner-take-all approach to the electoral process, candidates only have to garner the support of a number of key states to win an election. Presidential nominees thus typically target states like Florida, California, Michigan, Texas, and Pennsylvania, which have a total of 154 electoral votes among them.[5]

And the consequences are severe. We don't have candidates who focus on goals and objectives of national importance like the economy or the budget. No, what is happening is that *the electoral system itself is influencing the presidential policy platforms*. Is this any way to be running an election?

Presidential candidates who should be setting a national agenda and appealing to the nation's great middle class are effectively being forced to adopt political agendas in order to appeal to the local interests of a handful of states that have a significant number of electoral votes. To get elected, they can't target the most voters with a platform that focuses on improving the economic well-being of the nation. Instead these candidates target their campaigns to appeal to a specific number of states that are needed to win the electoral college. Florida, for example, is a great state, and I am not suggesting otherwise. But historically much of the vote in Florida has been driven by U.S. policy toward Cuba and where candidates stand on the embargo. Why should that one issue have such a disproportionately large influence on who gets elected to the White House?

The electoral college was developed and incorporated into the Constitution before the development of the modern-day political party system. At the time, there was no equivalent to the modern two-party system. When electors were chosen on behalf of their state, they were supposed to vote for a presidential candidate who promoted the best interests of the nation. Instead, electors now vote along party lines.

Surely with the brightest and most innovative minds in the world we can develop an electoral system that reflects the wishes of the American people and independents like me who want to see priority placed on the country's economic well-being rather than prioritizing very particular issues like agricultural subsidies.

Independents

If independents could compete equitably on a national basis during election campaigns, none of these issues would matter. We could let the Democratic candidate target the left-wing extremists and the Republican candidate focus on the religious right. An independent candidate who wanted to focus on national economic issues for the overall good of the nation could address the rest of us, those of us in the middle who consider ourselves fiscal conservatives and don't really care about what is going on in the bedrooms of the nation.

But the electoral system not only favors the two-party system; it limits the ability of independent candidates to effectively compete in it. There is no national election with a national ballot. Each independent candidate must get on the ballot in each state to compete for the electoral college. And the rules vary by state.[6]

From an organizational perspective, this is a tough challenge. Each state must develop its own local organization to get the candidate on the ballot. There is no national process whereby individuals can directly vote for the president. And since the rules and balloting differ state by state, it is hard for national candidates to develop national platforms that target middle America desperate for a candidate who supports reducing the federal deficit and less government without the trappings of social-programming initiatives.

Informally, these independent candidates also face other barriers. The media seems fixated on the two-party system. There is a mind-set that independents can't be taken seriously. Independents don't get the same kind of media coverage. They don't always get the same kind of exposure at the political debates at either the local or national level. In effect, we are kind of doing ourselves in. We lock out people who can challenge the status quo, because the two-party system has a monopoly on the electoral process.

In recent times, Ross Perot has been the most successful candidate to run for president as an independent. In the 1992 election, he received almost 20 percent of the popular vote, but because of the way the system is set up, he received no votes from the electoral college.[7] While it is true that Perot might have been his own worst enemy—he resigned partway through the campaign, then later reemerged in it—running as an independent has a number of distinct disadvantages. There is no real funding base, meaning that a successful independent must have a considerable fortune either personally or through support to initiate the process. Unlike the Democrats or Republicans, who build war chests throughout the nonelection years, there are no similar alternatives for independents.

The Tea Party Movement

The Tea Party movement, despite all its controversy, may prove the exception. For the most part, its members emphasize fiscal responsibility and limited government.[8] Arguments are made in favor of liberty and the need to restrict government involvement in the day-to-day activities of the American people.

Its greatest hurdle, like that of any movement, is that it is just a movement of grassroots activists. It is not a political party and there is no political leader. Maybe that's why its message is often muddled by extremists.

The questions going forward are twofold. First, how do you make sure that the core message of limited government gets out without being hijacked by social issues? Can it keep its message focused without attracting candidates who carry the family-values baggage?

Sarah Palin's initial appearances at Tea Party events raised some eyebrows. Her support suggests that the Tea Party movement may well be reverting to the Republican Party, which is currently focused on telling Americans how to live their lives. Don't get me wrong: Sarah Palin is a force. But her presence suggests politics as usual. The problem the Tea Party will face is that it needs to keep promoting its ideas and values without getting off message. Liberty and economic freedom need to remain its core focus. But the structure of the current electoral system will make this a challenge.

Second, how does the movement translate its core values into political action for change? How does a leaderless movement get legislators and the executive to consider its policy alternatives seriously? Do they need to transform themselves into a political party? Do they need to appoint a leader or group of leaders? How do they go forward? The Tea Party movement has a viable message, but let's see how they put their words into action.

The current system seems akin to a mad hatter's tea party. We need to go forward and not backward. How do we transform the electoral process to allow for new and viable alternatives like those being advocated by the Tea Party movement without the baggage of extremists on either side of the political spectrum? We need a system that allows for a candidate that represents me and people like me.

You know I'm right.

— Afterword —

Fiscal Responsibility
Is Social Responsibility

I told a friend of mine that I was writing a book about my ideas for fiscal fixes for the country. He laughed and told me I should call it *Every Man, Woman, and Child for Themselves*. I hear that sort of incredulousness a lot when I talk about limited government. People like my friend think I don't care about the poor or else I would know that government has to have *some* role in the nation's social woes and issues.

You know what? They are right. The government does have to have a hand in social issues. But here's the bottom line: Fiscal issues *are* social issues. Achieving a balanced budget *is* a social issue. Being fiscally responsible allows a government to deal more effectively with the social woes of the poor and struggling.

Look no farther than Europe for evidence that big government means social disaster. The entire European continent is teetering on the financial edge as country after country within the Euro zone comes up short on its social obligations. Governments there are telling citizens that they cannot deliver on what they have promised: lifelong protection, cradle-to-grave financial security, and income fairness.

Ironically, one of the European Union's slogans is "A Europe That Protects." Right now a lot of people are asking what happened to that protection. Here's what happened: countries there are running out of money and cannot pay for social programs they have promised their citizens.

Now, many citizens on the verge of retirement are being told they have to work for more years than they'd expected. When they do finally get to retire, their checks will be lower than they'd thought. Without warning, the standard of living they'd been experiencing is going to fall dramatically, particularly in countries such as Greece and Portugal. You call that protection? The governments there can blame only themselves though, after years of spending and bloated initiatives.

In fact, many economists think it is so bad that Greece will go through an actual depression. The country will have no choice. Its budget right now is so out of whack and its coming spending cuts so drastic that Greece will see a massive decline in its economy, which will lead to a dramatic rise in poverty.

That is a social issue.

Economists on CNBC say, "The fiscal adjustments in Europe will be painful." That's antiseptic-speak for "life is going to be horrendous for a very long time."

If you want a preview of what Greece and some of the other weaker countries in Europe could look like, take a look back at Argentina in the late 1990s. Argentina borrowed and borrowed from banks and investors so the government could keep on spending. When the bills came due, it couldn't pay, and it defaulted on its debts. It was no different from a consumer who racked up a big mortgage and credit-card bills and then couldn't keep up with the payments. Argentina overextended itself.

In Argentina's case, the country had borrowed so much that nobody in the world would lend to it anymore. Its credit had dried up, and just like when an individual gets cut off by lenders, Argentina was forced to work with just the money it had and to live within its means. It had no choice. There were deep and painful budget cuts nearly overnight. There were bank holidays—meaning days of closure when money is not accessible to anyone. Citizens were allowed to withdraw only a certain amount of money from their banks each week. Their money wasn't their own. The poverty rate in Argentina soared to 50 percent, despite the country's once having had a thriving middle class. Parents couldn't feed their families, and children were picking through the garbage. People went to the store and couldn't afford a bottle of olive oil, but just a capful, because of hyperinflation.

Sounds like a social issue to me.

Let me put Greece's fiscal adjustment into perspective for you. Argentina had to cut its budget by 1 percent of its GDP. Greece must cut its budget by 14 percent of its GDP, which is a much greater hurdle. Even if Greece doesn't default, in order to meet the payments of banks and lenders, the country will have to make cuts so drastic it will be devastating to its citizens. There will be massive layoffs, huge salary cuts, and a huge reduction in all that so-called protection the government was going to provide. Entire government agencies employing thousands of workers will be shut down and people in Greece will struggle.

That's a social issue.

Being fiscally responsible is socially responsible. Period. Fiscal responsibility is job one for a government. Guaranteeing citizens five weeks' vacation in a year is not. Look at France, which made so many promises to its citizens back in the year 2000: long vacations, short workweeks, and an early retirement. By doing so, France has done anything but guarantee protection for its citizens. In fact, it has done just the opposite. France has guaranteed a budget crisis that will lead not only to some angry citizens but also to widespread poverty. People there were bamboozled into thinking they'd be taken care of by the government.

Europeans are facing massive stagnation and austerity over the next few decades. French unions are protesting having to work beyond sixty years of age and having to work more than a thirty-five-hour workweek.

In the coming years, these issues will be the least of their problems.

A *New York Times* headline from May 2010 read "Crisis Imperils Liberal Benefits Long Expected by Europeans." It should have read "Crisis *Caused* by Liberal Benefits Long Expected by Europeans." It's not necessarily the people's fault, but the fault of the politicians who made unrealistic promises to get elected.

So what does all of this strife in Europe mean for us as Americans? One day, if something doesn't change soon, the same could happen here. We should see Europe as a crystal ball. It's rare we're given the gift of being able to see into the future so clearly. We are at a very critical juncture here in the United States. We will face the same fiscal mess the Europeans are facing now if we don't put the brakes on bloated government. Let's look at Europe as an opportunity and know that right now we're at a fork in the road. We must take the right road: the road to less spending.

If you think I'm exaggerating, let's talk about New Jersey. The state's governor, Chris Christie, wants state workers to assume one and a half percent of their health-care costs. Up until now, they haven't had to pay for it themselves. The taxpayer has footed the bill. Here's what he told his constituents in early 2010 when he explained why the state employees' benefits needed reform: He talked about a New Jersey state worker who retired at 49 (yes, you read correctly—49!) and contributed $124,000 over the years toward both his pension and health-care benefits. That contribution served him well. Over the course of the rest of his life he will get $3.3 million in pension payments and nearly $500,000 in health-care benefits.

Christie also talked about a retired New Jersey teacher who paid $62,000 toward her pension and zero for her and her family's health-care benefits. She will get $1.4 million in pension payments and the state will foot the bill for another $215,000 in health-care premiums.

A quick heads-up to those protesting union members: stop and look at what is happening in Europe. Just like the angry French citizens who want their entitlements, New Jersey state employees are fighting for theirs, even though what Jersey employees are getting is better than most of the workers in the private sectors get. But make no mistake: government-sector unions and the European welfare state are facing the same fate.

New Jersey is significant because the state's previous leader, Democrat Jon Corzine, was the only incumbent governor up for reelection in the fall of 2009. President Obama even campaigned heavily for him. Corzine's loss to Christie, despite White House backing, was a hint of what was to come. Voter discontent with big government was being heard at the New Jersey polling stations. This tells me people are slowly getting it.

If more governors get tough like Christie, we can avert the mess that Europe now faces. That's the good news. There is hope for us here because we have time.

But we have to start changing now, while we still do have

time. Leadership is going to have to make some tough decisions, and maybe some politicians will have to forfeit a second term to get the job done right.

Let me give you an example of the success of letting the free markets take their course: Latin America. I've covered the region for years and have witnessed firsthand the heartbreaking poverty there caused by government spending run amok. Child beggars, sewage in the streets, the disabled left on the side of the road to rot: vivid images I have from my time there.

But now, there are some successes. Brazil, for example, has become a star of the global economy. The country adopted free-market principles and started shoring up its reserves. The country wasn't nearly as badly damaged by the latest global downturn as many other countries were.

The explosive growth of mobile-phone use in Central and South America is a good real-world example at how fostering competition improves the lives of the poor. It is a lesson in how generous capitalism can be when governments allow it to grow.

For years, the governments of Latin America were the ones in charge of providing telephone service to their populations. The conventional wisdom was that something as crucial as phone service should not be only for the rich, so of course the government must provide phone service to all. But in country after country, governments didn't have the will or the money or maybe the know-how to actually make it happen. Wait times for phone lines in people's homes were years and years—or never.

We see this over and over again. Government deems something important and decides it must ensure that everyone has access to it, and then guess what: whatever is being provided is provided poorly.

We're going down that road with health care right now.

Luckily, when wireless arrived, most governments let the private sector handle it. Maybe mobile phones were seen as a luxury for only the rich, and governments didn't want to be seen dealing with something only for the wealthy. Instead, they let the free market step in and handle the wireless world, and guess what happened: Mobile-phone penetration sky-rocketed, even in the poorest parts of the world.

Naturally, the first wave of customers was wealthy and living in the most developed parts of the world. They had the money. But in the search for growth and profits, telecom companies started expanding in all parts of the world. They went to areas of the globe where people were hungry for the ability to communicate—where there were no phones. So many companies were competing for customers that they kept lowering prices. A mobile phone is now affordable and available in a way that landlines never were.

In the poorest continent of all, Africa, there were never more than 12 million fixed landlines or less than 2 lines for every 100 inhabitants. But there are now 295 million mobile phone subscribers in Africa or 37 mobile phones per 100 inhabitants. In developing countries there were never more than 13 landlines per 100 inhabitants. Now, there are more than 57 mobile phones per 100 inhabitants.[1]

When I worked at Univision News, we frequently received letters from women in Central America and Mexico with a frayed or fading picture tucked inside. They were usually photos of their sons who had left for the United States in search of work. The women hadn't heard from their children since they'd left. Their letters were filled with desperate pleas to put precious photos on television to see if anyone knew of a child's whereabouts or if he was still alive. We got phone calls too, from women who'd walked to town or saved up for a trip to the pay phone to make that one call to find their children.

Now cheap wireless has penetrated even the poorest parts of Latin America. Here in the U.S., there are cheap prepaid phones at every convenience store. Mothers don't have to put faith in the hands of a monthly landline phone call anymore. In a country like Guatemala there are more than 1,000 mobile phones per 1,000 people (some folks have two). Yet there are still only 100 landlines per 1,000 inhabitants.

Mothers can now sleep at night knowing that in an emergency their children can call with a prepaid phone card from the 7-Eleven, and they can have a phone by their bedside to receive that call. The government had no hand in that.

With the proliferation of apps, mobile phones are now being used as teaching devices in places like Mexico. Soon, I hope, apps will serve as mobile bank accounts, giving the poor access to banking in a way they didn't have before. The wireless industry improved the lives of many people in a way the government could not.

Wireless in Latin America is dramatic evidence that intense competition makes people's lives better and can provide far more than a well-intentioned government can. Freedom for companies to invest in technology and then charge enough for the service they are providing improves standards of living.

Competition, animal spirits, and entrepreneurialism are not to be decried. They are to be embraced.

Yes, Michael Moore, capitalism is a love story. Government needs to get out of the way.

We are at an inflection point in America: Between skyrocketing government spending and the oil leak in the gulf, we have been left feeling impotent. We have lost faith in our government's ability to fix what ails us. But our first mistake was to believe that the government could fix all of our problems. Our nation's strength comes from our belief in, and our reliance on, the individual.

Reminders of the power of the individual happen to me at the oddest moments. I was moved when I stumbled across a quote in the *New York Times* from a woman who was distilling absinthe, of all things. Cheryl Lins, a computer programmer and a watercolorist, was inspired by a *New Yorker* article to distill the no-longer-prohibited liquor and sell it to local stores and bars. But she couldn't start her business until New York state issued her a license. It took forever and she cried as she sent yet another email to Albany, desperate for a response.

She told the *New York Times*, "All I wanted was a chance to fail or succeed on my own merits, not because they were holding me up."

That quote stopped me in my tracks. It defines the American spirit so perfectly. She readily acknowledged that she could fail in her endeavor, but she was willing to take that risk. She knew it was up to her if only the government would get out of the way.

We are relearning the lesson that government isn't going to save us the hard way right now.

I saw a key moment of national self-discovery live on CNBC in May 2010, during President Barack Obama's first large-scale press conference following the BP oil spill—his first such news conference in ten months. I watched the White House press ream the president repeatedly for not doing enough. There were many questions and yet nearly all of them were the same: Why wasn't *he*, the president, doing more? Why hadn't *he* taken control of the situation? Why hadn't *he* fixed this problem yet? The anger in the room was palpable.

Immediately following the news conference I interviewed two Washington-based guests, one of whom told our audience that he thought the press's anger demonstrated that they don't give the president a pass on everything. They, of course, being the same members of the media accused of having given Obama a pass during the election. But I disagreed with the guests' interpretation.

Those journalists were angry with the president because they felt betrayed. After all, this is the man who came into office and said there are some problems so big that only government can fix them. He is the one who told them more government was needed in nearly every aspect of our lives to fix things such as health care, education, and energy. And yet, here he stood, *not* fixing the oil spill. They were flabbergasted. They had believed his big-government rhetoric during the campaign and during his battle with Wall Street.

Disappointment in the government's ability to stop the leak was inevitable. The BP fiasco is a glaring example of our overreliance on regulators and regulatory agencies to protect us. I'll go even further: what the BP disaster shows us is that the very act of creating an agency to protect us actually leads to *less* protection. When an industry has to answer to the *market,* it is forced to please many, many people. When an industry has to answer to a big government agency, it can focus all of its lobbying guns right at it and keep those regulators at bay. We saw it with Bernie Madoff and the SEC. We are seeing it now with the Minerals Management Service, the regulatory agency keeping an eye on big oil.

Long before the leak, back in 2008, the Office of the Inspector General found that nearly one-third of the entire staff dedicated to monitoring the industry socialized with, and accepted gifts from, oil and gas companies with which they were conducting official business. The report written on this relationship was nothing short of scathing. It said that the office had discovered a culture of substance abuse and promiscuity. Employees "accepted lodging from the industry after industry events because they were too intoxicated to drive home or to their hotel." These same employees "also engaged in brief sexual relationships with industry contacts. Sexual relationships with prohibited sources cannot, by definition, be arm's-length."[2]

Wonky economists have a term for what happened in the case of the MMS: *regulatory capture*. The regulators become, quite literally, captured by the very industry they are supposed to police. Industries will always try to seduce those who are supposed to regulate them.

That inspector general's report from 2008 wasn't enough to stop the massive leak. But the market regulation of BP has been far more brutal, swift, and just.

BP's punishment by the market has been furious, with the company's stock and bonds selling off dramatically as the mess continued on unsolved. That of course does nothing to bring back those who died in that tragic accident and brings no solace to the family members left behind. It does nothing to bring back the businesses in the gulf region forced to shutter and the families left jobless as a result.

But obtaining justice either through jail time or financial judgments is far more likely to happen here than in many other countries because of our free-market system. That's because the oil industry is not an arm of the government here. The affected families will have both criminal and civil legal recourse.

I know it doesn't sound like much, but ask yourself, What would happen in countries where the oil industry is essentially an arm of the government? In Venezuela, Russia, and Saudi Arabia, do you think the victims' families would have any hope of justice? Or of transparency? Of learning the truth about what happened? In those countries the incentives are for the government to hide the truth because the government and the industry are one and the same. In the United States that conflict doesn't exist.

And in the future, when it comes to protecting the safety of other workers still out there, fear of punishment by the market is a much greater threat to executives than punishment by the regulators. As crass as this will sound, we all know that watching their fortunes decline will be the biggest reason CEOs choose to act more cautiously in the future. No regulator will ever instill as much fear in them as a possible bankruptcy will.

And for those who say the incident proves we need more regulation, remember: *Drilling, along with banking, are two of the most regulated industries in America.*

I think it's fair to say the less-government mantra is gaining momentum. I can feel it. I used to feel alone in my viewpoints, but I'm hearing a lot of frustration and desperate concern for our future stability lately.

Look at CNBC's Rick Santelli's rant-heard-round-the-world in November 2009. He exposed a very raw national nerve when he shouted out his frustration with government spending and the government's attempt to reward people who shouldn't have been rewarded. He lambasted overextended homeowners and big banks and gave those of us who believe in small government a voice we'd been searching for. More than a million people clicked onto CNBC.com to watch Rick and to cheer on his rallying cry. He unleashed a tidal wave response that is driving the national debate still today.

People are speaking up with their votes too. In June 2010,

the unions were handed a huge defeat in the Democratic primary in Arkansas. They didn't back incumbent Blanche Lincoln because they felt she had abandoned them when she didn't support "card check," which would make unionization easier. But Blanche Lincoln won even though the unions there blew $10 million on her opponent. I don't blame the unions—if you back candidates based on a set of principles and they don't live up to them, you have a right to be angry. The unions are no different from the fiscal conservatives who felt betrayed by President George W. Bush.[3]

Blanche Lincoln didn't support a public option for health-care reform either, something also cherished by the liberal components of the Democratic Party. Her victory over a union-backed opponent tells me the electorate doesn't want to move that far toward government control of our lives. For that I am relieved.

There are more signs of less-government momentum we can draw on in South Carolina. Nikki Haley, running for governor, came out on top in her primary despite two accusations of infidelity, both of which she denied. Maybe the voters of South Carolina care more about small government than a candidate's personal life? I'm hoping we see more instances like this one, where voters embrace a candidate for his or her message about small government and low taxes, and not the peripheral garbage. That would be change I can believe in.

As journalists, we are taught that we are the voice of the voiceless. One of my goals in writing this book was to give a voice to the free markets, which have no voice. It was also to share my viewpoint that free markets can make us freer, happier, and better equipped to provide for our families.

Politicians always have a voice. They appear in the media all the time. They get to make their case about why we need more of what they make: *laws*. Regulators too frequently appear on television to tell us why it is so important that we get more of what they make: *regulation*.

Corporations and big business have plenty of voice, too. You might think they are a voice of the free markets, but frequently they are not. They aren't the underdog or the voiceless, because they generally have millions of dollars ready to lobby Washington.

I think the tides are about to turn for this country. F. A. Hayek's *Road to Serfdom* is soaring on the bestseller lists, even though it was written in the forties. It is a classic treatise on the connection between economic liberty and democratic liberty and on the dangers of planning the economy. It resonates with people who are fed up and unhappy with bloated government.

If you are frustrated with the way government is spending, growing and overregulating, you know I'm right when I say that it's time for *real* change.

If you are worried about saddling your children with your generation's debts, then you know I'm right when I say we need to buckle down now before it's too late.

If you want affordable health care and choice in education, then you know I'm right in my rally cry for letting the free markets take control on both fronts.

If you are for the free movement of capital, goods, and labor with immigration, then you know I'm right when I say stop being afraid and open the doors to the country.

If you are tired of debt and double-talk, then you know I'm right when I say there are too many government departments and too much spending.

And finally, if you believe in America, liberty, and individualism, then you know I'm right.

— Notes —

2. Ronald Reagan Had It Right

1. Bureau of Labor Statistics, "Labor Force Statistics from the Current Population Survey, May 21, 2010," Series ID LNS14, http://data.bls.gov/PDQ/servlet/SurveyOutputServlet?data_tool=latest_numbers&series_id=LNS14000000.
2. Joint Economic Committee, "The Reagan Tax Cuts: Lessons For Tax Reform," JEC Report, April 1996, http://www.house.gov/jec/fiscal/tx-grwth/reagtxct/reagtxct.htm.
3. Office of Management and Budget, "Historical Tables of the United States Government," Table 1.2—Summary of Receipts, Outlays, and Surpluses or Deficits (–) as Percentages of GDP: 1930–2015, http://www.whitehouse.gov/omb/budget/historicals/.
4. Cited in Daniel Mitchell, "Lowering Marginal Tax Rates: The Key to Pro-Growth Tax Relief," Heritage Foundation, May 22, 2001, http://www.heritage.org/Research/Reports/2001/05/Lowering-Marginal-Tax-Rates.
5. Cited in William J. Federer, "John F. Kennedy on Taxes," WorldNet Daily, July 19, 2004, http://www.wnd.com/news/article.asp?ARTICLE_ID=39517.
6. Sumeet Sagoo, ed., *Facts and Figures on Government Finance*, 38th ed., Tax Foundation, 2005, Chapter C, p. 105, http://www.taxfoundation.org/news/show/147.html.
7. Daniel Mitchell, "The Historical Lessons of Lower Tax Rates," Heritage Foundation, August 13, 2003, http://www.heritage.org/Research/Reports/2003/08/The-Historical-Lessons-of-Lower-Tax-Rates.
8. Ibid.; http://www.heritage.org/Research/Reports/1996/07/BG1086nbsp-The-Historical-Lessons-of-Lower-Tax; Bureau of the Census, *Historical Statistics of the United States: Colonial Times to 1970, Part 1* (Washington, D.C.: U.S. Government Printing Office, 1976).
9. Quoted in Mitchell, "The Historical Lessons of Lower Tax Rates."
10. Daniel Mitchell, "Lowering Marginal Tax Rates: The Key to Pro-Growth Tax Relief," Heritage Foundation, May 22, 2001, http://www.heritage.org/Research/Reports/2001/05/Lowering-Marginal-Tax-Rates.

11. Katherine Lim and Jeffrey Rohaly, "Variation in Effective Tax Rates," *Tax Notes*, February 8, 2010, http://www.urban.org/Uploaded PDF/412032_effective_tax_rates.pdf; Birgit Stein, interview by Amy Stelland, tape recording, August 16, 2005, Sausalito Branch Library, Sausalito, Calif.

12. Quoted in Mitchell, "The Historical Lessons of Lower Tax Rates."

13. Daniel Mitchell, "Flat World, Flat Taxes," *American*, April 27, 2007, http://www.american.com/archive/2007/april-0407/flat-world-flat -taxes/?searchterm=mitchell.

14. Tom Clark and Andrew Dilnot, "Long-Term Trends In British Taxation and Spending," Institute For Fiscal Studies Briefing Note, November 25, 2002.

15. "Remarks and a Question-and-Answer Session With Reporters on Signing the Veto Message for the Farm Credit and African Relief Bill," *Public Papers of the Presidents*, American Presidency Project, March 6, 1985, http://www.presidency.ucsb.edu/ws/index.php?pid=38293.

16. "Address to the Nation on the Federal Budget and Deficit Reduction," *Public Papers of the Presidents*, American Presidency Project, April 24, 1985, http://www.presidency.ucsb.edu/ws/index.php?pid =38536&st=&st1=.

17. Sagoo, ed., *Facts and Figures on Government Finance*, Chapter C, Table C6, "Federal Outlays by Major Category Fiscal Years 1962–2004," p. 70.

18. "Historical U.S. Inflation Rate, 1914–Present," InflationData.com, last updated May 19, 2010, http://inflationdata.com/inflation/Inflation_Rate/ HistoricalInflation.aspx?dsInflation_currentPage=2.

19. Author interview with Paul Volcker, air date June 11, 2004.

20. Tax Policy Center, "Tax Facts: Historical Amount of Revenue By Source: Receipts by Source" 1934–2015, May 3, 2010, http://www.taxpolicy center.org/taxfacts/displayafact.cfm?Docid=203.

21. U.S. Social Security Administration, "Automatic Increases," Social Security cost of living adjustments chart, http://www.socialsecurity.gov/ OACT/COLA/colaseries.html.

22. Interview with Milton Friedman, air date June 11, 2004.

23. "Message to the Congress Transmitting the National Energy Policy Plan," *Public Papers of the Presidents*, American Presidency Project, July 17, 1981, http://www.presidency.ucsb.edu/ws/index.php?pid=44096.

24. "Radio Address to the Nation on Oil Prices," *Public Papers of the Presidents*, American Presidency Project, April 19, 1986, http://www .presidency.ucsb.edu/ws/index.php?pid=37156.

25. "Message to the Congress Transmitting the Fifth National Energy Policy Plan," *Public Papers of the Presidents*, American Presidency

Project, March 26, 1986, http://www.presidency.ucsb.edu/ws/index
.php?pid=37062&st=&st1=.

26. Roger G. Noll, "Regulation After Reagan," *Regulation* 12, no. 3 (1988),
Cato Institute, http://www.cato.org/pubs/regulation/regv12n3/reg12n3
-noll.html.

27. Cindy Skrzycki, "Under Reagan, Scrutiny of Rules Became the Rule,"
Washington Post, June 8, 2004, E01, http://www.washingtonpost.com/
wp-dyn/articles/A23389=2004Jun7.html.

28. Joshua Green, "Reagan's Liberal Legacy," *Washington Monthly*,
January/February 2003, http://www.washingtonmonthly.com/features/
2003/0301.green.html.

29. "Farewell Address to the Nation," *Public Papers of the Presidents*,
American Presidency Project, January 11, 1989, http://www.presidency
.ucsb.edu/ws/index.php?pid=29650&st=&st1=.

3. My Second Favorite President

1. John Murphy, "NAFTA at 15: Assessing Its Benefits: Accord Has Boosted
Jobs, Exports Across the U.S.," U.S. Chamber of Commerce International Policy Backgrounder, February 2009, http://www.uschamber.com/
NR/rdonlyres/ee4a7ezykcijsb75ekqxiilw6ouy7px5xj7pzm55fwpygoy6c
uuqyudfdkrgqfxlysuyvxca32z6ofx7r3nsa2bn3mb/NAFTAat15.pdf.

2. Ibid.

3. Office of the United States Trade Representative, "NAFTA: An Annual Tax Cut and Income Gain for American Families," NAFTA Facts,
NAFTA Policy Brief, October 2007, http://www.ustr.gov/sites/default/
files/Quantification%20of%20NAFTA%20Benefits.pdf.

4. Office of Trade and Industry Information, International Trade Administration, U.S. Department of Commerce, "Industry, Trade, and The
Economy: Data and Analysis: New York: Exports, Jobs, and Foreign
Investment," updated March 29, 2010, http://www.ita.doc.gov/td/
industry/otea/state_reports/newyork.html.

5. Robert Rector and Sarah Youssef, "The Determinants of Welfare Casel-
oad Decline," Heritage Foundation, May 11, 1999, http://www.heritage
.org/Research/Reports/1999/05/The-Determinants-of-Welfare-Caseload
-Decline.

6. Ibid.

7. Robert Rector, "Welfare Reform and the Decline of Dependence," Heritage Foundation, September 9, 1999, http://www.heritage.org/Research/
Testimony/Welfare-Reform-and-the-Decline-of-Dependence.

8. Judith Havemann "Most Find Jobs After Leaving Welfare," *Washington
Post*, May 27, 1999.

9. Mary Corcoran, Roger Gordon, Deborah Loren, and Gary Solon, "The Association Between Men's Economic Status and Their Family and Community Origins," *Journal of Human Resources* (Fall 1992), pp. 575–601.

10. "The Clinton/Gore Administration: Largest Surplus in History on Track," White House, September 27, 2000, http://clinton4.nara.gov/WH/new/html/Tue_Oct_3_113400_2000.html.

11. Ibid.

12. Canadian Broadcasting Corporation, December 21, 1967, CBC Digital Archives, http://archives.cbc.ca/politics/rights_freedoms/topics/538-2671/.

4. Where the Right Went Wrong

1. Sasha Johnson, "Bush on auto bailout, war in Iraq, shoe-throwing reporter," CNNPolitics.com, video interview with Candy Crowley, December 16, 2008, http://www.cnn.com/2008/POLITICS/12/16/bush.crowley.interview/index.html.

2. Stephen Slivinski, "Bush Beats Johnson: Comparing the Presidents," *Tax and Budget Bulletin* no. 26, Cato Institute, October 2005, http://www.cato.org/pubs/tbb/tbb-0510-26.pdf.

3. Veronique de Rugy and Tad DeHaven, "The Mother of All Big Spenders: Bush Spends Like Carter and Panders Like Clinton," Cato Institute, July 28, 2003, http://www.cato.org/research/articles/dehaven-030728.html.

4. Veronique de Rugy and Tad DeHaven, " 'Conservative' Bush Spends More Than 'Liberal' Presidents Clinton, Carter," Cato Institute, July 31, 2003, http://www.cato.org/pub_display.php?pub_id=3184.

5. Citizens Against Government Waste, *2005 Congressional Pig Book Summary,* http://councilfor.cagw.org/site/DocServer/2005_Pig_Book.pdf?docID=1441.

6. Jonathan Williams, "Paying at the Pump: Gasoline Taxes in America," Tax Foundation Background Paper No. 56, October 2007, http://www.taxfoundation.org/files/bp56%20final.pdf; David Boaz, "Congress's Latest Christmas Tree Bill," Cato Institute, May 13, 2005, http://www.cato.org/pub_display.php?pub_id=3765.

7. Chris Edwards, "Obama's Budget and the $1 Trillion Mistake," Cato Institute, February 1, 2010, http://www.cato.org/pub_display.php?pub_id=11182.

8. Sheryl Gay Stolberg, "Bush Threatens Veto of Child Health Bill," *New York Times,* September 21, 2007, http://www.nytimes.com/2007/09/21/washington/21bush.html.

9. As quoted in Veronique de Rugy, "Facts Are Important," *National Review Online*, January 29, 2010, http://corner.nationalreview.com/post/? q=NzQzOGJjMmFmYjRlOWQ5ODRhYTY4OGI4MjAxNjQ3ZDM=.

10. U.S. Census Bureau, Housing Vacancies and Homeownership, Annual Statistics: 2007, "Table 5: Homeownership Rates for the United States: 1968 to 2008," April 2008.

11. "President Hosts Conference on Minority Homeownership," speech to George Washington University, Washington, D.C., October 15, 2002, http://georgewbush-whitehouse.archives.gov/news/releases/2002/ 10/20021015-7.html.

12. U.S. Department of Housing and Urban Development, "Community Planning and Development: American Dream Down Payment Initiative," http://www.hud.gov/offices/cpd/affordablehousing/programs/ home/addi/.

13. U.S. Department of Housing and Urban Development Archives, "President George W. Bush Speaks to HUD Employees on National Homeownership Month," Washington, D.C., June 18, 2002, http://archives .hud.gov/remarks/martinez/speeches/presremarks.cfm.

14. Ibid.

15. Ibid.

16. Lynn Adler, "Foreclosures soar 81 percent in 2008," Reuters, January 15, 2009, http://www.reuters.com/article/idUSTRE50E1KV20090115.

17. "Prescription Drugs and the Elderly: Policy Implications of Medicare Coverage," Rand Center for the Study of Aging Research Brief, 1999, http://www.rand.org/pubs/research_briefs/RB5028/index1.html.

18. Ibid.

19. Michael F. Cannon, "New Medicare Benefit Will Outspend Projections," CATO Institute, http://www.cato.org/pub_display.php?pub_id=3700.

20. Ellen E. Schultz and Theo Francis, "How Cuts In Retiree Benefits Falter Companies' Bottom Lines," *Wall Street Journal*, March 16, 2004, http:// online.wsj.com/public/resources/documents/SB107940131862956349 .htm.

21. House Budget Committee Democrat Caucus, Fiscal Year 2004 Budget Conference Agreement: "Republicans Dig the Deficit Deeper," http://bud gethouse.gov/congressional_budgets/fy2004/conf_summary\overview .htm.

22. 2009 Annual Report of the Boards of Trustees of the Federal Hospital Insurance and Federal Supplementary Medical Insurance Trust Funds, May 12, 2009.

23. Cannon, "New Medicare Benefit Will Outspend Projections."

24. Reuters, "Bush Imposes Steel Tariffs," *USA Today*, March 5, 2002, http:// www.usatoday.com/money/general/2002/03/05/bush-steel.htm.

25. Sarah Fitzgerald and Aaron Schabe, "Rusty Thinking on Steel Tariffs," Heritage Foundation, September 29, 2003.
26. Walter E. Williams, "The Argument for Free Markets: Morality vs. Efficiency," *The CATO Journal,* Volume 15.
27. Richard W. Stevenson and Elizabeth Becker, "Bush Avoids a Trade War by Lifting Steel Tariffs," *New York Times,* December 5, 2003.
28. Quoted in press release, "Bush Is No Champion of the Free Market," Ayn Rand Center for Individual Rights, November 14, 2008, http://www.aynrand.org/site/News2?page=NewsArticle&id=21939&news_iv_ctrl=1221.
29. Barry A. Kosmim and Ariela Keysar, "American Religious Identification Survey," Trinity College, March 2009.
30. Elisabeth Bumiller, "Bush Remarks Roil Debate on Teaching of Evolution," *New York Times,* August 3, 2005.

5. Fixing Unions

1. Michael Mishak, "Unplugged: The SEIU chief on the labor movement and the card check," *Las Vegas Sun,* May 10, 2009, http://www.lasvegassun.com/news/2009/may/10/stern-unplugged-seiu-chief-labor-movement-and-card/.
2. U.S. Bureau of Labor Statistics, "Union Members Summary, January 22, 2010," http://www.bls.gov/news.release/union2.nr0.htm.
3. U.S. Bureau of Labor Statistics, "Economic News Release, Union Members Summary, January 2, 2010," http://www.bls.gov/news.release/union2.nr0.htm; Conn Caroll, "Morning Bell: Government Unions Win, You Lose," The Foundry, January 25, 2010, http://blog.heritage.org/2010/01/25/morning-bell-government-unions-win-you-lose/.
4. James Sherk, "Majority of Union Members Now Work for the Government," Heritage Foundation, January 22, 2010, http://www.heritage.org/research/reports/2010/01/majority%20of%20union%20members%20now%20work%20for%20the%20government; U.S. Bureau of Labor Statistics, "News Release: Employer Costs for Employee Compensation—December 2009," March 10, 2010, http://www.bls.gov/news.release/pdf/ecec.pdf.
5. U.S. Bureau of Labor Statistics, "National Compensation Survey: Employee Benefits in Private Industry in the United States, March 2007," Table 1, August 2007, http://www.bls.gov/ncs/ebs/sp/ebsm0006.pdf.
6. Katherine Barrett and Richard Greene, et al., "Promises with a Price: Public Sector Retirement Benefits," Pew Center on the States, 2007, http://www.pewcenteronthestates.org/uploadedfiles/Promises%20with%20a%20Price.pdf.

7. "In Praise of Illinois," *Wall Street Journal*, April 8, 2010, http://online .wsj.com/article/SB10001424052702304539404575157650864015706 .html; National Taxpayers United of Illinois, "NTUI on WLS TV (ABC 7) and in The Wall Street Journal," April 12, 2010, http://www.ntui.org/ ntui-in-the-news/ntui-on-wls-tv-abc-7-and-in-the-wall-street-journal.

8. Chris Edwards, "Unions and Government Debt," Cato @ Liberty, April 5, 2010, http://www.cato-at-liberty.org/2010/04/05/unions-and-govern ment-debt/.

9. http://www.apwu.org/about/index.htm.

10. "Governor Schwarzenegger Delivers 2010 State of the State Address," Office of the Governor, Speeches, January 6, 2010, http://gov.ca.gov/ speech/14118/.

11. "California's College Dreamers," *Wall Street Journal*, March 10, 2010, http://online.wsj.com/article/SB10001424052748704187204575101461 287544470.html.

12. Jason Felch, Jessica Garrison, and Jason Song, "Failure Gets a Pass: Bar Set Low for Lifetime Job in L.A. Schools," *Los Angeles Times*, December 20, 2009, http://articles.latimes.com/2009/dec/20/local/la-me -teacher-tenure20-2009dec20.

13. "Fiscal Year 2011 Budget of Chris Christie, Governor of New Jersey, Transmitted to the First Annual Session of the Two Hundred Fourteenth Legislature," March 16, 2010, http://www.state.nj.us/governor/home/ pdf/budget_brief.pdf.

14. James Freeman, "New Jersey's 'Failed Experiment,' " *Wall Street Journal*, April 17, 2010, http://online.wsj.com/article/SB1000142405270230 33485045751841205467722244.html.

15. "New Milestone: Two Million American Teachers Now Corralled Into Unions, 1.3 Million Forced to Pay Dues," News Release, National Right to Work Legal Defense Foundation Inc., Washington, D.C., August 19, 2008, http://www.nrtw.org/en/press/2008/08/new-milestone.

16. Chris Edwards, "Public-Sector Unions," Tax and Budget Bulletin, Cato Institute, No. 61, March 10, http://www.cato.org/pubs/tbb/tbb_61.pdf.

17. Michael Mishak, "Unplugged: The SEIU chief on the labor movement and the card check," *Las Vegas Sun*, May 10, 2009, http://www.las vegassun.com/news/2009/may/10/stern-unplugged-seiu-chief-labor-move ment-and-card/.

18. Armand Thieblot, "Unions, The Rule of Law, and Political Rent Seek- ing," *Cato Journal*, Vol. 30, No. 1, Winter 2010, p. 39, http://www.cato .org/pubs/journal/cj30n1/cj30n1-2.pdf.

19. "Heavy Hitters, Top All-Time Donors, 1989–2010," OpenSecrets.org, Influence and Lobbying, updated May 16, 2010, accessed May 24, 2010, http://www.opensecrets.org/orgs/list.php.

20. Thieblot, p. 40.
21. Seth Michaels, "Union Members 25 Percent of Democratic Convention Delegates," August 21, 2008, http://blog.aflcio.org/2008/08/21/union-members-25-percent-of-democratic-convention-delegates/.
22. Joseph Carroll, "Sixty Percent of Americans Approve of Labor Unions," August 31, 2007, http://www.gallup.com/poll/28570/sixty-percent-americans-approve-labor-unions.aspx.
23. U.S. Bureau of Labor Statistics, "Union Members—2009," News Release, Table 3, January 10, 2010, http://www.bls.gov/news.release/pdf/union2.pdf.
24. "Obama Labor Day Speech at AFL-CIO Picnic," Huffington Post, posted September 7, 2009, updated October 23, 2009, accessed May 24, 2010, http://www.huffingtonpost.com/2009/09/07/obama-labor-day-speech-at_n_278772.html.
25. Nick Bunkley, "Some G.M. Retirees Are in a Health Care Squeeze," *New York Times*, November 9, 2008, http://www.nytimes.com/2008/11/10/business/10gm.html?_r=1.
26. James Sherk, "Auto Bailout Ignores Excessive Labor Costs," Heritage Foundation, November 19, 2008, http://www.heritage.org/Research/Reports/2008/11/Auto-Bailout-Ignores-Excessive-Labor-Costs.
27. Ibid.
28. Alex Taylor, "Behind Ford's Scary $12.7 Billion Loss," *Fortune,* January 27, 2007.
29. Sherk, "Auto Bailout Ignores Excessive Labor Costs."
30. Bryce G. Hoffman, "12,000 Paid Not To Work (UAW Union Alert)," *Detroit News,* October 17, 2005, http://www.freerepublic.com/focus/f-news/1503982/posts.
31. Flight Attendant Union, asanet.org (phone call with press agent at ASA).

6. Fixing Health Care

1. Dr. Merrill Matthews and Victoria C. Bunce, "Small Steps to Big Reform," The Council for Affordable Health Insurance, Shortcuts and Answers," #146, Aug. 2007, http://www.cahi.org/cahi_contents/resources/pdf/n146SmallStepstoBigReformB.pdf.
2. Victoria Craig Bunce and JP Wieske, "Health Insurance Mandates in States 2008," Council for Affordable Health Insurance.
3. Ibid.
4. "Individual Health Insurance 2009: A Comprehensive Survey of Premiums, Availability, and Benefits," AHIP Center for Policy and Research, October 2009.
5. Congressional Budget Office, "Health Care Reform and the Fed-

eral Budget," June 16, 2009, http://budget.senate.gov/democratic/documents/2009/CBO%20Letter%20HealthReformAndFederalBudget_061609.pdf.

6. Congressional Budget Office, "Long-Term Budget Outlook," CBO Summary, June 2009, http://www.cbo.gov/ftpdocs/102xx/doc10297/summaryforweb_ltbo.pdf.

7. Regina S. Rockefeller, "Massachusetts take-away messages for national health care reform," Nixon Peabody, http://web20.nixonpeabody.com/healthcare/sitepages/Massachusetts_take-away_messages_for_national_health_care_reform.aspx.

8. Liz Kowalczyk, "Across Massachusetts, Wait to See Doctors Grows, Access to Care, Insurance Law Cited for Delays," *Boston Globe,* September 22, 2008.

9. Liz Kowalzyk, "ER Visits, Costs in Massachusetts Climb, Questions Raised About Healthcare Law's Impact on Overuse," *Boston Globe,* April 24, 2009.

10. Aaron Yelowitz and Michael F. Cannon, "The Massachusetts Health Plan Much Pain, Little Gain," CATO Institute, p. 10, January 20, 2010.

11. "The Myth of the Underinsured Crisis," The Council for Affordable Health Insurance's Issues & Answers, July 2007.

12. Roy Ramthun, "Only Consumers Can Bend the Health Care Cost Curve," The Council for Affordable Health Insurance's Issues & Answers, July 2009.

13. Ibid.

14. Ibid.

15. Congressional Budget Office letter to Harry Reid, March 11, 2010, page 6.

7. Fixing Immigration

1. Melissa Lafsky, "The Case For Immigration: A Q&A With Philippe Legrain," *New York Times,* Freakonomics blog, October 17, 2007.

2. Vivek Wadhwa, AnnaLee Saxenian, Ben Rissing, et al., "America's New Immigrant Entrepreneurs," Master of Engineering Management Program, Duke University; School of Information, U.C. Berkeley, p. 4, January 4, 2007.

3. Bill George, "Attracting the Next Generation," Huffington Post, May 19, 2010, http://www.huffingtonpost.com/bill-george/attracting-the-next-gener_b_582595.html.

4. Compete America, "Overall H-1B Cap Not Yet Reached; Proves Market-Based Approach Is Justified," FY 2010 Filings Show U.S. Companies Trying to Retain U.S.-Educated Talent, April 28, 2009, http://www.competeamerica.org/fact_of_week/032906.html.

5. "Bill Gates written transcript from today's congressional testimony," NetworkWorld, p. 8, March 12, 2008, http://www.networkworld.com/news/2008/031208-gates-testimony.html?page=8.

6. Ibid.

7. Nicole S. Stoops, "A Half-Century of Learning: Historical Statistics on Educational Attainment in the United States, 1940 to 2000," U.S. Census Bureau, Table 1, http://www.census.gov/population/www/socdemo/education/phct41.html.

8. U.S. Census Bureau, American FactFinder, American Community Survey, Subject Tables S1501, "Educational Attainment, 2006–2008 American Community Survey 3-Year estimates," http://factfinder.census.gov/servlet/STTable?_bm=y&-geo_id=01000US&-qr_name=ACS_2008_3YR_G00_S1501&-ds_name=ACS_2008_3YR_G00.

9. Peter B. Dixon and Maureen T. Rimmer, "Restriction or Legalization? Measuring the Economic Benefits of Immigration Reform," Cato Institute, Center for Trade Study Policies, No. 40, August 13, 2009, http://www.cato.org/pubs/tpa/tpa-040.pdf.

10. Daniel Griswold, "Immigration Law Should Reflect Our Dynamic Labor Market," Dallas Morning News, April 27, 2008, http://www.dallasnews.com/sharedcontent/dws/dn/opinion/points/stories/DN-griswold_27edi.ART.State.Edition1.46527e0.html.

11. Steven A. Camarota, "Amnesty Under Hagel-Martinez: An Estimate of How Many Will Legalize if S.2611 Becomes Law," Center For Immigration Studies, June 2006, http://www.cis.org/Hagel-Martinez-S2611-Amnesty.

12. U.S. Department of Homeland Security, "Prepared Remarks by Secretary Napolitano on Immigration Reform at the Center for American Progress," November 13, 2009, http://www.dhs.gov/ynews/speeches/sp_1258123461050.shtm and http://www.dhs.gov/journal/theblog/2009/11/three-legged-stool.html.

13. Romano L. Mazzoli and Alan K. Simpson, "Enacting Immigration Reform, Again," Washington Post, September 15, 2006, http://immigration.procon.org/viewanswers.asp?questionID=000797.

14. U.S. Citizenship and Immigration Services, "USCIS Continues to Accept FY 2010 H-1B Petitions," April 8, 2009, http://www.uscis.gov.

15. U.S. Census Bureau, American FactFinder, American Community Survey, Subject Tables S1501, "Educational Attainment, 2006–2008 American Community Survey 3-Year estimates," http://factfinder.census.gov/servlet/STTable?_bm=y&-geo_id=01000US&-gr_name=ACS_2008_3YR_G00_S1501&-ds_name=ACS_2008_3YR_G00.

16. U.S. Department of Agriculture, Economic Research Service, "Food CPI and Expenditures, Table 7—Food expenditures by families and indi-

viduals as a share of disposable personal income," June 17, 2008, http://www.ers.usda.gov/briefing/CPIFoodandExpenditures/Data/table7.htm.

17. Jeffrey S. Passel and D'Vera Cohn, "A Portrait of Unauthorized Immigrants in the United States," Pew Research Center, April 14, 2009, http://pewresearch.org/pubs/1190/portrait-unauthorized-immigrants-states.

18. Ibid., Table B4: "Detailed Industries with High Shares of Unauthorized Immigrants, 2008."

19. Steven Mintz, "Landmarks in Immigration History," Digital History, Updated May 24, 2010, http://www.digitalhistory.uh.edu/historyonline/immigration_chron.cfm.

20. "U.S. Immigration Since 1965," History.com, accessed May 24, 2010, http://www.history.com/topics/us-immigration-since-1965.

21. Philip J. Hilts, "Landmark Accord Promises to Ease Immigration Curbs," *New York Times*, October 26, 1990, http://www.nytimes.com/1990/10/26/us/landmark-accord-promises-to-ease-immigration-curbs.html.

8. Fixing Education

1. U.S. Department of Education, National Center for Education Statistics, *Digest of Education Statistics, 2008* (NCES 2009-020), chapter 2 and table 179, http://nces.ed.gov/fastfacts/display.asp?id=66.

2. Ibid.

3. http://nces.ed.gov/nationsreportcard/naepdata/.

4. *Digest of Education Statistics*, chapter 2 and table 179.

5. David C. Miller, Anindita Sen, et al., "Comparative Indicators of Education in the United States and Other G-8 Countries: 2009," National Center for Education Statistics, March 2009, p. vi, http://nces.ed.gov/pubs2009/2009039_1.pdf.

6. Ibid.

7. 2009 Compensation Survey, A Survey of Professional, Scientific and Related Jobs in State Government Prepared by AFT Public Employees, p. 81, http://aft.org/pdfs/pubemps/pecompsurvey0909.pdf.

8. That salary puts them as individuals above 54 percent of all households in America when it comes to income. http://en.wikipedia.org/wiki/Household_income_in_the_United_States.

9. "2009 Compensation Survey: A Survey of Professional, Scientific and Related Jobs in State Government Prepared by AFT Public Employees," p. 81, http://aft.org/pdfs/pubemps/pecompsurvey0909.pdf.

10. Miller, Sen, et al., "Comparative Indicators of Education in the United States and Other G-8 Countries: 2009."

11. Molly Peterson, "Kipp: Learning a Lesson From Big Business," *Bloomberg Businessweek*, February 4. 2010, http://www.businessweek.com/magazine/content/10_07/b4166056302366.htm.

12. Louisiana Recovery School District, "Information at a Glance: District Snapshot," http://www.rsdla.net/infoglance.aspx.

13. Louisiana Department of Education, Recovery School District, "2009 School Measurements Show Marked Improvements in Recovery School District Schools," Press Release, October 14, 2009, http://www.rsdla.net/Media/Pressrelease.aspx?PR=1340.

14. Sarah Carr, "School Choice is a real test for parents in New Orleans," *New Orleans Metro Education News*, November 8, 2009, http://www.nola.com/education/index.ssf/2009/11/post_42.html.

15. New York City Department of Education, "Parents' Guide to Charter Schools," http://schools.nyc.gov/NR/rdonlyres/51A7C088-CC06-48E3-8FF8-B0C47BFC3C30/42574/FactSheetCharterSchools.pdf.

16. Caroline M. Hoxby, Sonali Murarka, and Jenny Kang, "How New York City's Charter Schools Affect Achievement," New York City Charter Schools Evaluation Project, September 2009, http://www.nber.org/~schools/charterschoolseval/how_NYC_charter_schools_affect_achievement_sept2009.pdf. It is important that the statistical comparison is between students who got into a charter school and students who *wanted* to get into a charter school so you can eliminate "self-selection" bias. One can assume any parents entering their student in the lottery are taking an active interest in their child's education already. You can't make that assumption about the student population at large.

17. Ibid.

18. Ibid., page ii-2.

19. Ibid., page i-5.

20. Ibid., page v.

21. "Encouraging the spread of charter schools, *The Washington Post*," Blackboard Pulpit, June 22, 2009, http://www.washingtonpost.com/wp-dyn/content/article/2009/06/21/AR2009062101783.html; Brian Ewing, "Grant may play role in teacher pay issue," news-record.com, November 13, 2009, http://www.news-record.com/content/2009/11/12/article/grant_may_play_role_in_teacher_pay_issue; "Charter School Profile," The Center for Education Reform, http://www.edreform.com/charter_schools/maps/.

22. Lindsey Burke, "How Members of the 111th Congress Practice Private School Choice," Heritage Foundation, April 20, 2009, http://www.heritage.org/Research/Reports/2009/04/How-Members-of-the-111th-Congress-Practice-Private-School-Choice.

23. "U.S. Names Education Grant Winners," Sam Dillon, *New York Times,*

March 29, 2010; Department of Education Overview Information Race to the Top Fund Federal Register, April 14, 2010.

24. Dillon, "U.S. Names Education Grant Winners."

25. Amanda Paulson, "How Race to the Top Is Recasting Education Reform in America," *Christian Science Monitor,* June 1, 2010.

26. Jennifer Medina, "New York State Votes to Expand Charter Schools," *New York Times,* May 28, 2010.

9. Shrinking the Budget

1. Milton Friedman, "Balanced Budget: Amendment Must Put Limit on Taxes," *Wall Street Journal,* January 4, 1995.

2. Congressional Budget Office, Kate Kelly and John Skeen, eds., "An Analysis of the President's Budgetary Proposals for Fiscal Year 2011," March 2010, http://www.cbo.gov/ftpdocs/112xx/doc11280/03-24-apb .pdf.

3. Tax Watch, "Rich to Poor: Will Redistribution Soar Under Obama Policies?" Tax Foundation, Winter 2010, http://www.taxfoundation.org/ files/tw-winter2010.pdf.

4. "An Analysis of the President's Budgetary Proposals for Fiscal Year 2011."

5. Total Debt: number comes out once a month.

6. Gene L. Dodaro, "Ensuring Accountability in a Time of Financial and Fiscal Stress," NASACT 2009 Annual Conference, August 17, 2009, p. 22, http://www.gao.gov/cghome/d09952cg.pdf.

7. Veronique de Rugy, "What Unsustainable Looks Like," *American,* March 3, 2010, http://www.american.com/archive/2010/march/what-unsustain able-looks-like/?searchterm=de%20rugy.

8. "Budget of the United States Government, Fiscal Year 2011, Table S-1," http://www.whitehouse.gov/omb/budget/fy2011/assets/tables.pdf.

9. Tony Crescenzi, "Sovereign Credit Risk Is the Risk Factor Du Jour," Pimco Viewpoints, February 2010, http://www.pimco.com/LeftNav/ Viewpoints/2010/PIMCO+Viewpoints+Crescenzi+Feb+2010.htm.

10. William Ahern, "Can Income Tax Hikes Close the Deficit?" Tax Foundation, Fiscal Fact No. 217, March 12, 2010, http://www.taxfounda tion.org/publications/show/25984.

11. Budget of the U.S. Government, Fiscal Year 2011, "Historical Tables, Table 4.1—Outlays By Agency: 1962–2015," p. 84, http://www.federal budget.com/HistoricalTables.pdf.

12. Jonathan Williams, "Gasoline Taxes: User Fees or Pigouvian Levies?" Tax Foundation, November 27, 2006, http://www.taxfounda tion.org/research/show/2048.html.

13. Robert Puentes and Ryan Prince, "Fueling Transportation Finance: A Primer on the Gas Tax," Brookings Institute, Center on Urban and Metropolitan Policy, March 2003, http://www.brookings.edu/reports/2003/03transportation_puentes.aspx.
14. Jonathan Weisman and Jim VandeHei, "Road Bill Reflects the Power of the Pork," *Washington Post,* August 11, 2005, http://www.washingtonpost.com/wp-dyn/content/article/2005/08/10/AR2005081000223.html.
15. Ibid.
16. Paul Basken, "Big Raise for Pell Grants, Despite Austerity," *The Chronicle of Higher Education,* February 1, 2010, http://chronicle.com/article/Big-Raise-for-Pell-Grants/63848/.
17. "Renewable Energy R&D Funding History: A Comparison with Funding for Nuclear Energy, Fossil Energy, and Energy Efficiency R&D," Congressional Research Service.
18. Congressional Budget Office, "The Budget and Economic Outlook: Fiscal Years 2010 to 2020," Pub. No. 4095, Table 3-1: "CBO's Baseline Projections of Outlays," January 2010, http://www.cbo.gov/ftpdocs/108xx/doc10871/01-26-Outlook.pdf.

10. Good-Bye, Social Security; Farewell, Medicare

1. Jagadeesh Gokhale and Kent Smetters, "Playing Good Cop Bad Cop," Forbes.com, August 4, 2009, http://www.forbes.com/2009/08/04/health-care-good-cop-bad-cop-opinions-contributors-jagadeesh-gokhale.html.
2. U.S. Social Security Administration, "2009 Annual Report of the Board of Trustees of the Federal Old Age and Survivors Insurance and Federal Disability Insurance Trust Fund," House Document 111-41, May 12, 2009, p. 64.
3. Ibid., p. 69—36.4 trillion part A, p. 111—general revenue contributions line $37 trillion for part B, and p. 127—general revenue contributions for $15.5 trillion for part D.
4. Ibid., p. 18.
5. Pamela Villareal, "Social Security and Medicare Projections: 2009," National Center for Policy Analysis, June 11, 2009, http://www.ncpa.org/pub/ba662.
6. Andrew G. Biggs, "Social Insecurity? Personal Accounts and the Stock Market Collapse, American Enterprise Institute," November 2008.
7. Robert J. Shiller, "The Lifecycle Personal Accounts Proposal For Social Security: A Review," National Bureau of Economic Research, May 2005.
8. "It's Your Money: A Citizen's Guide to Social Security Reform," Cato

Institute Project on Social Security Choice, page 24, http://www.cato .org/pubs/books/itsyourmoney.pdf.

9. Milton Friedman, "Speaking the Truth About Social Security Reform," Cato Institute Briefing Papers, April 12, 1999, http://www.socialsecu rity.org/pubs/articles/bp46.pdf.

10. Feldstein, Martin, "Did Wages Reflect Growth in Productivity?" *Journal of Policy Modeling* 30(4): 591–94, 2008, http://harvard.edu/urn-3:HUL .InstRepos:2794832.

11. The Tragedy of Fannie and Freddie

1. Congressional Budget Office, "CBO's Budgetary Treatment of Fannie Mae and Freddie Mac," Table 2: "Summary of CBO's August 2009 Budget Projections for Fannie Mae and Freddie Mac," January 2010, http://www.cbo.gov/ftpdocs/108xx/doc10878/01-13-FannieFreddie.pdf.

2. Ibid., p. 9

3. Rebecca Christie and Jody Shenn, "U.S. Treasury Ends Cap on Fannie, Freddie Lifeline for 3 Years," Bloomberg, December 5, 2009, http:// www.bloomberg.com/apps/news?pid=20601208&sid=abTVUSp9zbAY.

4. Alistair Barr, "Fannie, Freddie CEOs get $6 Million Pay Packages," Market Watch, December 24, 2009, http://www.marketwatch.com/ story/fannie-freddie-ceos-get-6-mln-pay-packages-2009-12-24.

5. "Facts on Policy: Homeownership Rates," Hoover Institute, Stanford University, August 19, 2008, http://www.hoover.org/research/factson policy/facts/26963064.html.

6. "The State of the Nation's Housing 2008," Joint Center for Housing Studies of Harvard University, Table A-4, p. 37, and Chapter 4, p. 16, http://www.jchs.harvard.edu/publications/markets/son2008/son2008 .pdf.

7. "Fannie Mae—Company Profile, Information, Business Description, History, Background Information on Fannie Mae," Reference for Business: Company History Index, http://www.referenceforbusiness.com/ history2/29/Fannie-Mae.html.

8. U.S Department of Housing and Urban Development, "Home-ownership: Progress and Work Remaining," Issue Brief No. III, December 2000, p. 1, http://www.huduser.org/Publications/PDF/homeowner ship.pdf.

9. Catherine Brock, "Hard Times for Bad Credit Mortgage," Mort gageLoan.com, http://www.mortgageloan.com/hard-times-for-bad-credit -mortgage-1526.

10. U.S. Department of Housing and Urban Development, "Highlights of

HUD Accomplishments 1997–1999," content archived January 20, 2009, http://archives.hud.gov/reports/acc97-00.cfm.

11. Steven A. Holmes, "Fannie Mae Eases Credit to Aid Mortgage Lending," *New York Times,* September 30, 1999, http://www.nytimes .com/1999/09/30/business/fannie-mae-eases-credit-to-aid-mortgage -lending.html.

12. "Highlights of HUD Accomplishments, 1997–1999."

13. Terry Jones, "Crony Capitalism Is Root Cause of Fannie and Freddie Troubles," *Investor's Business Daily,* September 22, 2008, http://www .investors.com/NewsAndAnalysis/Article.aspx?id=487182.

14. U.S. Department of Housing and Urban Development, "President George W. Bush Speaks to HUD Employees on National Home-ownership Month, Washington D.C., June 18, 2002," http://archives .hud.gov/remarks/martinez/speeches/presremarks.cfm.

15. As quoted in: House Committee on Financial Services, "House Republicans Ought to be Embarrassed about their Record on Fannie and Freddie," press release, April 28, 2010, http://www.house.gov/apps/list/press/ financialsvcs_dem/pressREP_04282010.shtml.

16. Jones, "Crony Capitalism Is Root Cause of Fannie and Freddie Troubles."

17. Carol D. Leonnig, "How HUD Mortgage Policy Fed The Crisis," Montana Department of Commerce, June 10, 2008, http://housing.mt.gov/ Includes/HCT/HowHUDMortgagePolicyFedTheCrisis.pdf.

18. Committee on Oversight and Government Reform, "Committee Holds Hearing on Collapse of Fannie Mae and Freddie Mac," http://oversight .house.gov/index.php?option=com_content&task=view&id=3467&Ite mid=49.

19. Ibid.

20. Eduardo Porter and Vikas Bajaj, "Mortgage Trouble Clouds Homeownership Dream," *New York Times,* March 17, 2007, http://www.nytimes .com/2007/03/17/business/17dream.html.

21. "Making Sense of the Foreclosure Crisis," Paul Solman interview with Alyssa Katz. Transcript of interviews originally aired October 15, 2009, http://www.pbs.org/newshour/bb/business/july-dec09/fore closures_10-15.html.

22. David Sreitfeld and Louise Story, "F.H.A. Problems Raising Concern of Policy Makers," *New York Times,* October 8, 2009, http://www.ny times.com/2009/10/09/business/09fha.html.

23. Ibid.

24. Ilyce Glink, "FHA Increases Down Payment for Some, Mortgage Insurance Premium for All," Moneywatch.com, January 20, 2010, http://

moneywatch.bnet.com/saving-money/blog/home-equity/fha-increases
-down-payment-for-some-mortgage-insurance-premium-for-all/1539/.

12. In Defense of Defense

1. Benjamin Friedman, "The Four Percent Folly," CATO @ Liberty, February 22, 2008, http://www.cato-at-liberty.org/2008/02/22/the-four
-percent-folly/.
2. Max Boot, "ObamaCare and American Power," *Wall Street Journal*, March 25, 2010, p. A21.
3. David Isenberg, "About That Non-Discretionary Spending," Cato Institute, January 26, 2010, http://www.cato.org/pub_display.php?pub_id=11170.
4. Kitty Donaldson, "UK Faces $54 Billion Defense-Spending Shortfall, Panel Says," *BusinessWeek*, March 22, 2010; Richard Norton-Taylor, "Defence budget facing £36bn black hole, says MPs," *Guardian*, March 23, 2010.
5. Donaldson, "UK Faces $54 Billion Defense-Spending Shortfall"; Norton-Taylor, "Defence budget facing £36bn black hole."
6. Edward Cody, "France Boosts Spending on Military," *Washington Post*, October 20, 2008 (divide $230 billion by 5), http://www.washington
post.com/wp-dyn/content/article/2008/10/29/AR2008102902589.html.
7. Slobodan Lekic, "NATO: Europe Must Upgrade Defenses," ABC News International, March 27, 2010, http://abcnews.go.com/International/
wireStory?id=10217646.
8. Christopher Preble, "The FY 2010 Defense Authorization," Cato @ Liberty, October 23, 2009, http://www.cato-at-liberty.org/2009/10/23/
the-fy-2010-defense-authorization/.
9. Boot, "ObamaCare and American Power."
10. "The Defense Budget," in *CATO Handbook for Policymakers*, 7th ed., p. 205, http://www.cato.org/pubs/handbook/hb111/index.html.
11. Benjamin Friedman, "The US Should Cut Military Spending by Half," *Christian Science Monitor*, April 27, 2009, http://www.csmonitor.com/
Commentary/Opinion/2009/0427/p09s01-coop.html.
12. Friedman, "The Four Percent Folly."
13. Doug Bandow, "Military Spending—For What?" CATO Institute, January 19, 2010, http://www.cato.org/pub_display.php?pub_id=11143.
14. Ibid.
15. Friedman, "The US Should Cut Military Spending by Half."
16. Tini Tran, "China Rejects US Criticism over Military Strength," *Guardian*, May 6, 2009.

17. Ibid.
18. Michael Forsythe, Frederik Balfour, and Chua Kong Ho, "China's Defense Spending to Rise at Decade-Low Pace," *BusinessWeek,* March 3, 2010, http://www.businessweek.com/news/2010-03-03/china-s-defense-spending-to-rise-at-decade-low-pace-update1-.html.
19. *SIPRI Yearbook 2008: Armaments, Disarmament and International Security* (Oxford: Oxford University Press, 2008), Appendix 5A, available at http://www.sipri.org/yearbook/2008/05.
20. "The Defense Budget," p. 205.
21. "Modernizing China's Military: Opportunities and Constraints," RAND Corporation, May 19, 2005, http://www.rand.org/pubs/monographs/2005/RAND_MG260-1.pdf.
22. Jim Yardley and David Lague, "Beijing Accelerates Its Military Spending," *New York Times,* March 5, 2007, http://www.nytimes.com/2007/03/05/world/asia/05military.html.
23. Preble, "The FY 2010 Defense Budget Authorization."
24. "Modernizing China's Military: Opportunities and Constraints."
25. Daniel Griffiths, "Fears Over China Military Build-Up," BBC News, February 15, 2007, http://news.bbc.co.uk/2/hi/6365167.stm.
26. Manu Pubby, "US Admiral: China to have first aircraft carrier by '15," *Indian Express,* December 5, 2009, http://www.indianexpress.com/news/US-Admiral—China-to-have-first-aircraft-carrier-by—15/550247; David Lague, "An Aircraft Carrier for China?" *New York Times,* January 30, 2006, http://www.nytimes.com/2006/01/30/business/worldbusiness/30iht-carrier.html.
27. "Modernizing China's Military: Opportunities and Constraints."
28. "An exorbitant privilege? Implications of reserve currencies for competitiveness," McKinsey Global Institute, December 2009, http://www.mckinsey.com/mgi/publications/reserve_currencies/index.asp.
29. Ibid., p. 14.
30. Ibid.
31. Representative Ron Paul of Texas, "The End of Dollar Hegemony," February 15, 2006, http://www.house.gov/paul/congrec/congrec2006/cr021506.htm.
32. "US Navy thwarts Somali pirate seizure of ship," Agence France-Presse, April 16, 2010, http://www.google.com/hostednews/afp/article/ALeqM5joD59OWPUeo9MCkFnbgeem2j4Thw.
33. Benjamin Friedman, "Defense Spending Correction," CATO @ Liberty, February 5, 2009, http://www.cato-at-liberty.org/2009/02/05/defense-spending-correction/.
34. Boot, "ObamaCare and American Power."

13. Rating the Ratings Agencies

1. Mark Pittman, "Moody's, S&P Defer Cuts on AAA Subprime, Hiding Loss," Bloomberg News, March 11, 2008, http://www.bloomberg.com/apps/news?pid=20601109&sid=aRLWzHsF161Y.
2. "AAA Oligopoly," *Wall Street Journal*, February 26, 2008, http://online.wsj.com/article/SB120398754592392261.html.
3. Lawrence J. White, "The SEC's Other Problem," *Regulation* (Winter 2002–2003), pp. 38–39, http://www.cato.org/pubs/regulation/regv25n4/v25n4-10.pdf.
4. Ibid.
5. Ibid.
6. Ibid.
7. "The Role and Impact of Credit Rating Agencies on the Subprime Credit Markets, Chairman Christopher Cox, U.S. Securities and Exchange Commission," testimony before the U.S. Senate Banking Committee on Banking, Housing, and Urban Affairs, September 26, 2007, http://www.sec.gov/news/testimony/2007/ts092607cc.htm.
8. White, "The SEC's Other Problem," p. 40.
9. "AAA Oligopoly."
10. White, "The SEC's Other Problem," p. 40.
11. Ibid.
12. Richard Sylla, "A Historical Primer on the Business of Credit Ratings," Department of Economics, Stern School of Business, New York University, prepared for conference on "The Role of Credit Reporting Systems in the International Economy," World Bank, Washington, D.C., March 1–2, 2001, http://www1.worldbank.org/finance/assets/images/Historical_Primer.pdf.
13. "AAA Oligopoly."
14. White, "The SEC's Other Problem," p. 40.
15. Ibid.
16. "The Role and Impact of Credit Rating Agencies on the Subprime Credit Markets," testimony by Cox.
17. Pittman, "Moody's, S&P Defer Cuts on AAA Subprime, Hiding Loss."
18. Gretchen Morgenson, "Marketwatch: Post Enron, All Eyes on Ratings Agencies," *New York Times*, December 16, 2001, http://www.nytimes.com/2001/12/16/business/market-watch-post-enron-all-eyes-on-rating-agencies.html?pagewanted=1.
19. Kreag Danvers and Anthony Billing, "Is the SEC Going Soft on Credit Rating Agencies?" *CPA Journal*, May 2004, http://www.nysscpa.org/cpajournal/2004/504/perspectives/nv6.htm.
20. Jonathan Laing, "The $2 Trillion Hole," *Barron's*, March 15,

2010, http://online.barrons.com/article/SB126843815871861303.html#articleTabs_panel_article%3D2.

21. Gretchen Morgenson, "When Bond Ratings Get Stale," *New York Times*, October 10, 2009, http://www.nytimes.com/2009/10/11/business/economy/11gret.html.

14. The Insecure SEC

1. Report of Investigation, United States Securities and Exchange Commission, Office of the Inspector General, Case No. OIG-509, Investigation of Failure of the SEC to Uncover Bernard Madoff's Ponzi Scheme, p. 1, http://www.sec.gov/news/studies/2009/oig-509.pdf.

2. Ibid., p. 5.

3. Report of Investigation, United States Securities and Exchange Commission, Office of the Inspector General, Case No. OIG-509, Investigation of Failure of the SEC to Uncover Bernard Madoff's Ponzi Scheme, pp. 4–5, http://www.sec.gov/news/studies/2009/oig-509.pdf.

4. Ibid.

5. Robert Bryce, "From Enron to the Financial Crisis, with Alan Greenspan in Between," *US News & World Report*, September 24, 2008, http://www.usnews.com/articles/opinion/2008/09/24/from-enron-to-the-financial-crisis-with-alan-greenspan-in-between.html.

6. Jesse Westbrook and Ian Katz, "Lehman shows gaps in law examiner says; firm stands by work," *Dallas Morning News*, March 21, 2010, http://www.dallasnews.com/sharedcontent/dws/bus/stories/DN-lehmanernst_21bus.ART0.State.Edition1.3db9609.html.

7. Peter J. Henning, "Why Did Ex-Lehman Executives Talk to Examiner?" DealBook, *New York Times*, March 15, 2010, http://dealbook.blogs.nytimes.com/2010/03/15/why-did-ex-lehman-executives-talk-to-examiner/.

8. Ibid.

9. Antony Currie, "Asleep in the Kennel," Reuters Breaking Views, March 15, 2010 http://www.breakingviews.com/2010/03/15/lehman.aspx?sg=nytimes.

10. Commissioner Harvey J. Goldschmid, U.S. Securities and Exchange Commission, "Post-Enron America: An SEC Perspective," Third Annual A. A. Sommer, Jr. Corporate Securities & Financial Law Lecture, Fordham University School of Law, December 2, 2002, http://www.sec.gov/news/speech/spch120202hjg.htm.

11. Donald J. Boudreaux, "Learning to Love Insider Trading," *Wall Street Journal*, October 24, 2009, http://online.wsj.com/article/SB10001424052748704224004574489324091790350.html.

12. Ibid.

13. Ibid.

14. Triennial Central Bank Survey of Foreign Exchange and Derivatives Market Activity in 2007, final results, December 19, 2007, Bank for International Settlements, http://www.bis.org/publ/rpfxf07t.htm.

15. Conversation with my CNBC colleague Steve Liesman, March 31, 2010.

15. Regulation in the Air

1. Kim Strassel, "Alternative Fuel Folly," *Wall Street Journal*, April 17, 2009, http://online.wsj.com/article/SB123993344387627879.html.

2. Christopher Sheffield, "Black Liquor Turns Solid Gold, Memphis Firms Reap Billions in Federal Tax Credits," *Memphis Business Journal*, January 22, 2010, http://memphis.bizjournals.com/memphis/stories/2010/01/25/story2.html.

3. Strassel, "Alternative Fuel Folly."

4. Christopher Hayes, "Pulp Nonfiction," *Nation*, April 2, 2009, http://www.thenation.com/doc/20090420/hayes.

5. Strassel, "Alternative Fuel Folly."

6. Hayes, "Pulp Nonfiction."

7. Sheffield, "Black Liquor Turns Solid Gold."

8. International Paper, Annual Report, 2009, p. 31, http://investor.internationalpaper.com/phoenix.zhtml?c=73062&p=irol-reportsAnnual.

9. Smurfit-Stone Container Corporation, "Comments Submitted for the Record, U.S. Senate Committee on Finance, Prohibition on Alternative Fuel Credit and Alternative Fuel Mixture Credit for Black Liquor, July 10, 2009, Christopher J. Brescia, Vice President Government Affairs, Smurfit Stone Container Corporation."

10. Gordon Hamilton, "Canada fights back over 'black liquor' tax on pulp and paper industry," *Vancouver Sun*, May 21, 2009, http://www.vancouversun.com/business/Canada+fights+back+over+black+liquor+pulp+paper+industry/1617370/story.html.

11. International Paper, Annual Report, 2009, p. 58.

12. Michael Wolff, "AT&T Sucks," Newser, December 29, 2009, http://www.newser.com/off-the-grid/post/363/att-sucks.html.

13. Jenna Wortham, "Customers Angered as iPhones Overload AT&T," *New York Times*, September 3, 2009, http://www.nytimes.com/2009/09/03/technology/companies/03att.html.

14. L. Gordon Crovitz, "Better Broadband is No 'Joke'—What the FCC Can Learn from Ronald Coase," *Wall Street Journal*, March 22, 2010, http://online.wsj.com/article/SB10001424052748704550004575133802210396886.html.

15. Drew Clark, "Spectrum Wars," *National Journal*, February 18, 2005, http://www.nationaljournal.com/about/njweekly/stories/2005/0218njsp.htm.

16. Hugh J. Aitkin, "Allocating the Spectrum: The Origins of Radio Regulation," *Technology and Culture* 35, no. 4 (October 1994), p. 688.

17. Grant Gross, "FCC's National Broadband Plan: What's in It?" *PC World*, March 12, 2010, http://www.pcworld.com/businesscenter/article/191438/fccs_national_broadband_plan_whats_in_it.html.

18. "Broadband Blockage," *Wall Street Journal*, Review & Outlook, December 30, 2009, http://online.wsj.com/article/SB10001424052748703278604574624481258303334.html.

19. Dale Hatfield and Phil Weiser, "Toward Property Rights in Spectrum: The Difficult Policy Choices Ahead," Cato Institute, No. 575, August 17, 2006, http://www.cato.org/pubs/pas/pa575.pdf.

20. Adie Tomer and Robert Puentes, "Expect Delays: An Analysis of Air Travel Trends in the United States," *Brookings*, October 2009, p. 2.

21. Ibid., p. 4.

22. Steve Chapman, "Don't Blame the Airlines," *Reason*, December 24, 2009, http://reason.com/archives/2009/12/24/dont-blame-the-airlines.

23. Robert W. Poole, Jr., and Viggo Butler, "Airline Deregulation: The Unfinished Revolution," Cato Institute, http://www.cato.org/pubs/regulation/regv22n1/airline.pdf.

24. Tomer and Puentes, "Expect Delays," p. 2.

25. Ibid., p. 3.

26. Department of Transportation, Bureau of Transportation Statistics, Press Release, "Airline On-Time Performance Improves in January," March 9, 2010, http://www.bts.gov/press_releases/2010/dot045_10/html/dot045_10.html.

27. Tomer and Puentes, "Expect Delays," p. 16.

28. Ibid., p. 14.

29. Ibid.

30. Department of Transportation, Federal Aviation Administration, 14 CFR Part 93, Congestion Management Rule for John F. Kennedy International Airport and Newark Liberty International Airport, Final Rule, December 2008, Federal Register.

31. Ibid.

32. Michael E. Levine, "Airport Congestion: When Theory Meets Reality," New York University School of Law, 2008, http://lsr.nellco.org/cgi/viewcontent.cgi?article=1163&context=nyu_lewp.

33. Tomer and Puentes, "Expect Delays," p. 14.

34. Justin Bachman, "Buckle Up? Airlines, Fliers Brace for Flight-Delay Rule," *Bloomberg Businessweek*, March 24, 2010, http://www.busi

nessweek.com/bwdaily/dnflash/content/mar2010/db20100323_742386
.htm.

35. Ibid.

36. Tomer and Puentes, "Expect Delays," p. 14.

37. Federal Aviation Administration, "What is NextGen?" April 20, 2010, http://www.faa.gov/about/initiatives/nextgen/defined/what/index.cfm.

38. Tomer and Puentes, "Expect Delays," p. 17.

39. U.S. Department of Transportation, Office of the Inspector General, "FAA's Process for Awarding ARRA Airport Improvement Grants," August 6, 2009, http://origins.recovery.gov/News/press/Documents/AIP+ARRA+Advisory+08-06-09.pdf.

40. Ibid.

41. Ibid.

42. Stephen Moore and Dean Stansel, "Federal Aid to Dependent Corporations: Clinton and Congress Fail to Eliminate Business Subsidies," Cato Institute, Briefing Paper No. 28, January 28, 1997, http://www.cato.org/pubs/briefs/bp-028.html.

43. U.S. General Accounting Office, "Factors Affecting Efforts to Improve Air Service at Small Community Airports," January 2003, p. 7, http://www.gao.gov/new.items/d03330.pdf.

44. Senate Report 111-069, "Transportation and Housing and Urban Development, and Related Agencies Appropriations Bill, 2010," http://thomas.loc.gov/cgi-bin/cpquery/R?cp111:FLD010:@1(sr069).

16. Private Banking

1. Gretchen Morgenson, "Death of a Loophole and Swiss Banks Will Mourn," *New York Times,* March 26, 2010, http://www.nytimes.com/2010/03/28/business/28gret.html.

2. Rone Tempest, "China Changes Its Role in Recurring Scene: Indonesia: As Ethnic Chinese Are Persecuted Again, Beijing Stays Silent," *Los Angeles Times,* February 28, 1998, http://articles.latimes.com/1998/feb/28/news/mn-23871.

3. Darcy Crowe and A. D. Pruitt, "Hugo Chavez Nationalizes Swanky Beach-Side Resort," *Wall Street Journal,* October 14, 2009, http://blogs.wsj.com/developments/2009/10/14/hugo-chavez-nationalizes-swanky-beach-side-resort/; Dan Molinski and Norihiko Shirouzu, "Venezuela's President Threatens Toyota, GM," *Wall Street Journal,* December 27, 2009, http://online.wsj.com/article/SB10001424052748704039704574615990386867578.html; Simon Romero, "Chavez Seizes Assets of Oil Contractors," *New York Times,* May 9, 2009, http://www.nytimes.com/2009/05/09/world/americas/09venez.html; Gerri Smith,

"A Food Fight for Hugo Chavez," *Bloomberg Businessweek*, March 11, 2010, http://www.businessweek.com/magazine/content/10_12/b4171046603604.htm; "Venezuela seizes top food producer's property," Associated Press, March 11, 2010, http://seattletimes.nwsource.com/html/businesstechnology/2011318476_apltvenezuelaexpropriation.html.

4. Jorge Castaneda, "Latin America's Deafening Silence," *Newsweek*, December 8, 2008, http://www.newsweek.com/id/171313.
5. Tax Justice Network Financial Secrecy Index, 2009, http://www.financialsecrecyindex.com/2009results.html.
6. "Mapping the Faultlines," Jurisdiction Report, Secrecy Jurisdictions, Delaware, Financial Secrecy Index, September 29, 2009, http://www.secrecyjurisdictions.com/.
7. Organisation for Economic Co-operation and Development, Center for Tax Policy and Administration, List of Unco-operative Tax Havens, http://www.oecd.org/document/57/0.3343.en_2649_33745_30578809_1_1_1_1.00.html.
8. Organisation for Economic Co-operation and Development, Center for Tax Policy and Administration, Summary of Outcomes of the Meeting of the Global Forum on Transparency and Exchange of Information for Tax Purposes Held in Mexico on 1–2 September 2009, http://www.oecd.org/site/0.3407.en_21571361_43854757_1_1_1_1_1.00.html.
9. Dan Mitchell, "The Liberalizing Impact of Tax Havens in a Globalized Economy," Cato Institute, March 23, 2009.

17. A Mad Hatter's Tea Party

1. "Independents Take Center Stage in Obama Era: Trends in Political Values and Core Attitudes: 1987–2009," Pew Research Center for the People and the Press, Survey Reports, May 21, 2009, http://people-press.org/report/517/political-values-and-core-attitudes.
2. Jesse McKinley, "California Voting Change Could Signal Big Political Shift," *New York Times*, June 10, 2010.
3. U.S. National Archives and Records Administration, Frequently Asked Questions, U.S. Electoral College, http://www.archives.gov/federal-register/electoral-college/faq.html#process.
4. Ibid.
5. U.S. Federal Election Commission, Distribution of Electoral Votes, http://www.fec.gov/pages/elecvote.htm.
6. National Center for State Courts, Court-Community Election Law, Election Divisions and Election Codes, http://www.ncsconline.org/wc/CourTopics/StateLinks.asp?id=26.

7. David Leip, Atlas of U.S. Presidential Elections, 1992 Presidential General Election Results, http://uselectionatlas.org/RESULTS/national .php?year=1992.
8. "Tea Party Patriots Mission Statement and Core Values," http://docs .google.com/View?id=dhsxmzm7_19fcdzskg5.

Afterword: Fiscal Responsibility Is Social Responsibility

1. International Telecommunications Union.
2. http://www.doioig.gov/images/stories/reports/doc//RIKinvestigation.txt.
3. "Comebacks and Comeuppance," *Economist*, June 10, 2010.

— Acknowledgments —

Those of us in the TV news business know how much work goes into putting a show on the air every day. Anchors like me have a lot of behind-the-scenes help from some wonderful producers and technical staff. Long days and extra hours are the norm for them. My team on *Power Lunch* is top-shelf, and I want to thank them all for their effort and dedication. Special thanks to CNBC's Mark Hoffman, Jeremy Pink, Andy Yonteff, Brian Steel, and Nik Deogun for supporting this project, and to Tyler Mathieson, thank you for reading as I wrote and for being a great editor and co-anchor.

Hard work isn't reserved for the television business. Writing a book, while very glamorous in the movies, is insanely challenging. I'm glad I had help. I couldn't have completed this project without the encouragement of my too-far-left-leaning, misguided friend Stephanie Krikorian. Thanks for arguing over health care and the use of quotations, and thanks for not panicking at the same time I did. Jessica Shapiro, thank you for being a meticulous fact-checker.

Writing was the hard part, but what felt easy was making a proposal into a book, and that's because of some fabulous people who are really good at what they do. *You Know I'm Right* was just an idea on a few sheets of paper until Maura Teitlebaum at Abram Artists Agency got her hands on it.

Thank you for making this book a reality. Mitchell Ivers, my editor at Simon & Schuster, you were a delightful part of the process. Thanks for the encouraging words and the amazing edits. Thanks to the rest of the Simon & Schuster team as well—Anthony Ziccardi and Kristin Dwyer. Your zeal from the beginning has been amazing.

Thanks to my parents, Kenneth and Maria Caruso, who had the great sense to move from Taxachusetts to New Hampshire, as close to a libertarian state as exists. There's a reason it says *Live Free or Die* on the license plate and why J. D. Salinger chose to hide out there. No nosy neighbors. No income tax. No sales tax. No services either. And that's how we like it. Would you please just leave us alone now?

To all my family and friends who were ignored for nearly six months straight: thank you for your understanding.

Of course, there is no way to repay CNBC for what turned out to be a seminal event in my life as a result of my employment: interviewing Milton Friedman. It was meant to be a short interview on school vouchers. It turned into four days of coverage, and we had huge ratings. Dan Clark, my producer at the time, backed my desire to do the interview, while everyone else thought I was nuts. Thanks, buddy. Meghan Reeder, you too.

Speaking of Milton Friedman fans, if you've read the book, you know how much I depended on the folks at the Cato Institute. People such as Veronique du Rugy and Tad deHaven, who relentlessly toiled away to expose just what a profligate spender George W. Bush was. If only the rest of the conservative world had been listening. Michael Cannon, Dan Mitchell, Chris Edwards, David Boaz, Benjamin Friedman, Dan Griswold, and Leigh Harrington all work tirelessly to preserve our freedoms.

Brian Riedl at the Heritage Foundation helped me find the $150,000 stop light buried deep somewhere on a government budget line.

Thanks to Bill Griffeth, who pushed me to finish writing at the very moment I was about to give up. Thanks to Gina Saudino for a hand early on. Thanks to Alex Kroke for his photography; to my lawyer, Elizabeth Corradino; to the Monday Night Club, and to the Saturday Supper Club.

— Index —